Empower Me

Tantric Awareness

2

Beautifully Illustrated

Collection: Sex Stories Mythology

By Jean-Claude Carvill

To Charisma, who allowed me to get her out of her "box" on becoming empowered. Her brightest smile light up my heart forever.

ISBN-13: 978-1511602150

ISBN-10: 1511602155

CONTENTS

PROLOGUE

I opened the windows to let in a chilled Parisian breeze. The crisp December temperatures pressed their tendrils of reality into my dream world: I was actually here. I breathed deeply: the air seemed even cleaner after one of Paris' temperamental downpours.

I know the nickname is an old one, but I couldn't help but chuckle at the irony: here I was, Freya Moreton, in the City of Love… and yet very much alone.

Only a few months before, I was snuggled into a comfortable life. I owned a yoga studio in Greenwich Village. My best friend, Daniela, and I had struggled to make something of the studio and it paid off. Our clientele became more exclusive as our reputation grew, and the business was more than afloat: it was thriving. I loved what I did, and was grateful that each measure of success put more distance between my life and my difficult childhood.

Enter hotshot defense attorney Tristan Lucas and a zero-to-sixty relationship. It was too easy to believe his confident advances were actually love. So, when he flew me to London and proposed, it didn't really occur to me to say no.

And while it played a part in the break up, I have to be honest: his jealousy and arrogance- not to mention his bull-in-a-china-shop attitude toward sex- had nothing to do with my instant attraction to his childhood friend, Corey Wallace. I believe that even if I never met Corey, I would have eventually broken it off with Tristan. But Corey showed me what tender, honest love really was, and that was hard to ignore.

It was impossible not to compare Corey and Tristan. Not only did my fiancй come up short in comparison, but as his possessive nature tightened around me, I realized I was only a possession to him. To say it was a toxic breakup would be an understatement, and not only because his secretary was… um… servicing him… when I went to

i

his office. Things escalated from there: Tristan went to confront Corey and somehow, I became the agreed-upon prize for a motorcycle race between the two.

How, how, how did this all happen? I couldn't help asking myself that question once again, gazing out the window of Corey's gorgeous Parisian apartment where he suggested I go until after the stupid race was finished. It wasn't hard to leave. I was disgusted at those two squabbling over me like two dogs with one bone. Corey soothed me, explaining that he only agreed to the race because beating Tristan was the only way to convince him to let me go.

But what if Corey lost?

And what if he won?

Where would either outcome leave me?

My silent contemplation was shattered by a knock at the door.

CHAPTER ONE

Anywhere With You

In khaki chinos, a navy polo shirt and a black Cerruti jacket, Corey stood with a single red rose in one hand a paper bag in the other. The smell wafting from the bag left no mystery as to its contents: fresh pastries.

His hair neatly swept off his forehead as always, he seemed remarkably fresh-faced and wore a cheerful smile.

"I… I..." I stuttered, wanting to throw my arms around him, but too numb to force any part of my body to budge. "Are you...?"

"I'm fine," he replied, sensing the only half-spoken question. "And Tristan is fine, too," he added, with a subtle arch of his eyebrow. "It's all over, Freya," he whispered. "I won."

"I don't care about the stupid race," I told him, coming to my senses enough to step forward and toss my arms eagerly around his neck.I caught him off guard, and he chuckled as his breath left his lungs.Even with his hands full, he embraced me in return.

In his arms, I felt a rush of sensation. Heat pulsed through me, thrumming to the elevated and the uneven beat of my heart. Liquid fire settled in my core, making me want to scream with a desire that I didn't understand. Startled by the power of it, my instinct was to immediately retreat. However, a far greater force was compelling me to cling on to him for dear life.

"I don't care about any of that," I mumbled my face buried somewhere near his clavicle.

"It's over, Freya," he said soothingly, the words gently spoken into my hair. "It's all over."

1

Feeling myself begin to tremble, I was unsure whether that was the effect of him or the tension of the last twenty four hours suddenly coming to the surface. I would be a fool to say that it hadn't been an emotional roller coaster, and it was possible that my nerves were now manifesting themselves physically. But I felt like there was something much deeper causing my tremors, and Corey seemed to notice it too.

Carefully, Corey pulled back a little, not completely relinquishing me.He leaned back just enough that he could look into my face. His eyes burned me, a spontaneous combustion of my soul.

"Corey," I breathed. I was surprised that I still had the ability to speak.

"Yes?"

"Corey, please," I whimpered.

"What, Freya?" he asked quietly.

"Kiss me," I whispered.

Thankfully, he didn't make me ask twice. Dipping his head slowly forward, I watched as his eyes slipped closed before I surrendered to the heavy pull of my own. His lips claimed me so softly, so gently, with a feather-like graze. The tease caused me to mewl as my body instinctively pressed against his solid form more firmly. My fingers swept up to the nape of his neck, and then a little higher, gripping his thick hair as I urged him to deepen the kiss.

That tongue, which had tormented me in Florida, slipped playfully forward, tasting my lips. My own tongue responded intuitively, tripping from the confines of my mouth and following the path his had taken. He left a sweetness in his wake, the remnants of chocolate from one of the pastries.

I moaned, a sound of delight and deep longing. He took advantage of my open mouth to slip his tongue inside..

As if my mouth and sex were connected, I felt it as surely as if he'd tenderly lapped at my that tender spot between my legs.

"Ugh," I groaned into him as my lower half convulsed.

"Mm," he moaned warmly.I heard the soft thump of the pastry bag hit the ground behind me. His hands were on my hips then, edging my back into the apartment before he kicked the door closed with the heel of his brown loafer.

Lusty dampness flooded my underwear and I writhed against him. Desperate to feel him inside me, I wasn't aware that my hands had darted forward and grabbed the tan leather belt at his waist. With shaky hands, I grappled with the buckle, until his sure fingers stopped me with a firm, but not ungentle, grasp of my wrists.

Tearing his lips from mine, he looked down at me, a little breathless.He smiled a a sweet smile. "Not yet," he breathed,

"Wh... what?" I asked, panting in an effort to tame my thunderous heartbeat.

"Not yet," he repeated, shaking his head.

A sinking nausea threw ice water over the fire that had been raging in my lower abdomen, and I continued to gulp in air. "You..." I whispered. "You don't want me?"

His soft smile widened and his eyes took on a lascivious expression I'd never seen in them before. "I want you, Freya. God, I want you."

My cheeks burning under that unapologetically libidinous gaze, I traced my tongue over the roof of my mouth, which still tasted distinctly of him. I averted my gaze, not sure what to make of the situation.

"I don't understand," I eventually murmured.

"I want to make love to you, Freya," he softly replied. "I want it to be like nothing you've ever experienced before."

"I'm sure it will be," I informed him quietly, hoping that my response to him would prove just as potent when it came to the act itself.

"I mean, I want it to be perfect," he added. "I want it to be just right: at the right time and in the right place."

Confused, my eyes moved over his face, finding only the same openness and sincerity I'd always seen. "We're in Paris," I reminded him. "The most romantic city in the world, right?"

Cocking his head to one side, he hummed. "Maybe," he hedged. "Maybe not."

"Corey, it doesn't have to be in the perfect place," I told him. "I... I just want to be with you." Cheeks flaming at the brazen way I'd announced my need, I cast my gaze quickly to the floor again.

Not letting me off the hook, he smoothly slipped his index finger beneath my chin and raised my face to his. "I want to be with you, too," he told me earnestly. "But I can wait."

"I'm not sure I can," I blurted. The statement was purely and unequivocally honest statement came tumbling out of my mouth before I had a chance to hold it back.

Lips quirking with a half-smile, his tender eyes drifted sensually down the length of my body and, then back up. "Well," he breathed, "I'm sure there's something we can do about that."

"Huh?" I asked.

Gently pushing me against the wall, he grinned. "We don't have to make love to make love, Freya," he chuckled. "And I certainly don't want to leave you frustrated," he added.

The words didn't make sense, but it didn't matter: Corey was pressing against me and I was lost in another world. Unsure what any of his words meant, I simply relished the feeling of his strong hands, pinning me to the wall.

Slowly his face drifted down to mine. In expectation, I offered him my lips, but he dipped a little lower, caressing my chin instead. Then, gradually, with butterfly kisses, he trailed up my jawbone to the base of my right ear.

My eyes drifted closed and I focused on the sensations: the heady smell of him, the teasing play of his mouth, the texture of his shirt as my hands dove inside his coat and clutched at his back. I had never felt so in tune with my own body, and so aware of someone else's.

Gently, he took my lobe between his teeth, sucking it into his sensual mouth.

"Oh, God," I whimpered, rubbing my lower half against his hard hip.

His hands, which still grasped me, made no effort to stop my movement. Instead, he began to suck harder on the soft flesh held captive in his mouth.

Electricity almost crackled between us, and I suspected he would not have the self-control to stop what he'd started. Against my thigh, I could feel the bulge of his excitement. The knowledge that his erection was for me, and me alone, caused me to climax right then and there.

Spikes of pleasure rocked through me, and I bucked and squirmed between the wall and his equally firm figure. "Oh, God," I mumbled. "Oh, God!"

"You're so beautiful, Freya," he whispered, releasing my lobe and allowing his tongue to trace the outer curve of my ear. "You're so very beautiful," he added slowly. "Do you know that?"

Barely able to register his words, much less provide him with a response, all I managed was a "Huh?"

"I'm sure men have told you that before," he continued, whispering the words sensually and intimately. "But do you really know it?"

"Corey," I wheezed, my body still quivering with the force of the orgasm.

"You will know," he promised. "I'm going to make sure you know exactly how beautiful you are."

Later, as we lay in bed, tangled in each other's arms, I could feel the steely length of his erection through the pajama bottoms he wore. Yet, he did nothing about it. He wouldn't even let me stroke him.

"It's okay," he assured me.

"But-" I began to argue. I wondered if he knew just how much I wanted to feel his solid presence between my thighs. Did he know how desperate I was for him to fill me, move within me, push my body to its limits? Did he realize how much I wanted to be helpless against his thrusts, my body demanding more, deeper, harder?

"I can be a very patient man," he said, smiling. "And you, my darling, are going to be worth the wait."

A surge of panic crashing over me, I stiffened. The sudden tension in my body didn't escape his notice.

"Are you okay?" he asked. The fingers that rested at my elbow began to caress me gently.

"Yes," I lied. "I'm just...what if I'm not?"

"What?" He chuckled, shaking his head.

"What if I'm not worth the wait?" I clarified. "What if I'm a disappointment?"

His face taking on a weighty expression, he stared at me intently.

True to form, I began to babble as my nervousness grew. "I mean, you've been with a lot of women. I'm sure some of them have been incredible lovers... and I'm.... Well, I'm..."

"You're gorgeous," he supplied quietly, still looking at me with the same unflinching gaze. "You're sexy," he added. "You're full of life, and passion, and love," he continued.

I wanted to tell him that he didn't know what he was getting himself into. He didn't realize that I had been completely frigid with every other man I'd slept with. Of course, 'frigid' wasn't a word that could be used to describe me while I was with him. But, maybe sex would be different. His foreplay blew my mind, but would I be just as eager for him? A primal voice told me that I already knew the answer to that question: the fact that I ached to feel him inside me was proof enough. Nevertheless, the insidious doubt would not let me be. It kept picking at my mind, like drops of water on sandstone.

6

"Freya, trust me," he urged. "When I'm with you, I'm not comparing you to anyone else."

"Are you sure?" I asked, my mind wandering to the picture of his mom that dominated the room.

"Yes," he insisted. "You're you," he said firmly, "unique and wonderful."

Snuggling deeper into his shoulder, I didn't argue with him. I had no desire to talk about it anymore.

We spent three days at his apartment. During the day, we'd scour the city; he showed me some of the famous landmarks and then we'd explore the flea markets in search of pieces of furniture for Nirvana. The Clignancourt was a treasure trove of stunning pieces. But none of it quite seemed right for the room he'd asked me to decorate.

Peering at a lamp he liked, he asked, "You don't like the décor at the apartment?"

"I love it," I quickly corrected him. "It's beautiful, but it's very Parisian. I'm not sure if it would work in Florida."

"Hmm," he nodded. "I know what you mean. See, this is why I'm leaving it in your hands. I have absolutely no idea what to do with the room."

And for the following three nights, we spent time quietly together. One night, we just sat curled up on the sofa with a glorious fire burning. The other two nights, we did a lot of kissing, some of which turned intensely passionate, so much so that I thought I would be able to convince him to abandon his patience. However, he remained unshakable.

Both times, though, he refused to leave me insatiate. He touched me, kissed me, and caressed every inch of my body until I was whimpering in ecstasy.

At the end of the best – and most frustrating – three days of my life, as we sat in the dining room eating a sumptuous continental breakfast, he asked if I'd go somewhere else with him.

I didn't bother to ask where, and I didn't bother to ask when or for how long. My answer was instinctive. "I'll go anywhere with you."

"Hmm," he beamed. "What do you say to Monaco?" he asked.

"Monaco?" I replied, matching his smile with one of my own. "I... I'd love to." I chuckled excitedly.

"Good," he replied. "I was hoping we could spend a week down there on my yacht."

"Over Christmas?" I asked.

"Yeah," he nodded. "Is that a problem?"

"No," I replied. "No, but don't you want to spend time with your family?"

"Actually, my foster parents are in Austria for the holidays," he said. "But I guess that was selfish of me not to ask you if you had plans," he added, his features growing somber. "I guess, you do have family you want to be with, right?" he added.

My own face fell and I clutched my fork a little more firmly. "Um... Daniela's the closest thing to family I've got."

"Oh," he replied. "I..."

Suddenly, the man who was usually so smooth seemed lost for words. "I'm sorry."

"Don't be," I responded, forcing a smile. "It's okay. And as families go, I couldn't ask for better than her." I continued to push unpleasant memories aside and compel some happiness on my face, but I could tell he wasn't completely buying it.

"You want to talk about it?" he asked.

Without bothering to ask how the hell he managed to see right through me, I gratefully shook my head. "No," I whispered.

"You know, you can talk to me," he said, reaching out and placing his fingers over my hand.

"I know," I replied sincerely. "Maybe someday," I shrugged. "Just... um... not right now."

"All right," he smiled.

***

Despite the length of the drive, Corey decided to travel down to the French Riveria by car. I didn't mind how long the journey lasted. All that mattered to me was that I was in his company.

During the trip, while Corey was too busy keeping his eyes on the road to pay my body the kind of attention he'd been paying it back at his apartment, I checked my phone, which had lain untouched for the previous three days.

The first message was from Daniela. 'Tristan was pretty angry about losing the race. The next morning, he came by the studio looking for you. I didn't tell him where you were, but he seemed pretty intent on finding you.'

The next text was from Tristan. 'If you think you can hide from me, think again! I will find you and I will bring you back. You're mine and I'm sure as hell not letting him take you from me.'

"I take it Tristan wasn't exactly a good loser?" I asked quietly, still staring at the message.

"Hmm?" Corey replied, keeping most of his attention on the road.

"He's looking for me, and he's pretty pissed by all accounts," I told him.

Lifting my eyes, I noticed that a tiny muscle in his jaw was flexing. "You're safe with me," he said eventually.

"I know," I smiled. "I don't think he'd do me any harm anyway, it's just..." When I heard the words that came from my lips, I was forced to assess them in a way I hadn't when they were just in my head. Did

9

I really think he wouldn't do me any harm? He'd hurt me on more than one occasion, while claiming that he loved me. Now, he was angry: could I really be sure that I knew his temperament well enough to say what he was or was not capable of?

"He won't be able to find us on the yacht," he continued, seeming to sense that I was second guessing myself. "And, in a week's time, we'll be in the middle of nowhere, and nobody will be able to find us."

Offering him a questioning gaze, I watched the knowing smile crease the corners of his mouth. "Where are we going?" I asked.

"The roof of the world," he replied gleefully.

"Huh?" I mumbled.

I was clear he had lost it. Perhaps the ordeal with Tristan had affected him emotionally as well?

Removing his eyes from the road momentarily, he twisted his face to the right and winked at me. "Wait and see," he said. "Wait and see."

When we arrived in Monte Carlo, Corey navigated the narrow streets like the back of his hand, eventually pulling to a halt at the Port Hercule. Vastly different from the below freezing temperatures in Paris, Monaco was offering a temperate fifty-five degrees.

The sun was making welcomed appearances every few minutes, despite the thick clouds that masked its face.

"New Horizons," Corey said, getting out of the car. He walked around the hood to open my door, but I beat him to it and by the time, he reached the passenger side, I was already standing beside the car.

Blinking up at the refreshing sun, I cast my eyes over the clean blue water and the light that reflected off of it. "New Horizons?" I asked.

"It's my boat," he nodded. Pointing to a massive yacht moored a few yards from us, he smiled. "Sort of my new toy, really," he added a little self-deprecatingly. "What do you think?"

10

I'd never seen anything quite like it in real life. It was over a hundred and fifty feet in length with three tiered decks at the stern. I could see the lower deck was kitted out for fishing, with lines secured to a rack and high-backed chairs anchored at the very rear of the boat. The main deck above seemed to be a living space, with patio furniture and what looked like a barbeque grill.

"It's a Diana Yacht, a Mystic," he told me, enthusiastic about his purchase. "Has five cabins," he added, "so you don't need to worry about us being on top of each other."

With a wry smile I quirked an eyebrow at him. "You being on top of me isn't something I'm worried about," I said matter-of-factly.

"Really?" he asked with a mischievous glint in his gorgeous eyes. "Because I was thinking about you being on top of me," he added, playfully nudging me with his hip, before smoothly lacing his fingers with mine and leading me toward the boat.

I was happy to follow him, regardless of the destination

Greeting a couple of crew members, who smiled warmly and seemed pleased to see their employer, Corey took me aboard and began to show me around the three decks.

With a living room, small cinema room, and even a gym, it was bigger than my studio and apartment combined. It was like a miniature cruiser. And then, on the very top, he showed me the sun deck, complete with its very own pool. When I sardonically pointed out that there was water all around us, he chuckled in agreement.

"You gotta admit, it's nice, though," he added.

"It's very nice," I nodded, smiling at his boyish excitement.

"What?" he asked.

"Nothing," I replied, still grinning. "I didn't think I liked the little boy in you," I added by way of explanation. "You already know I wasn't crazy about you racing. But I like to see you like this," I told him softly.

"Like what?" he chuckled.

Shrugging, I tried to find the right words. "I don't know," I muttered. "A little giddy," I suggested.

"Giddy?" he echoed eyebrows shooting upward. "I'll have you know, Miss Moreton, that I am never giddy." With that, he stepped forward and swept me up to his arms. "Well..." he added doubtfully. "Being around you does have a certain effect on me," he said softly.

As the gentle breeze wafted over the two of us and ruffled his usually neat hair, my gaze scanned his face: those gentle features, combined with a strong masculine contours. God, he was sexy.

"Corey," I whispered. "Make love to me."

"Soon," he replied. "I promise it won't be much longer now. But you're going to have to bear with me a little longer."

"You're going to kill me like this," I informed him in a grave tone.

Laughing at my dramatic statement, he tossed his head back.

"I'm serious," I added. "I've never wanted anyone like I want you."

His chuckles abating, he brought his face back down before gently kissing the top of my head. "Really?" he asked lips still resting in my hair.

Slightly embarrassed by the confession – although not as embarrassed as I would have been a week before – I nodded silently.

"So...?" he sighed. "Tristan?"

Immediately, I stepped back. "What is it with you two? Is this some kind of competition? Am I just an object in your 'who's better in bed' race?"

"No," he said firmly. He took hold of my hand and prevented me from moving any further away from him. "I'm sorry I brought him up: I shouldn't have. I just..."

"You what? You have to be better than him?"

12

"When it comes to you?" he countered. "Yes. I want to be better than him. I want to love you more than he did. I want you to love me more than you loved him. And when we do make love, I want it to be the most incredible experience of your life."

"I..." I began, knowing that I couldn't stay angry with him. "I just don't want to talk about my relationship with him," I said mournfully. "And you don't want to hear about it."

Looking chagrined he released my hand and put his own in his pockets. "I'm sorry," he said, his face dipping to his shoes.

"I'm sorry, too," I echoed closing the gap between us and snaking my arms around his waist.

It was hard being so close to him. It was always hard. Every touch, every slight brush of hands was enough to take me to the heights of arousal. While hugging him felt so very, very good, it also felt like I was teasing myself with something that he wasn't prepared to offer... at least, not right then and there.

"I won't bring him up again," he stated.

"I'd appreciate that," I sighed I was greatful that he dropped the subject so easily. I pressed my cheek against the hard, warmth of his chest. "You told me there was no comparison between me and your exes, right?" I added, thoughtfully.

"Yeah," he agreed reluctantly, knowing where I was heading.

"What makes you think it's different for me?" I asked.

"Okay," he acknowledged with a small sigh.

"But for what it's worth," I mumbled, lifting my face and kissing the underside of his chin, "I already love you more than I've loved anyone. You've already loved me better than anyone, and I can't wait for you to show me how good sex can feel."

"Oh, Freya," he breathed, his hands sliding down to my buttocks and claiming them in his muscular hands. With a sturdy tug, he pulled me to him, and the solid swell of his groin prodding at my navel.

13

Eyes fluttering, I slowly rolled my hips, rubbing myself against him. "Corey, I want to feel you."

"I want to feel you, too," he responded quickly.

"Touch me," I begged softly, not caring that we were out in the open, still in front of the dock, and there were at least half a dozen crew members on board who could have disturbed us at any moment.

Corey, on the other hand, hesitated. He lifted his face and looked about him before slowly, allowing the index finger of his right hand to trace the waistband of my jeans. When he reached the brass button, he flicked it open with expert precision and gently slid his hand inside.

As his fingers glided over my underwear, stroking my mound through the thin fabric, he kept his gaze solidly on me. His eyes studied mine, watching for the subtle changes in my pupils.

Gradually his touch shifted lower, exploring my outer lips, which were plump and tender with expectation. Still caressing me through my underwear, he drew his finger carefully between my damp folds. Pulling back up, he found the unmistakably distended bud.

I shivered violently as the pad of his finger rolled over my inflamed clitoris and fluid gushed from my center, flooding my panties and soaking into my outer garments. "Oh, Cor-" I began to say, the strength of the sensation taking my breath away before I was able to say his name.

"Mr. Wallace," a male voice from behind him said suddenly.

Using his own broad frame to keep me shielded from view, Corey twisted his head over his shoulder. "Yes?"

"We're ready to leave, sir, if you give us the word," the man uttered.

Clinging to the short sleeves of Corey's shirt, I buried my flaming face in his chest. I knew that what we'd been doing must be as plain as day to the crew memberthat I, mercifully, couldn't see.

"That's fine, Gregg," Corey replied calmly. "Thanks."

"Sir," Gregg replied efficiently before leaving as quickly and quietly as he'd arrived.

Smoothing his hand out of my shorts, Corey deftly buttoned them before rubbing both hands down the length of my trembling arms. "Are you okay?" he asked.

"Yeah," I breathed. "I guess. Do you think he-"

"He didn't see anything," he quickly replied.

"But he saw enough to guess," I countered, hanging my head as I wondered how the man before me had the power to transform the usually restrained and withdrawn version of me into the reckless, brazen woman whose desire for him wiped out all other considerations.

"It's all right," he gently said. "Gregg's not the kind of man to spread gossip," he assured me. "Besides, Freya, neither of us has anything to be ashamed of."

Accepting his point with a reluctant nod, I partially agreed. On some level, I did know that Corey and I weren't doing anything wrong or dirty. But old conditioning dies hard, and I couldn't shake the connection between sex and shame. The strings of men my mother had bedded, and the seedy way they'd come and gone, had taught me certain things about physical love. Those lessons weren't easy to dismiss.

"Freya?" Corey nudged, sensing that my mind had wandered. "Honey, are you okay?"

"Honey?" I replied, curious.

His hands still clutching mine, he smiled. "You don't like it?" he asked.

"No, it's not that," I responded, finding myself grinning as the thoughts of my mother, and what Gregg may or may not have seen, faded into the background. "It's just the first time you've called me that."

"And?" he asked, hopefully.

"And I like it," I told him quietly. "I like it a lot."

"Good, because I-" his smile halted along with his thought when the sound of my cell phone cut him off.

Grumbling, I apologized to him as I reached around to my rear pocket and pulled the phone from my pocket. "It's Blake," I told him, a crinkle in my brow as I brought the phone to my ear. "Hello," I said, watching the puzzled expression on Corey's face.

"Hey, Freya," Blake said, sounding more downbeat than his usual energetic self.

"Is something wrong?" I instantly asked.

"Freya, Tristan is going berserk," he sighed. "I've never seen him like this. I wanted to warn you. He knows you're out of the country and he's swearing that he's going to find you and bring you back."

Pulling the phone from my face, I put the call on speaker so Corey could listen in. "I don't understand," I breathed. "I told him that I don't want to marry him," I added.

"I know," Blake replied. "I know, he's just not willing to let it go."

Lifting my free hand, I swept the hair from my face. "Look, Blake," I began, "tell your brother that I'm just a nobody from Fresno. He can have his pick of women: models, actresses, singers… he doesn't need me."

Blake released a slow breath, "He wants what he can't have," he countered. "He's determined to get you back because he doesn't want you to be with Corey."

"Tell Tristan he needs to stop seeing Freya as a commodity. She's made her choice," Corey chimed in.

"Hey, Core," Blake greeted, his voice glum. "I've tried, man," he grumbled. "He's not listening to a word I say."

16

"Well, let him do what he has to do," Corey announced, shrugging as he protectively wrapped an arm around my shoulders. "He's not going to get to Freya, so he can throw his fit if he wants to."

"That's the other thing I wanted to talk to you guys about," Blake added ominously. "He's sworn he's going to get even with you, too."

Corey's eyes met mine briefly and a silent question passed between us. "What do you mean?" he said aloud.

"I don't know what he's scheming, but you can bet your life he's up to something," he explained.

As if on cue, Corey's cell beeped. While he pulled the phone from his pants pocket and studied the text message, I continued to speak with Blake.

"He'll cool down," I tried to convince him... or maybe I was trying to convince myself. In truth, I was concerned by the power that Tristan's money could buy him. Despite Corey's assurance that I could not be found, I was concerned about the reach Mr. Lucas and his cohorts wielded.

"I don't know," Blake muttered. "Like I said, I've never seen my brother like this. I can't help thinking he's gonna do something really stupid."

Corey gently cupped my cheek, gaining my undivided attention. "I'm just going down to the office," he softly told me. "I'll be back in a moment."

"Everything okay, Freya?" Blake asked, having heard Corey's voice.

"Not sure," I replied, watching Corey jog to the stairs and go down to the main deck. "Corey's just gone to check on something," I added.

"Is that Freya?" I heard Daniela's voice in the distance on the other end of the line.

"Yeah," he replied, no longer talking to me. "You want to talk to her?"

I didn't hear her make any reply, but her body language must have been a yes, because within moments, Blake was gone and her softly lilting voice was yammering excitedly in my ear.

"I hope this guy is worth it," she giggled. "Because it's causing a big pile of shit back here."

"So I've heard," I mumbled.

"So?" she uttered, expecting that one syllable to make sense to me.

"So?" I repeated, elongating the vowel.

Chuckling, she lowered her voice. "Is he worth it?"

"Oh," I breathed, finally comprehending the stilted line of questioning. "Well... yeah, yeah, I think he is."

"So, where are you now?" she asked.

"At the moment," I began, as the engines burst into life, and I felt the slight rumble through the soles of my feet, "I'm on a yacht in Monte Carlo."

"Who would have thought, huh?" she laughed. "When we were just teenage girls, working in a factory to help our families pay the bills, would we ever have imagined we'd be dating millionaires?"

A tiny part of her question caught in my mind. "We?" I asked. "We're dating millionaires?

Pitching her voice a little lower still, I sense she was moving away from Blake as she spoke. "I don't want to speak too soon," she hesitated. "But we've been seeing a lot of each other over the last few days, and I think... maybe there's something there."

Genuinely pleased for both of them, I didn't have to fake the grin that graced my face. "That's great," I said.

"And, I've gotta tell you, he is a wild man in bed," she enthused. "I wasn't expecting that from a clean bred, uptown boy," she added, giggling. "But, wow, the man has another side to him."

Still smiling warmly, regardless of the fact she couldn't see it, I listened quietly to her A-rating of Blake's sexual prowess.

"So, how about you and Corey? Have you guys hit the sheets yet?"

I opened my mouth to speak, but nothing emerged. I didn't exactly know how to answer that question. Yes, we'd been in bed together. No, we hadn't made love. Although we had sort of made love, I supposed. After all, he'd given me a number of orgasms over the previous days. But for sex, as in actual intercourse, then the answer was no. The situation was a little too complicated. Or maybe her question was too simplistic. Either way, I had no reply.

Thankfully, I wasn't coerced into giving her a long, drawn out explanation, because Corey came back up onto the sun deck with a tablet computer in his hand a sullen expression on his face.

"Uh, listen," I said into the phone. "I've got to go, but keep in touch if you've got any more news."

"Will do," Dani replied. "Take care."

"You too," I responded before bidding her goodbye and ending the call. Stuffing the cell back into my rear pocket, I looked questioningly at Corey. "What's wrong?"

"I'm not sure yet," he sighed, holding out the tablet for me to take. "But Blake's right: Tris isn't going to let this go without trying to destroy me."

"Destroy you?" I repeated, sure he must have been adding a melodramatic spin. However, as I took the computer and scanned the email sent from Tristan's account, I began to realize he wasn't exaggerating. Between ranting about how Corey must have 'cheated' during the race, he had sworn to get even one way or another.

'Bring Freya back now, or I swear to God you're going to wish you'd never met her. I will take down your fucking company and you with it. I don't care if it costs me every penny I own, I will get even with you!'

Lifting my gaze from the screen, I took in Corey's thoughtful eyes. "You want to go head back?" I asked.

"Why?" he countered.

Finding his simplistic query strange, I shook my head. "So, you can sort this out. You know, stop Tristan from doing whatever it is he's planning to do," I explained.

Inhaling deeply through his nose before releasing the breath loudly through pursed lips, he peered over his right shoulder. When he turned back to me, he was smiling. "You ever seen Corsica?" he wondered.

"What?"

"It's beautiful this time of year. We can sail all the way up the Med-"

"Corey," I blurted, halting his tempting ramble. "What about your business?"

"Let him do his worst," he shrugged. "All I care about right now is taking you to paradise. And nothing on this earth is going to stop me from doing that."

CHAPTER TWO

The Roof of the World

For the next seven days, Corey and I enjoyed the serene beauty of the Mediterranean's azure waters. The yacht made its leisurely way around the striking coastlines of Corsica and Sardinia, and I spent most of the daylight hours savoring the sensation of the sun on my skin or taking a dip in the surprisingly warm waters that surrounded us.

To me, this was paradise. Well, it was almost paradise. There was one thing missing. And the longer we spent together, the longer I felt his eyes on me, the more I experienced his hands, and lips, and tongue: the harder it was to accept his refusal to take things further. Despite the fact that he was never completely depriving me – not like he was depriving himself.I found myself feeling restless and incomplete, and it began to erode me.

Even though the feelings he stirred in me were stronger and more satisfying than any I'd ever had before, somehow I knew that it could be so much greater. After all, if simple touches and caresses were enough to make me quiver, logic told me that more would be... well, more.

Regardless of the almost painful anticipation, I couldn't bear to be apart from him, even for a few minutes. It was as though he'd replaced oxygen to me. However, realizing how 'needy' I'd seem if I expressed that thought, I kept it to myself and silently suffered every time he disappeared into his office.

He was never gone for very long, fortunately. But he did make frequent trips to check his emails and make phone calls, which made me wonder whether he was truly as blasй about Tristan's threats as he'd claimed to be. I certainly wasn't: I was terrified that soon Corey would get a phone call and our world would come crashing down. But he seemed unworried.

Meanwhile, the only thing I heard from Daniela or Blake was a text from the latter. 'Am thinking about surprising D with a last minute trip to Belize for Christmas. Do you think she'll be up for it?'

Assuming that meant that things were calming down in New York, I didn't bother to badger him with questions in reply. I simply wrote, 'Go for it!'

Still, I wasn't able to quite surrender myself to the moment and the incredible beauty around me. In contemplative moments, as I lounged in the Mediterranean, floating on my back and allowing my body to be softly undulated by small waves, my mind drifted to Tristan. All the mistakes I'd made, and the fact that I wouldn't forgive myself if my stupidity resulted in harm coming to Corey or his company, left a pit of despair in my stomach.

One afternoon, as those worries plagued me, I suddenly heard a splash to my right. Bolting up, I snapped my head around. My heart pounded wildly for a moment, until I realized that Corey was off to the side treading water, his dark hair emerging from beneath the crystal blue sea. He took a few strong, strokes toward me, and was soon right by my side. I felt a wave of relief wash over me as he entered my presence: a reassurance of sorts.

"Hey," he said, coming to a stop just arm's reach of me. "You stay out here much longer you're gonna start to look like a prune," he chuckled, flicking his head to shift the hair that was damply clinging to his brow.

"You spend all afternoon in front of that computer," I grumbled good-naturedly. "I come out here to find some company with the fish."

With an amused hum, he reached out with both hands and grabbed me. Pulling me close, he pressed me against his bare torso. As I felt his warm, wet, sun-kissed skin against mine, I couldn't help but let out a small whimper: it escaped me without a thought.

"I've just been eager to find out when your surprise is ready," he told me, his deep voice rumbling through me.

My body, as it always had, responded automatically to his presence, filling me with warmth as it readied itself for him. "Surprise?" I asked, trying to focus on the conversation rather than the desire that had been inflamed in me.

"Yeah," he smiled. "How do you feel about taking another trip?"

Snaking my arms around his neck, I laced my finger at his nape. "That depends," I hummed thoughtfully. "Is it going to be the right place?" I asked, knowing he'd interpret the emphasis.

"Yes," he replied unequivocally. "Yes, Freya," he added, nodding. "It's the perfect place."

"Then, how can I say no?" I replied.

That very afternoon, the yacht altered course and headed to the coast of Italy. We docked at Piombino. When we stepped off the yacht, Pierre was waiting for us. The Parisian chauffeur's face was tipped up to the glorious sun as he stood beside the open door of a scarlet Ferrari 458 Italia.

"Morning, Pierre," Corey said, slapping his employee heartily on the shoulder before smoothly lifting the trunk lid and tossing the two bags he was carrying inside. "Pleasant drive?" he asked.

"Oui, Monsieur Wallace," Pierre beamed in reply. "You know, sometimes I can't believe you pay me for this. Mademoiselle," he added, nodding to me as he slipped his sunglasses from his face and met my eyes.

"Good morning," I replied, smiling in return.

"I trust you've been having a good time?" he asked.

"Yes, thank you," I responded.

"And I'm sure you're going to love-"

"Uh uh," Corey quickly uttered, stalling whatever Pierre had been about to say. Closing the trunk, he turned quickly, placing an index finger to his lips. "Miss Moreton doesn't know where we're going yet," he explained to his driver.

"Ahh," Pierre crooned, nodding gleefully. "A surprise, huh? Well, she is sure to love it."

Sharing a subtle glance with his employee, Corey made his way to the passenger side and opened the door. "Ready?" he asked, lifting his face to me.

With no need for words, I stepped forward. I was wearing a summer dress and sandals: just two of the items of clothing he'd bought for me before we left Paris. I peered up at the warm rays that Pierre had been so enjoying, and wondered how I could be so lucky. Grinning at the man who had quickly become my fixation, I nodded my gratitude at his chivalry before slipping into the car.

I couldn't help but notice that, before shutting the door, he took a long, appreciative look of the expanse of leg that was afforded his gaze by the slit in my dress, which ran up my outer right thigh.

When he felt the weight of my stare, he lifted his eyes and smiled brightly. "Have I told you how beautiful you are?" he asked.

Smiling a little bashfully, I shrugged. "Not today," I replied.

"Well, that was very remiss of me," he commented dryly, his hand sliding down the edge of the door as he dropped onto his haunches. Crouching beside me, he slipped a soft, smooth hand over my bare, bronzed knee. "You. Are. Beautiful." He emphasized each word, although they were intimately spoken.

Covering his larger hand with my own delicate fingers, I sucked in a breath that caught in the back of my throat. "If you're not going to ravage me right here and now," I said shakily, "you're going to have to stop that."

Chuckling, his gaze dipped back to my thigh. "I'm not going to ravage you, Freya," he almost whispered, making me wonder whether he really intended me to hear. "I'm not going to take anything from you," he added as he pulled his eyes slowly up my form, settling once more on my face. Smiling, his fingers moved subtly, massaging the curve of my knee. "I want to give you everything," he breathed. "I want to give you the world."

"I don't want the world," I countered. "I just want you."

"Well, you've got me," he promised.

Falling deeper and deeper, emotion swelling in me, my eyes filled with unshed tears. Habit made me feel vulnerable and embarrassed by the intensity of my feelings, and I hurriedly shook my head. "Come on," I sighed, squeezing the hand that continued to move beneath mine. "Let's get wherever it is we're going."

"Okay," he grinned as he leaned forward and kissed my cheek. Then, with a soft, almost regretful sigh, he straightened and quietly closed the door.

Everything with Corey was an adventure. He drove us from Piombino to Rome. The three-hour journey, much of it along the coast, afforded some beautiful scenery. He was as enthusiastic about the vista as I was, although I was sure he'd seen it many times before.

When we arrived in Rome, he decided to give me a quick tour, showing me the Piazza Navona, the Pantheon, and Nero's Aqueduct. He was clearly enjoying showing me the sights; however, I found that there was one monument I had yet to see. It had been in front of me for a long time, but I had yet to get a glimpse, and it was the only thing on my mind.

"I'm sorry that we can't spend longer looking at the city," he apologized as we settled back in the car and drove to Leonardo da Vinci Airport. "We'll come back another time," he added. "We can spend a week or two seeing everything."

"That sounds nice," I replied quietly, staring out the window.

"You okay?" he asked curiously. "You seem a little quiet."

"Just tired," I replied, offering him a small smile. It wasn't a complete lie: I was beginning to grow a little weary. But, more than exhaustion, my distraction was caused by my own thoughts. They were thoughts of Tristan. I couldn't help comparing my dates with him to the ones I had with Corey.

With Corey, where we went and what we did, regardless of how wonderful, wasn't as important as the fact I was with him. And that made me realize something: my infatuation for Tristan was, predominately, a shallow one.

I'd been dazzled by the places he took me, the things he bought, the cars he drove, the hotels we stayed at. It was all exciting and heady. It was a world I hadn't known and never thought I'd get a chance to. And it was that which attracted me to Tristan. I'd been, effectively, prostituting myself – he'd been right about me: there really wasn't anything I wouldn't be prepared to do.

Maybe it had been the same with my professor, John Lytton. Perhaps at an unconscious level, I had gotten into that highly inappropriate relationship because I knew I'd get something out of it.

No, I knew that wasn't true. I had wanted something from John, but it wasn't money or any other material item. I'd wanted love: the love of a father figure.

"Freya," Corey gently nudged.

Snapping from my thoughts, I lifted my head and found him standing by the open passenger door.

"We're here," he grinned.

'Here' was a private strip upon which stood the plane he'd told me about: the Dassault Falcon 7X. It was a business jet, with the Wallace Enterprises logo on the tail fin. As I gradually came back to myself, I got out of the car and took in the scale of the plane, which was larger than some of the domestic airlines jets I'd flown in.

"How many of us are going... and where we're going?" I asked, stunned.

"You, me and Andrew, the other pilot," he replied, smiling.

He neglected to answer my second question.

"Other pilot?" I repeated.

"I'm going to fly us some of the way," he explained.

"You fly, too?"

"Yeah." He grinned. "You ever been in a cockpit?"

I shook my head.

"It's an incredible feeling," he commented fervently. "You'll come up and sit with me, won't you?" he wondered. "For a little while, anyway?"

"Try and keep me away," I chuckled, walking side by side with him across the asphalt, our shoulders brushing as we stepped in perfect synchronicity.

Stopping at the bottom of the steps, Corey gestured for me to go first, but he remained close behind me: close enough, in fact, that I could feel his soft breath on the back of my neck and the heat of his groin against my buttocks.

I was about to twist my head over my shoulder when I was greeted at the cabin door by a pilot.He was dressed in a full navy suit, complete with a gold insignia and epaulettes.

"Good evening, Miss Moreton," he smiled, giving me a casual salute with his index finger.

"Hello," I replied, not stopping to ask how he knew my name.

"Mr. Wallace," the pilot added, giving him the same gesture. "We'll be ready to go in a few minutes," he continued. "Did you want to get us off the ground, sir?"

"Err, no," Corey replied. "I'm going to show Miss Moreton around, make sure she's settled in. I'll take over from you later," he said, smoothing his hand across the small of my back before curling his fingers around my waist.

The cabin was like nothing I'd ever seen. Light, airy, and with dazzling white walls, it had small windows dotted throughout the length. There were two cream leather couches with ruby red cushions. Then, further down, sat four seats: two on either side of the cabin. Each seat was spacious and, so Corey told me, reclined all the way back. In the back of the cabin was a door that led to three large bedrooms. Each of them housed a king-size bed, a large television screens and a private bathroom.

"You could play football in this thing," I commented dryly, as he showed me the last of them.

"Well, I made a few modifications," he replied, wandering toward the large bed and perching himself on the edge of it. "The plane was originally intended for up to nineteen passengers. But it's rare that I travel with that kind of entourage, so I decided to make it a luxurious space for the handful of people I do fly with."

With an understanding hum, I nodded.

A slight crackle came across the intercom, "Mr. Wallace, we're ready for takeoff, so make sure you're safely buckled up."

Getting up, he casually slipped his hand in mine, something that seemed to have become natural to both of us, and led me back out into the main cabin. Dropping into one of the couches, he buckled his belt with ease, while I fumbled slightly with my own. He watched me, with a slightly amused wiggle of his eyebrows, but he didn't patronize me by taking over.

A little annoyed at being rattled by such a simple device, I puffed a strand of hair out of my eyes. Eventually, with a satisfied sigh of victory, I mastered the thing and flopped back in the seat.

I think, shortly after that, I must have fallen asleep. And, I assume, Corey carried me to the bedroom, because I don't remember making it there under my own steam. Nevertheless, that's where I found myself as my eyes fluttered open. Still clothed, but beneath the warm covers, I blinked away my disorientation enough to realize it was dark. Pushing the bedclothes aside, I rubbed the backs of my hands over half-closed eyes and shuffled off the luxuriously comfortable bed.

Taking a detour to the bathroom, I splashed some water on my face, brushed my teeth and straightened my unruly hair before heading back out into the cabin. But I didn't find Corey there. In fact, I didn't find anybody.

I considered the possibility that he was getting some sleep, but couldn't figure out why he'd use one of the other rooms when we'd already spent ten nights in the same bed. My questions were answered nearly immediately.

"Freya." His silky voice filled the cabin over the intercom. "Come up to the cockpit. I want to show you the view."

Following his direction, I walked forward and found the cockpit door fractionally ajar. I pushed it open and saw him seated on the right, headset in place, hands on the control yoke.

Through the broad front windows, I could see dozens of lights glimmering beneath gossamer clouds. The moon, meanwhile, was dazzling bright. It was breathtaking.

"It's something, huh?" he chuckled, noticing the mesmerized expression in my eyes.

"Yeah," I breathed. "It's amazing. Is this what you were talking about when you said you wanted to take me to the roof of the world?" I asked him, feeling as if we were looking down on the entire planet, even though I knew that wasn't even close to being true.

"No," he chuckled. "No, we're not quite there yet. But not much longer."

"How long have we been in the air?" I asked, my feet stepping forward unbidden as I rested my hand on the back of his chair. My fingers barely brushed his shoulder, but I felt the spark as powerfully as ever.

"About six hours," he replied.

"And am I allowed to ask where we are?" I probed, trying to ignore the clawing impulse to slip onto his lap and rub myself to orgasm against him.

"I don't see why not." He shrugged. "We somewhere close to the border between Afghanistan and Pakistan," he told me.

"Pakistan?"

"Hmm," he confirmed with a nod and a mischievous smile. He clearly enjoyed keeping me in suspense... in more ways than one. I longed for the moment when the tension would release in every one of those ways.

"And how much longer to go?" I continued in my steady line of questioning. I knew that his answer would mean very little to me. I had no sense of how far we'd travel in an hour, nor did my sense of direction give me a clue as to where we were heading.

He paused for a moment, glancing at a couple of dials on the dash in front of him. "Three hours," he replied. "Maybe a little less."

"And..."

"Uh uh," he quickly said, laughing. "No more questions. You've been given all the clues you're going to get."

***

Annoyingly, he held as firm to that as he did to his vow not to make love to me until we'd reached the perfect place and time. On top of this frustration was the fact that I couldn't persuade him to leave the cockpit and come back to the bedroom with me. I wanted to drag him back to the bedroom myself, but it would be futile: I was no match for his gentle strength.

Regret evident in his eyes, he refused. "Andrew's only had an hour's sleep," he explained. "I can't ask him to come back and take over already."

30

"Doesn't this thing have some sort of autopilot?" I exclaimed in a last ditch effort.

His eyes shown amusement asI said it, and the corners of his mouth quirked upwards in faint a smile.

"It doesn't work quite like that, I'm afraid. Someone still has to be here."

Unable to hide my disappointment, I nodded silently.

"Soon," he added, smiling. "Soon, Freya."

Soon. The one word was enough to flood me with nervous excitement. It felt like I'd been waiting for him forever. And, I suppose, in many ways, I had. I'd been waiting my whole life for someone who made me feel the way he did.

The wait was almost over. And that thought filled me with both joy and dread. Dread, because I wanted so desperately to please him as much as he had already pleased me. He'd set the bar high... impossibly so.

Suggesting that I go back to the cabin and relax, Corey returned his focus to the task at hand.

Not wanting to be left alone with my thoughts, I asked him if I could stay a while longer.

"Sure," he replied, as if there was never any question. "Make yourself comfortable," he suggested, flicking his head to the seat by his side.

I slipped into the vacant copilot's chair, gazing at the silky clouds that passed below us. For a long time, we remained that way, sitting in companionable silence. Occasionally, my eyes were drawn to him and I find him staring back at me. Smiles were shared, but no words were spoken. They didn't need to be.

The better part of three hours passed incredibly quickly, and then Andrew disturbed the blissful silence.

"Are we ready to start the descent, Corey?" he asked, adjusting his tie with one hand as he straightened his jacket with the other.

"We'll be coming up on Paro in a few minutes," Corey replied.

Without needing to be asked, I autocratically vacated the seat, assuming that the pilot wished to sit down.

He smiled gratefully, as he slipped in behind me and gave the dials a cursory glance. "All looks good," he commented, predominantly to himself. "Right, let's get ready to put this baby down."

"It's okay, Freya," Corey grinned. "Go ahead and get comfortable in the cabin."

"You're not coming?" I wondered.

"No, I'm going to stay here, give Andrew an extra pair of eyes and hands. It's a tricky strip to put down on, even for someone of his caliber."

"Why, thank you, Corey," his pilot chuckled. "High praise indeed."

"All right," I mumbled, sensing that I'd just be in the way if I lingered any longer. Turning, I heard the two of them discussing the weather and the altitude before I left the cockpit and walked listlessly through to the cabin. It momentarily drifted through my mind to go back to the bedroom, but I figured sleep was beyond me – besides, I'd probably messed up my internal clock enough by having such a long nap. And then, of course, there was the change in time zone. I didn't even know what time zone we were in any more. However, through the small windows, I could see soft amber light beginning to emerge on the distant horizon.

Nestled in the eastern Himalayas between India and Tibet, Few are privileged to enter this Himalayan Kingdom, where a unique way of life is protected from the 21st Century. Long isolated from the world at large, Bhutan's landscapes are pristine and its traditional cultures fascinating. Thimphu, the capital of Bhutan, lies in a beautiful wooded valley, sprawling up a hillside on the banks of a river. All Bhutanese art, dance, drama and music is steeped in Buddhism and represent a struggle between good and evil.

Slumping into the couch, I could only watch as the earth began to loom closer. The first thing I could really make out of the terrain below was that there were huge snow-capped mountains. Gradually, green valleys came into view. Pulling my feet up, I twisted so that I could look through the window over my shoulder just as the wing began to dip that way.Apparently we were going to land in the mountains.

Confused, but trusting the men on the flight deck to know what they were doing, I watched with my heart in my mouth as we began to fly directly through one of the valleys. Rationally, I knew the oppressive mountainsides either side of us couldn't be that close, but it seemed frighteningly claustrophobic.

Craning a little, I tried to get a look at the landing strip below. There appeared to only be one. It was narrow and had very dull lights tracing it. No more than a few yards from the runway was a wide stream with a surface so still it could have been a sheet of ice.

Not realizing I was holding my breath, I waited for what I expected to be a ferocious bump. But, as we touched smoothly, I exhaled. Once we were on the ground, my gaze moved to the still closed cockpit door, waiting eagerly for Corey to emerge and finally tell me what was going on.

It was a long few seconds as the plane drew to a halt, and before the pristine white panel opened. But eventually, Corey opened the door to the cabin and stepped inside.

"See, told you." He grinned. "Is this guy good or what?" he chuckled, pointing a thumb over his shoulder at the pilot who was scribbling on a clipboard.

Andrew didn't bother to look up, but I could see the crinkle in the corners of his eyes that came with the broad smile.

"Well, here we are," Corey added, taking a long stride and standing before me.

"And where is here?" I asked, unfurling my legs and pushing myself from the seat.

"Bhutan," he smiled.

"Bhutan?" I replied, wide-eyed. "You.... Are you serious?"

His smile growing wider, he slipped one hand in his pocket and shrugged. "I think you're really going to love it," he said. "And I have a gift for you."

"Bringing me here is a gift," I said, feeling lightheaded.

With his free hand, he reached forward and gently took mine between his fingers. "No," he softly uttered. "You being here is a gift to me," he corrected me smoothly. "But, I promise, I'm going to spend all the time we share here making you feel as good as you make me feel."

"Oh, Corey," I sighed, shaking my head. How did he do that? How did he know exactly what to say, when to say it and how?

He was a romantic in every sense of the word, and he had an incredible knack for making me feel special. Really special. I didn't feel like some prize, a bauble that he liked to keep on his arm to improve his own image. Having me by his side didn't seem to have anything to do with image.

Paro international airport Bhutan

Paro international airport Bhutan

Paro international airport Bhutan

In fact, it had nothing to do with anybody, except us. Corey didn't need to make a big show: there was no need for ostentatious gifts to make me feel wanted. Just a few words… a few simple words… was all it took to make me feel like a queen in his eyes.

"Come on," he said suddenly, squeezing my hand and guiding me to the door that Andrew was opening.

"Have a good time," the pilot offered, as we walked past him and hustled down the steps.

"We will, " Corey called back, barely pausing in his stride.

I was mesmerized by the landscape around me. Even though we were in the middle of an airfield, the scenery was enough to rob the air from my lungs. Ironically, it was reminiscent of the way I'd felt when I first set eyes on Corey. Bhutan, like him, seemed to hold a special place in my heart, even though I'd never been there before. For some reason, they both seemed very familiar to me.

Below, on the narrow strip an attractive olive-skinned woman stood beside a silver Jeep Grand Cherokee. Even though the sun was just coming up, the air around us was dry and mild: not as hot as the weather we'd left behind in the Mediterranean, but much warmer than it would have been in New York.

The woman wore a pair of knee-length chino shorts with an open, light blue blouse over a camisole top. One thumb was stuck casually in her belt loop, while the other hand twirled a pair of sunglasses around and around.

I noticed the unmistakable smile she gave Corey, and tried to remind myself that everyone (even the men who worked for him) greeted him in a similar way. It didn't mean anything... did it? She was, after all, a real beauty. She had long black hair that cascaded down to her shoulder blades, and luxurious lashes that veiled mysterious dark eyes.

After gazing at her for a second, I looked up at the man by my side and tried to gauge his reaction to her.

"Srista," he smiled, keeping my hand tightly clasped in his. "Thanks for arranging everything. I really appreciate it. This is Freya," he added, introducing me.

She shifted her focus to me, smiled and nodded a greeting. "I'm SristaNawang," she said, her Indian accent more pronounced as she spoke her name. "But, call me Srista: we don't use last names here in Bhutan." Then, her attention swiftly moved back to Corey. "Your palace is ready," she informed him proudly, removing the thumb she'd hooked in her shorts and opening her palm to reveal two sets of keys: one of them was obviously for the car.

"Thanks," Corey replied, scooping them from her palm and slipping both into his pocket.

"Like you asked, there are some clothes in the back seat, specifically jackets. You might find it gets a little cold up there."

"Up where?" I asked, looking between the two of them in confusion.

"The palace," Corey said, with a half-smile. "Your palace," he added. Releasing my hand, he smoothed his palm over the small of my back. "It's my gift to you."

"A palace?" I asked incredulously. What the hell was he talking about?

"The builders worked around the clock to finish it," Srista piped up. "And my team has been toiling hard to ensure it is decorated and comfortable for you both." Leaning back against the Jeep, she looked very satisfied with herself. "I really think you're going to like it."

"Well... I... I'm sure I will," I breathed. Twisting my head to Corey, I stared at him. "A palace?" I repeated.

"It's a palace," he shrugged. "Hopefully, you will like it."

With that, too stunned to ask any more questions, I allowed myself to be steered toward the Jeep and helped up into the high passenger seat. Before getting into the driver's seat, Corey fumbled around in a large valise in on the back seat. After a few moments, he emerged with a thick sweater in his hands. Climbing behind the wheel, he gently laid the garment across my lap. "You're probably going to need this," he said. "We're going up to the Himalayas," he said, as if it was no big deal. "It's about 4,000 meters above sea level, so it can get pretty chilly, especially this time of year. But the view is worth it."

"Oh... Um...." Sure I was about to wake up and find myself alone, in bed in my apartment, still engaged to Tristan and pining over the man beside me, I shook my head. "Okay," I mumbled with a quirk of my shoulder. What else could I say?

"This is it," he softly said, taking my hand in his and lifting it to his face. "This is the start of an entirely new chapter in both of our lives," he added before kissing my knuckles reverently. "I have a feeling it's going to be a good one."

We're going up to the Himalayas

CHAPTER THREE

The Love Nest

The house seemed to be in an impossible location. Right on the edge of a mountainside, it was modern in its expanse of glass, but it was also traditional, with wooden beams and a butterfly roof. As we drove up the winding, craggy roads I couldn't help but wonder how equipment and materials had been transported to the site.

"What do you think?" Corey asked, pulling the car to a stop outside large double front doors.

"It's... it's incredible," I said, my eyes moving from the house to the stunning area surrounding it. We were high enough that we looked down on smaller mountains, and even smaller homes. In the distance, there were snow-capped mountain peaks, and sprawling, unspoiled blue skies.

"I hoped you would like it," he said softly. "It's our love nest, Freya," he added. "Our spot away from the rest of the world. Here, if we want to, we can get away from everyone and everything. It's just you and me."

"Sounds like paradise," I replied, smiling as I continued to gaze at the addictive view.

"That's my intent. Let me show you around," he grinned.

I climbed down from the jeep, following him as he took me around to the side of the building where there was a fire pit, some wrought iron furniture and a rattan pod chair, which was swinging from the overhanging roof that sheltered the outdoor living space.

Realizing how right he'd been about the change in temperature, I pulled the sweater over my head as he pointed to the mists that hung over the small mountains below. There was a chill in the subtle breeze, and a dampness that could chill to the bone that I hadn't felt

41

in the valley. The air around us was much thinner, too. I could feel the difference with every breath. My lungs were forced to work that little bit harder, but it was worth it.Every inhale was filled with incredibly fresh, clean air.

"See what I mean?" He chuckled. "Roof of the world."

He was right; it did feel like we were as high as it was possible to be, peering down on the rest of the planet. It was a sight that made me feel insignificantly small. Wrapping my arms around myself, I stared ahead of me, completely captivated.

Corey stepped closer, tenderly slipping his arm around my shoulders and pressing himself to me. "Too cold?" he quietly asked.

Not quite able to take my eyes from the view, I simply shook my head. "Thank you," I breathed. "Thank you so much for bringing me here."

His fingers moving smoothly over my arm, he tipped his head down to mine and kissed my hair. "Thank you for coming with me," he said, smiling. "You're freezing," he commented, rubbing my arm vigorously.

Reluctant to leave the addictive view, I resisted his attempt to steer me into the house. "I'm okay," I told him.

"You sure?"

Twisting my face to his, I blinked up at his concerned eyes. "I'm not ready to go in yet," I whispered.

"There are some beautiful views from in there, too," he countered.

"I can imagine," I replied, briefly turning to look at the three-story structure. "But I just want to linger here a little longer."

"Okay," he nodded.

Silently, he let me drink in my surroundings, gradually coming to the realization that everything around me was real. As the arm gently tightened around me, I was reminded that he was very real, too.

"So?" I eventually sighed. "This is it? This is the perfect place you've made me wait for, right?"

Softly smiling, he dropped his head until it was resting on mine. "I think so," he exhaled. "What do you think?"

For almost two weeks, I'd been waiting for this moment. I had been waiting for him to tell me that we'd reached that ideal place and time. Impatiently, I'd been counting the days, imagining what it would be like to finally be one with him. And now that moment had arrived, nervous anticipation had become something close to terror. It wasn't imagination any more, which meant things wouldn't play out as I could force them to in my mind. He'd waited for it all to be perfect, but what if it wasn't. What if I wasn't perfect?

Who was I kidding? I wasn't going to be perfect. I'd never been perfect in my life – not to Mom, not to my dad, not to any lover I'd ever had. Even Tristan had wanted to change me. It was no longer about "what if." I was certain that now that the moment was upon me I would fail miserably. Corey was going to be disappointed, and once again, when everything was going so well, my life was going to implode. I was almost ready to hyperventilate just thinking about it, and I considered just turning around and running away.

"Freya?" Corey murmured, lifting his head and turning to look at me. "Sweetheart, there's no pressure. If you're not ready, I can wait."

Shaking my head, I forced my focus to his eyes, knowing that something within them always had the power to still my rampantly questioning mind. "I am ready," I assured him confidently. "I feel like I've been ready all my life. I'm just..."

"Scared?" he offered.

"N-" I pressed my lips together firmly before I had a chance to deny it. I didn't want to lie to him. Although it was my instinctive self-preserving reaction to refute any sense of fear, it was equally natural to open myself completely to him. "Yes," I admitted quietly, "a little bit."

With a warmth that made me weak in the knees, he smiled at me. Then, slowly, he lifted both hands and cupped my face between them. "There's no need to be," he promised softly. "You can trust me."

Anxiously gripping my lower lip between my teeth, I warred with myself on just how open I should be: how open did I want to be? "I know," I eventually replied. "And I do trust you."

"Then everything will be okay," he responded simply. Gradually he stroked the pad of his thumb across my cheekbone, such an uncomplicated, unassuming gesture. Yet, it had the force to stir desire that banished all other concerns.

"Corey," I whispered, unconsciously leaning into his touch.

"Just let it happen, Freya," he quietly replied. "Just relax and let your body and soul tell you what they want."

My eyelids trembled, fluttering closed, and I craved the sensation of his lips on mine. I didn't have to ask for them. I felt the warmth of his breath caressing my face momentarily, a precursor to his touch. Delicately, he pressed his mouth to mine, melding to them as if for the very first time.

My hands slid forward, smoothing over his abdomen before slinking around his waist and tugging him close. My lips automatically parted beneath the pressure and I slowly extended my tongue. The tip tasted him lightly, but all too soon, his deliciousness was gone. Disgruntled, I groan as I forced my eyes open.

His gaze met mine and the dark pools of light twinkled as he chuckled. "Let's go inside," he suggested, reaching behind him and taking my hand in his.

Without complaint, I allowed him to lead me through the large glass doors into a sleekly decorated living area, with contemporary furniture mingled with traditional Bhutanese rugs. A large fireplace at one end of the room had two couches placed in a V in front of it.

He took me through the room to the first of two flights of stairs of bare mahogany wood. The staircase was easily wide enough for three people to walk abreast and the wall on the right hand side was covered with artwork.

The home was massive, even bigger than his Florida villa, Nirvana. We passed a large number of rooms, not stopping to explore any of them – he knew exactly where he was heading. Eventually, at the end of a hallway, he opened the door to the master bedroom. It was approximately the same size as the living room. And, like the living room, had windows all along the mountain-facing wall. He was right: the views from inside were just as striking, if not more so.

With the headboard against the opposite wall providing a ridiculously beautiful sight to anyone who woke up in it, the California king size bed was dressed in crisp, white linen.

Still holding my hand, Corey drew me further across the hardwood floor. Quietly, he opened a door on the right, which opened onto a large, marble-floored bathroom.

A corner tub sat at one end, and a large cubicle shower, which was easily large enough for four people, stood opposite it. Next to the shower was a long counter with two sinks and a pile of three small, ruby red towels beside each.

Despite the cold touch of the marble, the room was warm. There was a soft light that came from the dozens of tiny bulbs embedded in the ceiling. On the wall adjacent to the bath was a heated rail upon which hung a luxurious, large towel and a white, silk gown.

"Why don't you take a soak and relax," he suggested, his voice deeper and more commanding than I'd ever know it. Perhaps the anticipation was affecting him, too. Or maybe that timbre was simply in my imagination.

"Are you going to get in with me?" I asked, a playful smile teasing at the corners of my mouth.

Softly, he shook his head. "I want to get a few things ready."

"Ready?"

"Hmm," he confirmed. "I want to get the mood just right."

I didn't know exactly what that meant, but as he carefully removed his hand from mine, I didn't ask him to explain.

"You should find everything you need," he added, smiling as he took a step back. "But shout if you want anything else."

I remained almost motionless, only my upper half twisted so I could keep my focus on him as he gracefully backed out of the room. His dark eyes lingered on my face, and his generous smile beamed until he reached the door and gently tugged it closed behind him.

Suddenly very aware of my racing heart, I took a deep breath before twisting toward the tub and bending to turn the faucets on.

***

I suppose I must have been lounging in the water for about twenty minutes when it began to get tepid. During that time, I'd strained to hear any movement from the room next door. I'd tried to calm my frenzied mind, and had resisted the urge to allow my hand to slip between my legs. My body was ripe to be touched after two weeks of previewing his expertise. My core was pulsing, hot and needy with the overpowering expectation of a completion I'd yearned for.

Fingers trembling with excitement and nerves, I reached for the towel as I pushed myself from the chilling water. I hurriedly dried my body before slipping on the luxuriously smooth robe, which reached mid-thigh, and quickly tied the thin belt around my middle.

Swallowing an anxious lump in my throat, I moved to the door and opened it.

The first thing that struck me was the smell: an intoxicating scent of jasmine. It filled the room and danced across the air toward me. The next thing I noticed were candles: they were everywhere. Providing the only light in the room, they offered a clement glow.

The sheets were turned down invitingly and, at the foot of the sturdy, chrome bed frame stood Corey. He was bare-chested, wearing nothing but a pair of white silk pajama pants.

I was reminded of his chiseled physique: his broad shoulders, tightly toned abdomen and his hard, masculine pecs. My legs began to tremble and weaken, and I found that as much as I wanted to, I couldn't move.

Flashing a smile that showed all his perfect, dazzlingly bright teeth, he gazed back at me. Gradually his eyes moved down the length of my body, as if committing me to memory. My heart seemed to stop under the weight of his stare. I waited expectantly for some hint of disappointment to cross his features. However, the wide grin never faltered, not even for a second.

"You look incredible," he eventually murmured.

"So do you," I responded weakly, my voice catching in a tight, dry throat. Feeling overwhelmed by the flood of sensations that the sight of him stirred in me, I found myself unable to take him all in. Instead, my focus shifted to his thick, dark hair and a subtle curl in one strand above his ear.

"Freya," he said calmly, "come here."

Certain my legs wouldn't carry me, I remained frozen and silent. The only part of me that moved was the heavy thudding of my heart, which crashed against my chest violently.

Unperturbed, Corey stepped forward, keeping his movements steady and sure. As he reached me, both hands swept naturally forward, cupping my hips as if they belonged to him.

Blinking, I forced my eyes to meet his. My lips parted slightly as my need for oxygen increased. Shyly I lifted my fingers and with the lightest touch, brushed the palms of my hands along the smooth skin if his abdomen.

"I want to see you," he said, as he delicately gripped the belt of my robe and tugged it free.

I shuddered visibly as the air hit my exposed skin, but it was arousal rather than a chill that slid goose bumps over every inch of my flesh.

Corey smiled reassuringly as the backs of his fingers grazed my belly and he pushed the bathrobe aside.

"Oh, God," I hissed, grabbing his forearms for support as my feeble knees quaked and moisture heated my core with sparks of fire.

Somewhere in the back of my mind, where a few sane thoughts still dwelt, I wondered how it was possible for him to have such a profound effect on me with relatively little effort. However, those thoughts – and anything else that lingered in my brain – were quickly swept away when he leaned forward and pressed his lips to my neck.

He kissed my throat lightly, and then his tongue darted forward, tasting the delicate skin. Opening his soft lips, he sucked gently, moving his lips down to my collarbone.

Restlessly, I shifted my weight from one leg to the other, my thighs brushing and stimulating the electrical buzzing I felt between them. Meanwhile, my grip on his arms tightened.

"You smell so good," he mumbled softly, not lifting his head as his mouth continued to trail across my clavicle to the soft dip between them. His hands were slowly sliding over my flared hips, long fingers caressing the curve of my buttocks.

Unconsciously, I breathed deeply of him: sandalwood was wafting from his hair and merging with the jasmine.

The tip of his curious tongue danced in the concave flesh at the base of my throat before he began to lick his way down my sternum.

Whimpering, I clenched my thighs, desperate for relief from the disquiet that ached for pressure. My clitoris, painfully swollen with urgency, tingled. My sex, moist and eager, clenched expectantly.

Corey's hands clutched my ass in both strong hands, massaging the globes of flesh with self-assured hands. I bucked in response, pressing my lower half to the prominent curve that pushed at the smooth fabric of his pajamas.

"Ahh," I gasped, sucking in a large lungful of air.

I felt his lips quirk, but he didn't raise his face. His mouth was busy traversing the outer curve of my breast.

My right hand snapping up to the back of his head, I gripped his hair as he kissed and licked his way around the breast in ever decreasing circles. By the time he reached my nipple, it was achingly hard.

"Corey!" I cried out, arousal coating my inner thighs when he sucked the stiff peak into his warm mouth. Eyes slamming shut, I tossed my face to the ceiling, panting as my sex swelled. Unbidden my hips undulated and I rubbed myself whorishly against his thick, muscular thigh.

Slowly, with dilated pupils, he lifted his face to mine. "Still feeling scared?" he asked softly.

"I want you," I gasped. "Please, Corey, I-"

He silenced me with a deep and passionate kiss, his tongue sensually diving into my mouth and curling around mine with a low groan, which emerged from his chest and pulsed into me with intense vibrations.

"Hmm," I mumbled into his open mouth, both hands grasping the back of his neck and pulling him closer.

His naked chest pressed against my bosom, his hot skin branding me. "Freya," he whispered, pulling back from the kiss. "Oh, God, you're beautiful," he sighed, his eyes moving sensually over my face while his hands continued to mold my buttocks.

"Corey," I muttered, my voice so weak that sound barely crept from my lips. "I need you."

"I'm here," he replied simply and calmly. "I'm right here." With that, he gently removed his hands from my ass and took the thin robe in his fingers. Deftly, he pushed the silky material from my shoulders and let it drop to the hard floor.

My entire body quivering, I stood naked before him, waiting impatiently for him to put his hands on me again.

He remained temperate and cool, his eyes the only part of him that appreciatively ravished me. Starting at my long, dark hair he shifted his gaze down over my pale skin, lingering over my full breasts: the areolas dark and flushed with excitement, the turgid nipples straining for him. Leisurely, he moved lower, tracing my scooped waist and the curve of my hips before finally dipping to my long legs.

"Corey," I pleaded, my own gaze captivated by the swell at his groin, which tented his pajama bottoms.

"It's all right," he replied, smiling as he smoothly lifted his hand and offered it to me. "Just relax, Freya," he added calmly. "Breathe."

Following his instruction, I inhaled deeply as I placed my quivering fingers into his palm. He quickly wrapped his own strong hand around mine and pulled me toward him with a gentle tug.

I put up no resistance, stepping forward and feeling the surge of pleasure that accompanied the brushing of my thighs.

His dark and intense gaze still moving affectionately over my exposed skin, Corey smiled as he led me toward the bed. "Lie down," he whispered, placing his lips next to my ear and pressing his soft cheek to my face.

My tongue cleaved to the roof of my dry mouth, and I nodded my ascent.I sat down anxiously on the edge of the spacious, spongy mattress.

"On your front," he added, grinning.

"Wh...what?" I asked.

"Lie down on your front," Corey explained, slowly disengaging his fingers from mine and reaching for a bottle that sat on the bedside table.

Sudden panic struck me. What exactly did he have in mind? Was the bottle lubricant of some kind? Was he planning on anal sex? I'd never engaged in any kind of anal play before, let alone penetration.

"I... I..." I stammered. "I don't... um..." As I continued to babble fruitlessly, I watched Corey unscrew the bottle and pour a few drops of some scented oil into the palm of his hand.

"Something wrong?" he asked as he replaced the cap and rubbed the liquid between his fingers.

"It's just... I...."

"Relax," he urged. "Trust me."

Swallowing with difficulty, I nodded and scooted back onto the bed. Rolling over on the cool, clean sheets, I exhaled slowly as I twisted my face to one side and pressed my cheek into the plush, plump pillow.

I felt the mattress give as Corey climbed onto the bed. However, for several long moments, he didn't touch me. Then, just as I opened my mouth to speak his name, his hands, slick with oil, were on my shoulders.

A groan of release was pulled from somewhere deep in my belly as he began massaging me with firm, steady strokes. Sweeping the palms all the way down my spine, he stopped just short of my buttocks before sliding all the way back to the nape of my neck.

"Feel okay?" he asked quietly.

"Oh, God, yes," I whimpered, unsure how the movement of his hands across my back could be felt so profoundly at the juncture of my thighs.

"Tell me if you need it harder," he added.

At the mention of the word 'harder,' my brain was assaulted by the images of him on top of me; inside me; thrusting; stretching me; filling me. My body reacted in kind, pulsing and seeping yet more excitement from my heated sex.

As his hands wrapped lightly around my neck and his thumbs circled my nape, his mouth hovered over my shoulder, lingering close enough that I could feel the gentle play of his breath. But his lips still too far away to actually touch me.

"Breathe," he reminded me quietly before finally seeking my skin with his mouth.

"Ahh," I groaned, my hips quivering and jerking.

I heard him chuckle gently as the small spikes of pleasure rocked me. "That's right," he mumbled, lips still brushing my shoulder blade. "Relax and let it come."

"Corey," I mewled. "I'm so...." Desperate for you? Ready to feel you moving in me? Horny that I feel like I'm about to explode? Any of those would have been accurate descriptions of how I felt, but none of them made it further than my head. I succumbed to the pleasure on a visceral level.

"You're perfect," he commented calmly. "Do you have any idea?" His mouth trailed opened mouthed kisses down the length of my spine.

Each caress of his lips caused me to release a whimper of pleasure, and my need grew so potent it was painful. My body was no longer simply 'ready' for him. It was demanding him. It wanted him unequivocally. With a hunger I'd never felt before, I realized there was no question anymore. I had to feel him inside me. And I had to feel him no. I'd die without it.

"Corey, I can't wait any longer!" I insisted, the words croaked from my constricted throat.

With a motion so sudden that it caught by surprise, he grasped my hips and flipped me onto my back.

"Ahh," I gasped as I bounced lightly on the mattress springs. Blinking, I found him kneeling beside me, his palms on either side of my arms and his upper body leaning over mine.

"Freya," he said reverently, his eyes flashing with fiery, naked desire that made my insides melt. "I want to make this last," he whispered. "I want to linger over every second."

"Corey," I replied, my hips instinctively rising in invitation.

With a crooked smile, he dipped his head, his face sinking between my breasts and his lips playfully sliding down my torso.

Whimpering as I tossed my head back into the pillow, my lower half undulated restlessly while my hands moved unbidden to tangle into his hair. When he reached my naval and his tongue darted quickly in, intense spasms wracked me.A spike of heat shot down from my abdomen into my sex.

His right hand slid smoothly down the sheet, caressing my outer hip and thigh before reaching my knee. Gently, he nudged my legs apart and I happily opened myself to him.

However, he didn't position himself between my thighs as I'd expected him to. Instead, his head continued to move lower, kissing my mound.

"Corey, you don't have to-" I began to say.

Without removing his head, he lifted his face to me and I found him staring intently back at me. "I want to," he said earnestly. "Unless," he added quickly, "you don't want me to."

"It's not that," I muttered.

"Okay then," he smiled, twisting his face and kissing my inner thigh. Then his sensual tongue snaked forward and he licked upward.

Lifting myself from the pillow, I supported my upper body on my elbows and stared hypnotized by the movement of his dark head between my parted legs.

With seductive finesse, Corey pressed his mouth to my engorged labia. I bucked in pleasure and then, as if he were kissing me, his tongue drifted between the tender lips and lapped at the arousal between my folds.

"Ugh," I groaned, hips jerking.

His expert tongue slipped up until the sharp tip met my highly responsive bud.

That simple touch was enough to send blinding flashes of light across eyelids that had suddenly snapped shut. "God," I squealed, my fingers twisting the sheet beneath them while my thighs unconsciously clamped around his head. My sex pulsed and hips undulated in a rhythm of their own making.

Corey didn't stop, nor did he alter the speed with which he licked at my pounding clitoris. Slow and steady, he dragged the climax out until I was screeching his name breathlessly.

Gradually the tension began to leave my body and the sensation subsided, leaving only the warm ghosts of it behind. Weakened, my arms gave out from beneath me and I flopped back onto the bed.

As I struck the mattress, Corey began to lift his head. "I don't think I've ever known a woman quite as responsive as you," he commented, a smile evident in his voice.

My heavy lids struggled to open and, sure enough, I found him beaming at me. "I don't..." I began wearily. "It's never been like this before."

Seeming pleased with that revelation, he swept up my body and claimed my mouth. He tasted of me; a sweet and slightly salty mixture that was slick and caused our tongues to glide over each other. Sucking my lower lip into his mouth, he gently grazed it with his teeth before finally letting it go.

"You need a minute to recover?" he asked, one hand absent-mindedly massaging my thigh.

"No," I breathed, shaking my head. "I want you now, Corey."

"I want you," he echoed, his hands moving to the waistband of his pajama pants and edging them down.

As he removed his clothing, I pushed myself into a sitting position, fascinated by the sight of his solid, strong and large erection. Like the rest of him, it was beautiful. The soft, pink crest; the thick corona; the broad, smooth shaft with a subtle upward curve, and pulsing vein – everything about him was perfect.

While he slipped the pajamas off and tossed them aside, my hand was drawn to him. Unable to take my eyes from his manhood, I tentatively wrapped my fingers around the shaft, appreciating just how large and hard he was. Oblivious to the movement of my own hand, I stroked him from base to tip letting my thumb linger over the glans and the clear fluid that oozed from him.

"Hmm, Freya," he hummed, his free hands returning to my legs and molding the thighs with firm strokes. "That feels good," he groaned.

"You're big," I commented foolishly, my wide eyes still captivated by the erection I clutched in my slender fingers.

Corey chuckled in response. "Are you okay?" he asked.

"Yes," I quickly replied, forcing my gaze to his face.

"You ready?" he softly whispered, leaning closer and kissing my mouth.

"Yes," I repeated, the word muffled by his lips.

Tenderly, Corey leaned into me, coaxing me back down onto the bed as he lifted himself and placed his knees between my sundered legs.

My fingers automatically fell away from the scorching heat of his length and I wrapped my hands around his shoulders. Every movement that came next was natural. I didn't have to think, I didn't have to bid my body to what my head thought I should. Instead, every action was inherent and, strangely, familiar.

Placing my feet flat on the bed, I dragged them closer to my buttocks and opened myself more fully to him. Lifting my head from the pillow, I offered him my mouth and he quickly swept me up in a passionate kiss.

His tongue swept into every moist recess, seeking, it seemed, all of the unexplored depths of me. As I moaned in pleasure at his thorough charting of my mouth, I felt the bulbous tip of his manhood nudge at my sex.

My entrance was swollen in anticipation, and arousal eased the passage, inviting him in. Nevertheless, he did not sheath himself in a frenzied hurry to reach completion. His lower half moved steadily, shifting closer to mine in a casual inexorable drive forward.

I felt every flutter of my passage as it attempted to draw him deeper. I felt every flex of my muscles as they gave beneath the pressure of his strong presence. I could even feel the pulse of his heartbeat as it pounded throughout the length of his shaft. It was somewhat slower than my own rampant pulse, but it was a hardy beat.

Shifting back from my lips, Corey inhaled sharply and braced himself on hands he placed either side of my upper arms. My eyes fluttered open and I found him staring intently down at me, a calm, serene smile brightening his face.

"You feel so good, Freya," he murmured.

"Corey," I replied, my breath uneven as my hips jerked upward.

Slowly, he continued to stretch me, gently insisting an entrance that I was all too willing to offer him. The sensation was intense, almost painful, but the overwhelming sensation was pleasure and rightness. This was how it was meant to be. This was the man I was meant to be with.

"You're beautiful," he exhaled, giving one final push of his hips until he was finally buried within me.

"Ahh," I moaned, my whole body quaking. The sense of completion, the sense of belonging flooding over me so forcefully that it brought tears to my eyes. I was full, completely and perfectly filled, as if his body and mine had always been designed for the other.

"Oh, Freya," he groaned, his head dropping until it was resting against mine.

"Corey," I whimpered in response, closing my eyes and luxuriating in the sensation of togetherness. There was no he and I anymore: it was as if we were joined as a single unit. We were one: it was impossible to tell where I ended and he began. I had heard women talk about this kind of sex, I'd read about this kind of sex, but I had never experienced anything even remotely close to it. And I had begun to believe I never would.

Gradually opening my eyes, I realized Corey wasn't moving.

He was looking back at me, his soft gaze moving delicately across my face. "Feels so good," he murmured.

As heavy droplets escaped my eyes, I nodded.

"You okay?" he asked softly, his lips dancing across my cheeks and banishing the teardrops.

"Yes," I whispered, my voice thick with emotion I didn't understand. "I'm fine. I'm better than fine."

"Oh," he sighed happily, "I could stay like this forever."

Did he mean that? As wonderful as I found the sensation, I ached for him to move within me. I needed the age-old cadence of that primal dance.

"Corey," I quietly uttered, my hands smoothing over the tense, sinewy muscles in his back. "I need you to..."

"What? What is it, my darling? What do you need?"

"I need..." I added, my hips bucking against his much more solid, strong ones. "Please..." I whimpered.

"Can you wait a little longer?" he asked.

Confused, I blinked. "I...I don't..."

"It'll feel better like this, if you can hold off," he explained, seeming to understand exactly what I needed.

Still baffled, I shook my head. Didn't he want to thrust? Surely, that was the natural instinct of all men? The fact that he was able to 'hold off' for as long as he already had seemed improbable to me, so his encouragement seemed out of place.

"It's all right, Freya," he quickly added. "There's no pressure. Just tell me what you want."

"I want to feel you move inside me," I whispered, acutely aware that those words had never emerged from my mouth before.

"Okay," he replied simply, already pulling his hips back a little.

I hissed a sharp breath as I was once again reminded of how large he was.

Then, as slowly as he'd entered me, he slid himself back in until his neatly cropped, jet-black pubic hair was nestled against my distended folds.

Contentedly moaning at the now familiar feeling of fullness, I arched my back and writhed against him, enjoying the sensation of pressure on my exposed clitoris.

"Ah," Corey exhaled. "Freya."

"More," I begged, urging him on.

Without question, he fulfilled my request, pulling back and thrusting again with that same, steady control. Then, his motion became perpetual. Always measured, always tightly contained, but unending in its flow. In and out, he gently stoked the fire that raged in my center.

Bending his head, he took my nipple into his mouth as he continued to urge me to completion. But there was no sense of haste, no race to finish, no frenzy of brutal pounding action. Instead, our joining was causal, tender, and loving. It was about so much more than just the physical thrill of friction. Electricity crackled between us, and I felt completed by the experience.

Nevertheless, that physical thrill was very much alive and well. Bucking and gyrating, my hips wriggled beneath him, meeting his thrusts and hungrily rubbing myself against him.

"Corey," I mewled, feeling the tension grip me. I involuntarily held my breath as I waited for the wave to crash over me.

"Breathe," Corey urged.

Blinking up at him, my brow creased quizzically.

"Trust me," he smiled, his body never missing a beat. "Keep breathing."

In no condition to ask questions, I simply followed his direction, taking in a deep lungful of air and resisting the instinctual drive to hold my breath. I kept breathing deeply as he continued to move inside of me.

"That's right," he encouraged softly. "That's good."

"Faster," I whimpered, flashes of an orgasm just out of reach stirring in my loins.

"You don't need it," he replied calmly, his voice slightly hoarse. "Just let it happen, Freya."

I'd been sure he was trying to kill me with a lack of sex, now I felt confident he was trying to kill me with the fulfillment.

The nails on both hands digging into his sleek back, I concentrated on breathing and put my faith in him to know my body better than I did. I trusted him completely, and I knew that he wanted me to be fulfilled entirely: nothing he suggested was out of selfishness.

For long moments, I began to doubt him. However, with a rush so sudden and so violent it caught me completely by surprise, every muscle in my body clenched. Pleasure coursed through me, and then my limbs shuddered and jerked as if I'd been struck by an electric current. Oblivion surrounded me as I cried out his name. At least, I think I cried out his name. In truth, no sound ever hit my ears, but that might have been thanks to the deafening of blood pounding against my eardrums.

It seemed to last an inordinately long time, and when the shaking of my form finally subsided, and I opened my eyes. Corey had gone completely still above me, but he was smiling sweetly.

"Are you okay?" he asked.

"Oh, God," I huffed, almost unable to find the air to speak. "God, Corey, that was..."

"You're amazing," he commented gently, tipping his face down and kissing dampness from my cheeks.

Having been unaware of the silent tears that were streaming down my face, I blinked in confusion.

"It's all right," he assured me. "Just a release."

"Release?" I replied.

"Hmm," he nodded. "Physical and emotional release often goes hand in hand," he added.

Not really understanding what he was talking about, I remained mute.

"Has anybody told you how gorgeous you look when you come?" he asked, changing the subject.

"Um... no," I replied. It was an honest answer, even if it wasn't the full truth. However, the mention of orgasm bought me crashing down to the reality of the situation. Corey was still within me, still rock hard, unspent and unsatisfied. I was surprised, and a little worried.

"You..." I stammered, my brain still fogged by the intensity of my own climax. "You haven't-"

"It's okay," he said, shrugging one shoulder.

"But... but..."

"It's not necessary," he offered simply.

Dumbstruck, my mouth dropped open slightly. Was he serious? Well, I guess, when you get right down to it, none of it wasnecessary. But could he honestly come this far and not experience a release of his own. Or was there something even more concerning going on? Was it me? Had he been disappointed by time we'd spent together?

"Freya?" he said, noting, I suspect, the concern that had etched its way into my features.

"You don't want me?" I asked, sounding like a lost girl.

"It's not that," he quickly insisted, shaking his head. "But, if you're tired, or if you don't want me to climax while I'm still in you, then it's no big deal to me."

"I want you to come," I told him quietly, my thighs wrapping more solidly around his waist. "Please, Corey."

"Okay," he replied smoothly, dropping a tender kiss on my lips before his hips returned to their inexorable rhythm.

Drawn into a ceaseless world of pleasure by the movement of his body in mine, it felt like a long time before the quality of his groans indicated he was reaching the cusp of the pinnacle. I marveled at how he had not allowed himself to release until now: how he had managed to wait until I essentially gave him the permission to come inside of me. And, as he exploded with ecstasy, I climaxed again.

Unlike every other man, whose ejaculate had made me feel like little more than a vessel for it, Corey's warmth filled me with life and love. I had been loved. We'd made love, in the truest sense of the phrase.

As sleep tugged me into its warm embrace, I was certain of two things: Corey had ruined me for any other man, and I was only too happy to be ruined.

CHAPTER FOUR

Opening to You

When my eyes groggily fluttered open, I was surrounded by a complete darkness. The candles had all been extinguished, and the jasmine was now just a faint whisper on the air. A solid arm lay across my abdomen and a smooth chest was pressed comfortingly against my back. Smirking to myself at the realization that it hadn't been a dream, I twisted my face over my shoulder.

"Hey," Corey said, his bright eyes wide open and looking intently at me in the darkness. "You okay?"

"Okay doesn't even begin to describe it," I chuckled, swiveling in his arms so I could face him. Snaking my own hand over his hip, I nestled closer, sliding one leg between his and feeling lightheaded when the weight of his flaccid manhood draped across my thigh. "But, I'm sorry," I added sincerely, searching his handsome face.

Brow crinkling, he shook his head. "For what?"

"That it wasn't how you'd planned it," I replied softly.

"The only part I planned was being with you," he countered.

"But... you wanted to do things differently, and I..."

"Oh," he sighed, chuckling as he finally understood my meaning. "Freya, there was no plan. I just wanted to make you feel good."

"And you not moving would have made me feel good?" I asked, skeptically.

Tightening his embrace, he ran his hand across the small of my back. "I think so," he warmly said. "It's a Tantra technique," he added. "But I meant what I said, whatever you want, Freya. Whatever you want, I'll give you."

Those were words that I had never heard before, especially in this context. It was enough to make me lightheaded again.

"Tantra?" I echoed, sleepily. Finally some things were beginning to make sense. "That was what the massage was all about?"

"Yeah," he affirmed, smiling. "Felt good?"

"It was incredible," I assured him. I slid my left hand up between us and began to stroke his chest tenderly. "You are incredible," I stated matter-of-factly. "I've never met anyone like you, Corey. And I'm not just talking about the sex. You're.... Well, you're just..."

With a soft smile, he looked at me, waiting for me to finish my thought.

"I just didn't think men like you existed anymore," I sighed.

"So, you believe me, then?" he wondered. "You believe that this isn't just a game to me, and that I'm not using you to settle some petty score with Tristan?"

Hesitantly, I gazed into his sincere, candid eyes. "If it is," I slowly began, "you're the best actor I've ever seen." Tracing his jaw with my index finger, I smiled. "You're also the biggest asshole."

Laughing good-naturedly, he tossed his head back into the pillow.

"No," I quietly uttered, bathing in the warmth of his laugh. "No, I don't believe this is just a game to you."

Still grinning, his chuckles ceased and he set his steady gaze on me once more. "I'm glad," he said, the hand at my back moving up to my face and sweeping a strand of hair off my cheek. "Because it's important to me that you trust me."

"I do trust you," I reminded him. "I wouldn't be here with you if I didn't."

Drifting into peaceful silence, he ran his fingers through my hair, a wistful, contended smile quirking at the corners of his mouth.

"Can I ask you something?" I mumbled.

"Of course," he replied easily.

The pad of my fingers moved over the day-old stubble on his chin, and I exhaled slowly. "What did you mean earlier, when you said that an emotional release often comes with a physical one?"

Giving me a small shrug, he shook his head. "Just that," he whispered. "Sometimes, the release of an orgasm can bring out emotions... ones you might not have even known were there."

"So... I don't understand. You think I have emotional problems?" I asked quietly, wondering suspiciously if he was getting a little too close for comfort. Although I'd told him I trusted him, and that was the truth, there were some things I still wanted to keep to myself.

"No," he chuckled. "I'm not saying that at all."

"I was sobbing for no reason?" I wondered.

"I didn't say that, either," he countered gently. "A lot has gone on over the past few weeks," he suggested. "Whether you realize it or not, it has affected you, Freya."

Accepting his explanation and much preferring it to the one my own mind was conjuring, I nodded. "I guess you're right." Other wounds had long since healed, and there was no lingering trauma resurfacing when I was at my most vulnerable... was there?

"Besides, I guess we've all got our share of unresolved emotional issues," he added, conversationally. "Things we think we've dealt with, but haven't fully addressed, right? A very smart woman once told me that."

Remembering the conversation well, I lifted my eyes to his. "Yeah," I mumbled.

"You know, you can always talk to me," he softly urged, "about anything."

"I know."

"About your sister," he quietly added.

"I know," I repeated. "And I do want to talk to you about that. I want to talk to you about everything." That was true: I did. Contrary to spending my entire adult life pushing it all away and trying to ensure nobody knew about it, I wanted Corey to know my past. I wanted him to know me. The real, whole, complete me. The imperfect me. And that was scary.

"Just not yet?" he finished for me with no hint of impatience or annoyance.

"Not quite yet," I confirmed. "Sorry."

"Don't be," he insisted, curling his long finger around my chin and cupping it gently. "Don't ever apologize for that. If you're not ready, it's because I haven't made you feel safe enough yet. You have got nothing to be sorry for."

"But you have made me feel safe," I argued.

Smiling, he quickly tipped his head forward and kissed the tip of my nose. "It's just going to take some time," he explained softly. "I need to earn it," he added, grinning. "And I have no problem with that."

"What about me?" I countered. "Do I need to earn your trust, too?"

For a second his smile faltered and his eyes dropped away from my face. "I already trust you, Freya," he said. "More than I've ever trusted any woman, and more than I think you realize." His focus shifted back up and met my eyes. His gaze met mine solidly, and he continued. "You've already got something that I've never given anyone else, and, the darnedest thing is, I didn't give it to you. You took it somehow."

"I..." I mumbled, shaking my head. I had no idea what he was talking about and was reluctant to ask.

With a soft, self-deprecating chuckle, he closed his eyes. "Let's get some sleep, huh?" he suggested. "We can talk more about all this another time."

"Okay," I whispered. "Oh, Corey," I added, "can I just ask you one more thing?"

66

"Sure," he smiled.

"How long did it last?"

Brushing his thumb across the angle of my chin, he shook his head. "How long did what last?"

"How long were we making love for?" I asked, feeling my cheeks flush a little. "I don't need to know exactly," I added, in case he wondered what kind of strange person keeps a stopwatch going. "I just got caught up, and lost all track of time."

"Tell you the truth, so did I," he quietly told me. "But... um... I'd say it was only two hours or so."

"Two hours?" I echoed. "Only?"

"Give or take," he continued, with a small jerk of his shoulder. "Is... err.. is that okay?" he wondered, peering at me questioningly.

I wondered what kind of man asked if it was okay for incredible sex to last two hours. Then I supposed it was the same kind of man who could cause me to have incredible sex for two hours.

"Yes," I quickly insisted. "Yes, absolutely. It was the best two hours of my life," I told him sincerely.

"Mine too," he replied. His mouth swept forward and claimed mine in an ardent, but tender kiss, and he hummed in delight. "Get some sleep," he encouraged, slinking his arm back over my waist and tugging me close to the comfort and security of his chest.

Happy to be swept up in his embrace and be held tightly to him, I also allowed my heavy eyes to slip closed. Throughout the night, even in my dreams, I was aware of his warmth, his strong torso and his muscular, protective arm. I'm fairly certain that I'd never slept so well before that night.

***

The next morning, I awoke to the soft pattern of his breathing and the golden sunlight that streamed through the window. At first, I rubbed at my eyes, feeling very smug about exactly where in the world I was. Not just on 'the roof of the world' surrounded by the most incredible natural beauty I'd ever experienced, but also – and more importantly – I was in bed with Corey Wallace. I was in the arms of Corey Wallace: I had spent the night with his naked skin pressed against mine. Back in Florida, I would have killed for this.

Not wanting to wake him, I carefully lifted his arm and scooted out from beneath its weight. Not bothering to pick up the robe we'd left abandoned the night before, I wandered unashamedly naked to the large windows and drew in an amazed breath. The morning light bathed the mountains in the most amazing glow, as if a god was directing that celestial light to provide maximum impact.

That morning, there was a thin mist rising from the valleys below, masking the greenery in a gossamer-like sheet. I tired to blink away the dream I was clearly having: it all seemed so surreal. But it was very much happening to me. I took in the beautifulsight before me for a good ten minutes, just enjoying the silence and beauty of the morning. Then, twisting my face over my shoulder and catching a glimpse of the peaceful looking man behind me, I realized that was an equally surreal sight. Nothing about my life felt real: everything was too good to be true.

However, as the voice of doubt began to question whether this could all be ripped away from me as quickly as it had come, I shook my head. "Don't do this," I muttered to myself. "Don't overanalyze it or question it to death," I added, exhaling as I stepped toward the bathroom and quietly opened the door. "For once, just enjoy what it is and stop worrying about everything else," I sighed. I continued my pep talk a little louder once I was behind the closed door.

Catching a quick glimpse of myself in the mirror, I noticed that my eyes seemed brighter than they had for weeks. In fact, that haunted look that had been with me since the very first night I'd spent with Tristan was gone. That darkness and weight had been lifted. Perhaps

Corey had been right: the emotional release was nothing more than the stress and turmoil of the previous weeks.

Smiling at my own visage, I turned away from the mirror and jumped into the shower cubicle. It felt like another room entirely, not just a shower. As I lathered my body and hair, I even found myself singing gently, something I hadn't done for months. I was happy: genuinely and almost sickeningly happy. I could well imagine Daniela's voice if she could have seen me then.

"See, what did I tell you?" she would have said. "Good sex is good for the soul."

And part of me knew that it was thanks to the good sex. The orgasms I'd experienced with Corey had left my abdomen as sore as if I'd done crunches, but they had also filled me with a vibrancy... some of his vibrancy perhaps. Was that possible? Could some of his innate life energy and positive aura be transferred through intercourse? At first, it seemed like a ridiculous question, but the more I dwelt on the possibility, the more I wondered whether auras could share energy. After all, our auras had been connected for a very long time the night before.

Then, of course, there was the glorious realization that there was nothing wrong with me. I was more than capable of experiencing climax with a lover. In fact, in the hands of the right man, I was highly responsive.

But I also knew, and would have told Dani if she'd been in that bathroom with me, that it was about more than just sex. But then, sex between Corey and I hadn't been 'sex.' Not in any sense of the word I'd been familiar with up until that point.

It had been... I didn't know how to describe it. The limited English language just didn't give me the right words. It was just... well, more. So much more.

Eventually, I emerged from beneath the luxurious streams of warm water and wrapped myself in a large towel. Not bothering to dry my hair, I left it dripping on my shoulders and down my back as I ambled lazily into the bedroom.

Stopping when I saw that the bed was empty, my eyes quickly moved around the room. I found Corey on the balcony. He had his back to me and his cell phone was pressed to his ear.

His pajama pants hung at his hips, but he was naked from the waist up. His hair was tousled and much more relaxed than the carefully styled look he usually wore. For several minutes, I simply watched him, my eyes wandering over his broad shoulders and sculptured contours of his back. Catching sight of faint red marks from my fingernails that grazed his shoulder blades, I felt a strange mixture of guilt and arousal.

Unaware of the compulsion to move, I found myself stepping toward the window and carefully sliding the large door open.

Corey heard the brush of the tracks and flicked his face over his shoulder. He offered me a soft smile before turning his attention back to the mountains.

"Yeah," he said into the phone. "Well, I figured that he would."

Drawn to him, I gently stroked the marks I'd left on his otherwise flawless skin. The pads of my fingers didn't detect any real depth to the injuries. Nevertheless, I leaned in and kissed each of the wounds by way of apology. Noticing he was covered in tiny goose bumps, I wondered why he'd exposed himself to the cold air.

"I don't know when I'll be back," he continued calmly, one arm almost absently snaking behind him curling around my lower back. "No, no. I don't think that's necessary."

Only too happily, I let him tug me closer, pressing myself against his back before wrapping both arms around his waist and sharing the warmth of our bodies.

"I trust you to handle it," he added. "Besides, I can't drop things here. Not now."

I had been letting his words wash over me, but I was intrigued by that last part and I lifted my face curiously.

"It'll blow over," he uttered softly. "We just have to ride it out. I'm sorry that means you're on the front line, but-" he stopped and I assumed he'd been interrupted, because he began to chuckle. "I know you can," he agreed. "I have every faith in you."

My fingers gently explored the waistband of his pajamas, stretching the material slightly as I ventured a brief touch of the bare skin beneath it. However, my mind was only partly on the sensation of heat I found on his flesh. I wondered what he was talking about, and with whom.

"All right," he sighed. "Well, keep in touch. Bye." With that, he allowed his arm to flop to his side.

"Everything okay?" I asked, my lips teasing his spine.

"Hmm," he practically purred. "You keep doing that and everything is perfect."

Smiling, I tightened my grasp around his middle. "I meant the phone call," I explained.

"I know you did," he responded quietly. "It's..." Releasing a breath, he tensed. "It's fine, really. It's just Tristan."

My own body stilled and stiffened. "What's he done?" I asked ominously.

Sighing again, he tossed his cell into a nearby cushioned wood-frame chair and placed both hands on my wrists. Loosening my embrace, he turned in the circle of my arms and faced me.

"It's bad," I commented matter-of-factly.

"No," he insisted. "Well," he quickly added. "It's nothing really bad. It's... he's just trying to stir something up."

"What do you mean?" I wondered, looking up into his strong, handsome face with the certain knowledge that he would be honest with me. I don't know how I knew that. It wasn't as though I had much in the way of experience to go on, and I got the distinct impression he would protect and shelter me whenever possible. However, something in his eyes told me that, even if things were difficult to say, he would have the strength to say them.

"He's leaked a story to the tabloids," he said.

"What?"

"It must have come from him," he continued. "A few headlines are claiming that you and I were messing around behind Tristan's back and you left him at the alter for me."

"What?" I blurted. "That's.... But that's-"

"I know," he soothed, placing his hands on my upper arms and slowly running them down to my wrists. "I know. But it doesn't matter, does it? We know the truth, and that's what's important."

"But what about your business?" I countered. "People trust you. That's why he's done this, isn't it? He's trying to tarnish your reputation, to make you look like some..." I ran out of steam when words refused to come.

"Like I told Rebecca," he evenly replied, tilting his head toward the phone he'd tossed aside, "this will blow over."

"What if it doesn't?" I argued, concern rising. "What if people believe it?"

"Some people might," he conceded. "But most people won't. After all, we're talking about trashy supermarket tabloids here, Freya."

Staring deeply into his resolved face, I found no doubt: not even the slightest hint of worry. "Shouldn't you at least put your side of the story out there?" I suggested.

With a gorgeous half-smile, he shook his head. "I'm not going to dignify it," he said. "And I have much more important things to focus on right now."

"You do?"

Vigorously, he nodded as his fingers smoothed their way up to the towel held around my body with just a tuck of the thick fabric between my breasts. Carefully, he began to tease the material away from me. "Yes," he insisted. "I do."

"Corey!" I yelped, quickly covering his hands and preventing him from peeling the towel away from me. "What if somebody sees?"

"Nobody can see from here," he smiled. "We're completely secluded, I promise."

My eyes widening, I took a quick look around us. True, it did seem that we were in the middle of nowhere. But, could there be someone lurking with a telescopic lens? "Are you sure?" I asked, skeptical as I continued to study the uninhabited mountains around us.

"Well," he replied, chuckling. "If you hear a helicopter, I'd duck for cover, but other than that..."

Finding his playful smile annoyingly irresistible, my own lips tugged in a grin. However, I could not let thoughts of Tristan and the damage he was causing back in New York go with quite the same ease that Corey could.

"Hey," I urged, brushing the backs of my fingers across his stubble-covered cheek. "Are you sure you're not worried about what this is doing to your reputation?"

"This," he emphasized, "isn't doing any harm to my reputation."

"You know what I mean," I sighed.

"Freya," he said, managing to make my name sound intensely erotic. "I'm not bothered by some sordid, sensationalist story. Besides, I brought you here for a reason. I wanted us to get away from the rest of the world. And that's exactly what we're doing. Here, Tristan doesn't exist." Slowly, he began to pull the towel away from me and my weakened fingers put up no resistance. "Here, nothing exists, except you and me."

The chilly morning air struck my damp skin, and should have made me feel cold. However, beneath the raging heat of his eyes, I felt certain I was bathing under a scorching summer sun. I was vaguely aware that my skin broke out in goose bumps, and my nipples became hard from the temperature change. But that was far away, and Corey was very close.

Still holding the towel in both hands, Corey closed his eyes as he lifted the material to his face and inhaled deeply. I watched him savor the scent as gratification stretched the corners of his mouth.

Did he have any idea how sexy that made me feel? Such a simple gesture, but powerful beyond any words could ever be. He loved even the faintest scent of me.

As his eyelids fluttered open again and settled on my face, a little hazy and with just a tinge of self-awareness, I realized he hadn't done it for show. He probably hadn't even been aware of it. He certainly wasn't aware of what it was doing to me.

Content to stand bare to his gaze, an unbidden smile brightened my features.

His soft lips curled upward in mirror of the action. "It's..." he mumbled, "I don't...." With a self-deprecating chuckle, he shook his head. "I don't know exactly what it is you do to me," he quietly admitted, as if it were a confession. "But I've never felt like this before."

His words, or more specifically the sincerity with which he said them, prompted a rush of affection for him that made me want to throw my arms around him and squeeze him tight. However, I stood motionless, my eyes welling with emotion. His disclosure seemed to deserve a quid pro quo, and a desire in me – one that had been present from the day I met him - was screaming at me to give him more of myself.

"Corey," I whispered, carefully reaching for his hand and pulling it toward me.

"Hmm?" he replied, relinquishing his hand's hold on the towel and blithely letting me direct his palm to my chest.

Carefully, I smoothed my fingers over his, urging him to cup my breast. At first, he let me direct him. But, within moments, he responded to my silent request and continued the slow massage without my guidance.

Shocked by just how quickly my body reacted to him, I breathed deeply, realizing my sex was already preparing to grant him access.

"There's... um..." I began, a little breathlessly. "There's something I wanted to tell you last night, but I..." Struggling to concentrate on the words emerging from my mouth, I was overwhelmed by the glorious fervor that stirred in my belly and heightened the sensation of his soft fingers as they adoringly caressed the swell of my breast.

"Tell me," he encouraged quietly, tossing the towel on the chair behind him and taking the weight of my other breast equally gently.

Swallowing with difficulty, I let my eyes droop closed as I reveled in the joy of his hands. "God, that feels good," I whimpered.

"You feel good," he replied.

His thumbs flicked over my erect nipples, and I took in a sharp breath.

Eyes still loosely closed, I didn't see him lean forward, but I certainly felt the sudden presence of his tongue, lapping tenderly at one tightly peaked nipple. My whole body pulsed and throbbed, hips jerking as the sensation created a deep yearning in my center.

Delicately, he sucked on my tight bud, releasing a guttural moan. Then, as quickly as his glorious, warm mouth was on me, it was lifted. "What did you want to tell me?" he asked, huskily.

"Oh," I muttered. "I... um.... Last night was amazing, Corey."

"I know," he chuckled.

"No, I mean, it was really amazing. It was... I'd never experienced anything like that before."

"Hmm," he hummed joyfully, his fingers still moving sensuously over my breasts and his thumbs teasing at the erect nipples. "I'm glad."

"What I'm trying to say is that, I've never... I had never had an orgasm with anyone else."

Briefly, Corey's hands paused; but that split second's stillness was the only indication that he was surprised by whathe had heard. As his fingers began to move again, they slowly left my bosom and slid down my torso.

"I thought there was something wrong with me," I continued, mild embarrassment forcing me to keep my eyes closed. "But... uhh..." My breath was stolen, stalling my words, as one of his large palms slipped smoothly over my mound. "Oh, Corey!"

"Don't stop, Freya," he whispered.

"Uhh," I whimpered. As the tips of his fingers met my swollen folds, my own hand snatched down and pressed him more firmly to the juncture of my thighs.

"What did you want to tell me, Freya?" he asked, his index finger sweeping softly through the dampness toward my waiting core.

"The very first time..." I breathed. "The first time you touched me..." Gasping as he slowly inserted his finger, I clung to his wrist. "You made me come, Corey," I mumbled. "In the middle of the restaurant, with all those people around. All you did was take my hand, and I climaxed."

When Corey didn't respond to the revelation, I slowly opened my eyes, desperate to gauge his reaction. I found his deep, brown eyes gazing intently back at me. He smiled lightly as his finger slid inside me, stroking the yielding flesh along the front wall of my passage.

"Corey," I panted, lifting my left leg and curling it around his hip. My hands, meanwhile, grasped his shoulders for support.

"Don't stop talking, Freya," he said. His body was pressing against mine and the large swell of his erection made itself very evident at my hip.

Mewling, I tilted my hips, but he didn't need any assistance. He had already found a responsive spot and was placing pressure in exactly the right place.

"Cor..." I whimpered. "I'd never... felt anything like it... so powerful, it nearly knocked me off my feet." As he pressed harder against my G-spot and began to rub in firm circles, I squealed in delight. "And... and..." I stammered. "And, I'd never even... not even while making love... I..." No longer making sense, but sure he still understood me, I continued to babble. "Thought I was frigid.... Couldn't climax with a man...."

His mouth suddenly covered mine and his tongue slipped between my parted lips. Quickly and with fervent passion, he explored me thoroughly and stole what little breath was in my lungs. The movement of his finger remained incessant and strong, causing my hips to shiver with pleasure.

Tearing his mouth from mine, Corey's chest heaved. "You are far from frigid," he asserted confidently.

"It's you," I panted in reply. "It's you... I...." Feeling the ecstasy take me in its scorching hot grasp, I cried out. "You! No one else." My body was pulsing, and my sex clamped around his finger in rapid spasms. Blinded momentarily by the lights that flashed through my brain, I rode those moments of euphoria, uncaring of the fact that my cries were echoing off the mountains surrounding us.

Corey's free hand was wrapped around me, that one strong arm, holding me close and keeping me upright. His palm resting at the small of my back moved in small, comforting circles as he muttered in my ear. "I've got you, I'm right here."

"Ugh, Corey!" I screamed.

"It's all right," he crooned. "It's all right."

With my heart thudding wildly, I sucked in air through my open mouth, and was overcome with lightheadedness. For a moment or two, I was convinced I was about to faint. However, the intensity of the pounding in my brain eased. And then, gradually, I came back to my senses, back to my body, and back to reality.

"Okay?" he chuckled as he felt the tension seep from me and the rampant fluttering of my sex abate.

My head falling forward, I rested on his shoulder, catching my breath. "How... how do you know how to do things like that?" I whispered.

Palm still moving warmly over my back, he was quiet for several long moments. "I'll tell you about it sometime," he eventually said, an unusually serious quality to his tone. "I promise."

"On second thought, maybe I don't want to know," I said, lifting my heavy head. "I'll probably just get jealous," I told him with a straight face.

He smiled as the fingers still inside me continued to move in lazy strokes that spoke of relaxation and affection rather than any fresh attempt to stimulate more from my already drained body. I appreciated that he kept the connection going without rubbing me raw. I was unsure how he did it, but I admired him for it.

"I think it was probably a combination of things," he said.

Thrown by the change of subject, I shook my head.

"The fact that it's different with me," he offered in explanation. "It's probably partly to do with a lack of foreplay."

"I don't need any foreplay with you," I pointed out wryly. "Unless you count saying 'hello' as foreplay."

Grinning, he acknowledged the argument with a small shrug of his left shoulder. "Nevertheless," he insisted, "I think it played a part. Premature ejaculation may have also been involved. But mostly, it's because a lot of men forget, or just don't know, that the most easily aroused and responsive part of a woman's body is her mind."

Quietly, I considered that, allowing myself to digest his words. I became increasingly aware of the calm, gentle motion of his finger inside my passage. All of his points were valid: they were clichйs, but true nonetheless. It still didn't explain everything, though. "None of those things account for me climaxing at the touch of your hand, though," I whispered, pensively.

"That's true," he agreed. "I guess...." he offered, pausing to think briefly. "I guess, we just have a connection." Slowly, he removed his finger from my body and deliberately lifted it to his mouth. Sensually, he drew the long finger across his lips before sucking it into his mouth.

Watching him, my jaw dropped open.

Amused by my wide-eyed fascination with his action, he flashed me a mischievous grin. "Maybe," he mumbled, gradually removing the finger from his mouth and licking his lips, "it's something neither of us can explain."

My suddenly dry tongue was clinging to the roof of my mouth as I stared at the movement of his lips. "I..." I faltered. "I don't need to know why, I'm not sure I care anymore." I told him truthfully. "I just want you to know. I want you to know what you've done for me, I want you to know what I've never told any other man, and I want you to know how different I am with you."

"Thank you, Freya," he replied. "That means a lot to me."

"That you're the only man to make me come?"

"Well, I've gotta admit, it's flattering." He grinned. "But, no, I meant that you can tell me something like that. It means a lot to me that you can be open."

"I want you to know me Corey," I replied softly. "And I don't just mean know my body. I want you to know me."

"Sounds good to me," he replied. "Come on," he added, running his hand along my back. "Let's get inside, you're getting chilly."

Hopeful that he would lead me straight back to bed, I nodded and followed him back into the house.

CHAPTER FIVE

An Exploration in More Ways than One

Sometime later that day, when hunger won over both of us, we got out of bed and, untroubled by our nakedness, dashed downstairs like giddy teenagers, teasing each other with tickles and shared laughter. I hadn't felt this alive in a very long time.

In the kitchen, Corey rummaged through thecupboards, listing all of the many foods he had on offer. Unconcerned with exactly what I ate, I perched on a stool before the large center island and allowed my mind to wander as I watched each of his graceful, purposeful movements. The things that had captivated me about him right from the very start were the same things that now seemed so obviously indicative of his skills as a lover. He was extremely patient, gentle, respectful, and calm, and he was very considerate. He was also always very much in control of his reactions and behavior. That last one was something I felt sure he could stand to loosen up over, but I wasn't going to complain.

Tristan had shown me what uncontrolled desire looked like. There was no comparison between the pleasure Corey had given me and the discomfort I'd experienced during most of my encounters with Tristan, other than the fact that they were on opposite sides of the spectrum (if they were on the same spectrum at all).

As I sat quietly, thinking, Corey quickly threw together a couple of bowls of fruit and granola, placing one in front of me before settling in the seat directly opposite me.

"I was thinking," he started, "we could go and explore some of the scenery this afternoon." He picked up his spoon and enthusiastically began scooping up a large mouthful of our late breakfast.

With a knowing smile, I slipped a piece of mango into my mouth. "Scenery from right here looks pretty good to me," I commented, my eyes wandering over his bare chest.

"Well, it's not bad from here, either," he shot back, grinning. "But there's so much I'd like to show you," he added.

"I've been enjoying what you've been showing me in the bedroom," I pointed out dryly, lingering over another juicy mouthful of fruit.

"I've been enjoying that, too," he chuckled. "But we've got all the time in the world to enjoy each other." Chewing on a small mouthful of banana, he paused. "It's your call: if you want to hang around here, we can."

"No, no, I'd like you to see some more of Bhutan. There is just one problem, though," I reminded him. "Other than the clothes I came in, I haven't really got much to wear."

"Ah," he responded, "well, that's not altogether true."

Despite attempts to coax more from him, he refused to provide further explanation until after we'd eaten. We enjoyed our light breakfast, smiling and carrying on as though we had been together for years instead of days. When we were finished, Corey said he would show me what he meant by his comment. Leaving the bowls on the counter, we headed back up to the bedroom, and the double doors on the left, which opened into a large walk-in closet.

"Take a look," he urged with a cock of his head.

Peering quizzically at him, I stepped inside. On the right of the closet was a long line of beautiful, new clothes. Hanging on the opposite side were garments that looked very familiar. Reaching out with one suspicious hand, I grabbed the leg of a pair of jeans and pulled them a little closer to me. "These are my clothes," I mumbled, head flicking toward him.

"Well, I wasn't planning on wearing them," he laughed.

"No," I chuckled in return. "I mean, they're my clothes. How did you...?"

"I asked Daniela to pack a few things you might need. I hope you don't mind."

Shaking my head, I turned my eyes back to the rack of clothes. 'A few things I might need' looked to be my entire wardrobe. "Of course I don't mind," I whispered. "That was very kind of you."

Leaning against the doorframe, he seemed content to simply watch me. "There is one more surprise, but you're going to have to wait a little longer for that," he added.

"I don't suppose you're even going to give me a hint," I commented, not needing to look over my shoulder to know he was smiling.

"Nope," he responded. There was determination in his voice. "Otherwise, it wouldn't be a surprise now, would it?" Pushing himself away from the door, he stepped backward. "Give me a shout when you're ready and we'll get going," he added. "Bathroom's yours: I'll use the one in the room next door."

"It's a big bathroom," I pointed out, hoping to halt his movement. "And a big shower."

With a suggestive, almost tempted smile, he shook his head. "Hmm, you keep this up Miss Moreton, and we'll spend the entire day doing nothing but making love."

"You say that like it's a bad thing."

"No," he smiled, "not a bad thing. Although, I do worry that your body's going to get fed up with me."

"Impossible," I assured him, leaving my clothes and turning fully toward him. Stepping forward, I reached out, resting my hand on his hard pec. "Impossible," I repeated quietly.

Instinctively, Corey's hands came to my hips and cradled the curves gently. His eyes narrowed slightly as he studied my face. "You're not sore?" he asked skeptically.

"Well," I hedged, "a little bit." However, it wasn't the soreness I'd experienced in the past after intercourse. It was a strangely comforting sensation: a reminder that I had been completely and thoroughly loved. "Feels kind of nice, though," I whispered confidently.

With a soft smile, Corey dropped his head to one side. "Well, let's make sure it doesn't feel anything other than nice, huh?" he suggested. "Besides, I didn't bring you all this way to keep you cooped up."

As always, what he said made perfect sense. Logic told me that we couldn't carry on indefinitely the way we'd been going. My body – and his too for that matter – would begin to protest eventually. "You're right," I nodded. "I know, you're right."

"So, what do you say to Thimphu?" he asked, his fingers squeezing me lightly.

"Thimphu?" I replied.

***

As we drove down from our high spot tucked away from the rest of the world, I could feel the air changing; become drier and warmer. Soon, I decided it was too hot for the thin sweater I wore and peeled it off.

Heading west, Corey spoke informatively about the city we were about to visit.

"It's Bhutan's capital and the largest city in the kingdom, but it's still pretty small by our standards."

I listened to his deep, calming voice as I studied the landscape that passed on both sides. We were entering the Wang Chuu Valley and passing the Raidik River. As we approached the city, I instantly saw what Corey had meant: compared with the rustic area of the country we'd left, Thimphu was a metropolis, but it still maintained a charm that was simply not present in cities like New York, London or even

Paris. For one thing, Thimphu had glorious hills, and forests to the north and west.

Wang Chuu Valley and passing the Raidik River.

With the temperature a comfortable seventy degrees outside, I pushed the electric window down and breathed deeply of the fresh, clean air.

As we swept into the more built-up areas of the city, we passed numerous people: women all with vibrantly colored blouses, with patterned cloth wrapped around them to form dresses. The men wore knee-length, red checked robes tied with belts.

There were several other vehicles on the road, but none quite as shiny and new as Corey's Jeep, which caught the attention of a few locals.

When he finally pulled the car to a stop and we climbed out, I looked back in the direction we'd come from and marveled and the heavy mist that clung to the mountains. "Wow," I whispered.

Locking the doors with a quick jab of the remote on his keys, Corey strolled around the front of the car. "Never gets old, either," he said before gently lacing his fingers with mine.

I turned to look at him in his white linen shirt and khaki cargo pants. Clutching his hand in return, I smiled. "Hmm?" I asked.

"The views around here," he offered, glancing about him. "None of this ever gets old. I could drink it all in forever and not get bored with it."

"Yeah," I nodded. "I think I could, too."

"This way," he coaxed with a light tug of his hand. "You up for a walk?"

Women from Bhutan

"Sure," I replied, keeping step with him and remaining at his side.

Not bothering to ask where we were heading, I was content to absorb all that was around me. I'd never seen so much green in and around a city before; it was a strange mix of wilderness and civilization that I found captivating. We passed shops, with matriarchs giving instructions to their employees. We passed men pulling carts of fabric, and we passed a group of children laughing as they tossed a ball to each other.

"Up there," Corey pointed, encouraging me to look up to an old building on a hill ahead. It seemed lonely up there, and its white walls were stained from the weather. However, it stood grand and imposing, as though it was keeping a watch on the rest of the city.

"What's up there?" I asked.

"It's the ChangangkhaLhakhang," he replied, as we began the slight incline up to the ridge. "It's the largest and oldest temple in the city.It's been here since the twelfth century."

ChangangkhaLhakhang

I began to see the colorful arches and the golden cylinders that hung between them

From a distance, it looked more like a military fortress than a temple, but as we drew closer, I began to see the colorful arches and the golden cylinders that hung between them. "Bells?" I asked.

"Prayer wheels," Corey smiled. "The Buddhists believe that turning those spindles has the same effect as speaking a prayer."

"Oh," I responded, my focus drawn to the intricate markings that adorned those arches.

Entering the grounds, we passed a group of young monks wrapped up in their maroon robes. As we drew close, Corey slipped his hand free of mine and placed his palms together before dipping his brow until it touched his fingertips.

"Namaste," he offered quietly.

The men mirrored the greeting in reply and smiled before continuing on their way.

There were only a handful of pilgrims in the courtyard as Corey smoothly reclaimed my hand and strolled into its center. Then, grinning, he urged me to turn around and look back in the direction we'd come.

Thimphu was stretched out below in all her glory: the greens, the quiet way of life, a series of red roofs. And in that peaceful, serene moment, we just gazed at the incredible sight. We didn't say anything at all. We simply stood there and reveled in the air, the beauty, and the peace. We were content to just "be."

I was overcome with a sense that I had been there before. My mind wandered to strange place, and I felt certain that I had stood in that very spot before. Although I had never set foot in Bhutan, let alone Thimphu, I could have sworn that the vision before me was familiar. Equally familiar was the feel of the man by my side marveling at it with me.

Eventually, with a soft squeeze of my hand, Corey brought me from my strange musing. "You know it's weird," he mumbled. "My parents never brought me here as a kid; I didn't come for the first time until I was twenty-five, but I always think of my mom when I'm up here." With a quirk of his head, he continued. "Well, I think of my mom a lot wherever I am, but especially here."

"You think she would have liked it?" I wondered.

"Oh, God, she would have loved this." He grinned, thinking quietly to himself. "Yeah, this would have been her idea of heaven."

Not knowing what to say, I remained silent as I watched the cocktail of sadness and joy that crossed his face. Wanting to offer him some comfort, I did the only thing I could think of and leaned close to him. With my arm resting snugly against his, I tipped my face upward and brushed my lips across his cheekbone.

His mouth twitched in response.

"She loved you, Corey," I whispered. "I can see that in the pictures of the two of you. She loved you so much."

"I know," he replied quietly. "I loved her. I still love her."

Exhaling, I blinked back tears that weighed heavy on my lower eyelids. "It's never going to stop hurting," I told him, unsure exactly where the words came from. I hadn't been aware of an urge to say them, and they seemed directed just as much to me as they were to him.

"Not entirely," he agreed, twisting his face toward mine. His lips just a breath from mine, I expected him to close the gap between us, but he didn't. "It'll never stop hurting entirely. But the pain can ease. Some wounds never disappear, Freya, but they can be healed."

It struck me sharply that he wasn't just talking about his own situation, and a familiar panic rose up in me when I thought about my own mother. Silently, I reminded myself that this was Corey in front of me; the man I could trust, the man I intended to open my heart to. There was nothing to fear.

Slowly, Corey's eyes closed and he dropped his face forward. His lips melded delicately with mine, tenderly caressing. His kiss was filled with a sadness that bled into me. I thought about a young, vulnerable Corey, the fourteen-year-old who had lost his entire family. The desire to hold him tight overwhelmed me, even though I knew that there was nothing I could do to make him feel at peace.

Still clinging to his right hand, I wrapped my free arm around his back and pulled him fiercely toward me. I wanted to take that sadness from him: I wanted to absorb it all.

But there was more to the kiss. It also imbued comfort and reassurance. He understood my heartache and reminded me that I wasn't alone.

By the time he carefully pulled back, a single tear was weaving its way down my face. Corey's free hand rose to my cheek and he wiped the salty droplet away with the careful pad of his thumb.

"You okay?" he asked quietly.

"Yeah," I replied, the word wavering in a throat swelled with emotion. Blinking, I studied the eyes of the confident, capable and self-assured man before me and saw something else. What I saw was something that both surprised and concerned me. There was fear behind that sanguine exterior.

Surely, I was mistaken. Corey wasn't afraid of anything. He was strong and dependable. He was the unshakable force that I could rely on completely. He had no vulnerabilities, no weaknesses. That's why I was safe with him.

And then it occurred to me that I wasn't being realistic nor was I being fair to Corey. He was a human being, not some superman. Of course, he had fears and flaws. I'd been seeing the 'perfect' him: the persona that the rest of the world saw. Sure, the persona was a pretty close approximation of who Corey really was, but it wasn't all he was. It wasn't the real man.

Internally chiding myself for my selfish concerns, I realized that the 'real' Corey was exactly what I wanted. Yes, that was a little scary, because it meant he wouldn't always be the strong one, but that was okay. I wanted a relationship, didn't I? A proper, adult relationship, not one with a quasi-father figure. Those thoughts, which had been barreling through my brain at a hundred miles an hour came to a sudden, screeching halt.

A father figure. Was that what I'd been doing?

Looking back on every single one of my relationships, it seemed like a stupid question. Of course, that's what I'd been doing. I'd always been drawn to older men, none of whom had treated me as an equal: men who offered me the kind of affection my dad hadn't been able to give. I had only been with men who invariably called the shots in our short-lived relationships.

Here I was with a chance to change all that. And instead of embracing it, I was wallowing in self-induced panic, because it suddenly seemed that maybe I wasn't the only one that needed fixing.

Demanding that I get a grip, I closed my eyes and struggled to push my own fear aside. I was being childish. After all, I knew myself more than capable of being tough. Besides, how incredible would it feel to be the woman he relied on?

The hand I held at his back slowly moved up until it brushed the thick hair that almost reached his collar. "What are you thinking about?" I asked, meeting his eyes once more.

"I'll tell you later," he replied, seemingly brushing the question aside.

"Corey, you know this talking thing goes both ways."

Smiling, he leaned forward and kissed my mouth gently. "I know," he mumbled, lips still partly merged with mine. "And we will talk when we're back at the house. I promise."

Trusting him, I let it go and kissed him in return.

Running his hand over my hips, his long fingers strayed toward the curve of my buttocks as he finally broke free from my mouth. "I want to show you the rest of the temple before we head back down," he said.

"Okay," I whispered.

With that, the conversation was dropped. And although my concern over whatever he was bottling up didn't completely leave me, his mood quickly shifted back to the even one I'd come to know.

We lingered for another thirty minutes at the temple, while he showed me the statue of Avalokitasvara, with his thousand arms and eleven heads.

"He's a Bodhisattva," Corey told me, his arm draped around my shoulders, "an embodiment of enlightenment," he added. "Avalokitasvara specifically depicts compassion: the compassion of Buddhists."

The striking, ornate image hypnotized me for long minutes, until eventually, Corey pointed out that the sun was setting and we should begin the walk back to the car.

***

When we got back to the house, the sun had faded behind the mountains, creating a curious amber glow that dwelt on the very cusp of the mountains. In moments, that beautiful sight was only present for moments, before the bright orb disappeared from view.

Mourning the loss of that moment's perfection, I waited for Corey to delay the talk he'd promised, knowing that would be exactly what I'd do if there was something I didn't want to discuss. And sure enough, after tossing his car keys on the table by the gargantuan front door, which was easily twice the height of him, he suggested that we head outside to the patio.

"I thought you were going to tell me what was on your mind," I reminded him carefully, trying not to sound like I was nagging it out of him.

"I know," he smiled, approaching me and snaking his arms around my waist. Pulling me close, he continued. "And I am. I thought we could go out there and relax with something to eat and a glass of wine."

"All right," I said. Smiling, I untangled myself from his embrace and headed toward the living room.

"No," he called, stopping my broad, eager steps. "Not that one. This way," he added, jerking his thumb down the hallway to his right.

"Whe...?" I started to say, but he was already moving and I had to break into a slight jog to catch up to him.

He led the way to another large reception room. The north and east facing walls were glass panes from floor to ceiling and beyond them was another patio. But unlike the one Corey had shown me the day before, this one had a Jacuzzi built into the decked floor.

While sliding the concertina doors open with one hand, Corey was already unbuttoning his shirt with the other.

Steam was rising from the water's surface and as he stepped forward and dipped the tips of his fingers in, he hummed his approval of the temperature. "Just about perfect I'd say," he smiled, tossing his head over his shoulder and enticing me forward with a flick of his eyes.

My own feet moved forward, called as always by the his magnetism.

Standing straighter, he quickly peeled his shirt from his shoulders and tossed it aside. "I'll be back in a second," he said before dashing back into the house.

My upper body twisted to watch him leave, but I didn't ask where he was going. Instead, once he'd shot through the room and was no longer in sight, I turned my attention to the tub. Soft bubbles drifted upward and broke, creating a light rippling sound. Bending at the knees, I dappled my fingers in just as he had done, and had to agree: the temperature was just about perfect.

Unable to resist the call of it, I lifted my still wet hand to my shirt and pulled it up over my head. Then kicking off my shoes, I unbuttoned my jeans and slid them down my thighs. Reassured by Corey's promise that we were concealed from view, I had no reservations about shedding my underwear just as quickly. And, once I was naked, I stepped into the Jacuzzi with a soft sigh of contentment.

At first, the water seemed a little too hot on my air-chilled flesh. However, I quickly adjusted to the heat and, closing my eyes, I sank back into a comfortable corner of the tub. It was nice to just sit there and relax. The hot water contradicted the cool air in playful, relaxing way, and I felt very much at peace.

Releasing an unashamedly noisy breath, I felt every muscle in my body soften.

"Good?"

Forcing one eye open, I cast a glance at him. He stood by the doors, a bottle of wine and two glasses in one hand and a plate of crackers and cheese in the other.

"You have no idea," I smiled at him.

"Oh, I think I do," he crooned as he toed off his shoes and stepped forward.

As he set the food and drink by the edge of the tub, and both hands moved to the waistband on his pants, interest quickly prompted both eyes to open sharply. Intently, I watched as he unfastened his fly and pushed the pants off his hips. A bulge in his underwear was evident, but as he edged his boxers down, the erection popped up proudly and caused me to inhale a sharp breath.

One look at him in all of his masculine splendor was enough to incite a longing in me that was now more fervent than those long weeks spent in expectation. Now, I knew what awaited me, and there was no longer any fear. I wasn't worried about disappointing him, and I wasn't worried about being disappointed.

"Ohh, that's good," he commented as he slipped into the water and glided smoothly toward me. Stretching out with both arms, he placed his hands on the edge either side of my head.

Without hesitation, I parted my legs as he drew closer and welcomed him between my thighs. However, that's as close as he got. His hips pressed against the soft flesh of my inner thigh, his erection remained in the expanse of water that still existed between us.

At that moment, all thoughts of conversation had left me. My brain was centered on one thing and one thing alone. His, on the other hand, was still frustratingly clear.

"So," he began gently, "you asked me what I was thinking about while we were up at the temple?"

Thrown by the disparity between what I thought was about to happen and what actually seemed to be going on, I hesitated. "Uh... yeah," I replied.

"Well, I...." he breathed. "I... um..."

As he faltered, my memory drifted to that morning and the way he'd reassured me as I was trying to open my heart to him. Needing to show him my unconditional love and acceptance, I followed his example. Slowly allowing my right hand to slip beneath the water, I pushed through the resistance toward him. My fingertips met his chest and drew lazy patterns across his muscles. Allowing the water to ease the path, I let my hand glide down to his abdomen, pausing briefly to circle his naval.

"Freya," he whispered, his eyes focused on mine.

"It's okay, Corey," I soothed, venturing a little further south and stroking the neat thatch of coarse hair above his manhood. Tenderly, I circled him at his thick base and then smoothed up until I was clasping most of his shaft. Then, bringing my other hand into play, I rolled that palm over his tip, feeling him shiver.

"Oh, Freya," he groaned.

"Talk to me, Corey," I urged, allowing my fingers to move of their own volition, pleasuring him without overthinking exactly what I was doing, how I was doing it, or when. Instinct guiding me, I rubbed his heavy length and teased his tender head with the pads of my fingers.

"I...." he wheezed. "I was thinking about you... and about how I wouldn't want to lose you."

Smiling, I squeezed him more firmly as I pleasurably worked my hand from root to tip. "You're not going to lose me," I told him.

"I didn't think I was going to lose my mom, either," he pointed out, the muscles in his biceps flexing as he gripped the edge of the tub behind me. "Things happen, Freya. Life can do things that aren't fair."

"I know," I replied, offering the only words I could. How could I tell him that he's fears were irrational when they so obviously weren't? I knew what we had was something most people could only dream of. To lose that would be to lose one's self.

"And the thing is, Freya," he continued, swallowing heavily, "I've spent my whole adult life never getting close to women, never really trusting anyone."

Confused, I wanted to tell him that couldn't possibly be true. After all, I'd seen him with people: he was open, and he was overtly amiable. He didn't shut himself or his emotions away – quite the opposite, in fact. That was what drew people to him. However, conscious of the fact he was pouring his heart out, I just listened. Listened and let him knowthat I was there for him by continuing to slowly, rhythmically stroke his rock hard member.

"I always thought," he murmured. "That was because, deep down, I knew I wouldn't find anyone better than my mom.... I know that sounds Freudian, and I guess it is," he admitted. "But I know that I put her on a pedestal. I know that I measure every woman I meet against her, and it's not that they're 'not good enough' per se." He sighed. "I've known women that I've been... very fond of. Women that I thought I loved. But something always made me keep that at arm's length, you know?"

I wasn't sure I did know, but I nodded and encouraged him to go on.

"Oh, Freya," he gasped, eyelids fluttering as I rubbed my thumb across his frenulum. Sucking in a deep breath, he steadied himself. "Anyway, I realized weeks ago that the way I felt about you was different. For the first time in my life, I'd met a woman who I wasn't comparing with my mom," he forged ahead, his voice growing gravelly. "And when I discovered that you had feelings for me, I knew I was in trouble, because I'm not just fond of you, Freya. I don't just think I'm in love with you. I am in love with you. And this afternoon, I was suddenly struck by what it would do to me if...."

"Corey, I love you," I replied sincerely, leaning forward and pressing my mouth to his. The movement of my hand intensifying, the surface of the water between us lapped with the frantic motion beneath.

Easing his own hand away from the edge, Corey's fingers plunged down and stilled my rampant desperation to bring him to completion. Pressing his lips against mine, he shushed the beginnings of my protest before any sound left me. "It's all right," he soothed.

"I love you," I repeated. "And I'm not going to leave, I promise."

"We've known each other less than a month, Freya," he replied. "Neither one of us knows how this is going to turn out, and I thought I was okay with that."

"But you're not?" I wondered.

His eyes dropping slightly, he pensively inhaled. "I don't think I could bear losing you," he softly uttered.

"Well, I feel the same about you," I responded automatically.

It wasn't a lie. Just because it was automatic didn't mean that the words didn't hold the most truth I had ever felt in my life. I truly thought that if I lost Corey, I wouldn't be able to go on.

"Three weeks ago, you were engaged to someone else," he reminded me.

I tensed and opened my mouth to shoot back something defensive, but quickly realized he hadn't meant it as an accusation. He was simply stating a fact. From his point of view, from the whole world's point of view for that matter, I must have seemed fickle at best and nothing more than a money-grubbing slut at worst.

"That was different," I whispered, the hand that held him coming to a still but refusing to release him. "You said you thought you'd been in love before," I offered, hoping he'd understand.

"I was never ready to marry anyone though, Freya," he mumbled. "And getting to know you over the last few weeks, it's difficult to imagine you saying 'yes' to a proposal on a whim."

I was cornered, both literally and figuratively: trapped between the curve of the Jacuzzi and his large form, and facing questions that I couldn't easily answer. How could I ever make him understand when I wasn't entirely sure I understood it myself?

Yet, I knew only too well the significance of what came out of my mouth next. His trust in me was on the line, and if I wasn't very careful I could blow everything. For several minutes, I let sentences whirl around my mind, trying to latch onto one that would express my feelings for him and assure him that my whole relationship with

Tristan was a mistake. But how? How to ever explain that? A month ago, I hadn't even believed it myself.

With a quite sigh, I slowly relinquished my hold on his erection and let my hand drop limply by my side. There was no quick fix to this; there were no magic words that could simply dismiss his concern. There was only one thing I could offer him: the truth.

CHAPTER SIX

All of Me

Wanting to dispel the uncomfortable silence that separated us, Corey continued to tenderly enclose my wrist in his hand and brushed his thumb across my pulse. "Freya?" he softly whispered. "It's not... I mean, we don't have to talk about this right now."

Given the offer of putting it off, I was sorely tempted to grab it and run. But what lay at stake was too important. I wanted him to trust me. I needed him to trust me, and the only hope I had of gaining it was to tell him everything: all of the things I'd been too ashamed of, and all the things that were so painful I'd wanted to bury them. I had to tell him all of the things I'd hoped no one would ever know.

"It's... um..." I began haltingly, unable to meet his eyes. "It's difficult to explain," I said, unsure whether I was prefacing for the sake of forewarning him or simply as a delaying tactic.

"Freya, you don't-"

"I want to." I quickly cut him off. "I want to tell you, I just... I need you to bear with me."

"Sure," he responded assuredly.

"See, the thing with Tristan... the thing with every man I've ever been involved with was about me looking for something that I'd never had." I breathed, lifting my gaze to his. I found that he waswatching me closely: not staring but simply remaining interested and completely involved with what I was saying. I continued to talk, finding it a little easier to continue.

"I.... Tristan gave me that. At least, I thought he did. It wasn't love, not in the sense that I love you, but I'd convinced myself that didn't matter. I believed he'd make a good father, a good husband, and that I'd have stability and security with him..." Pausing, I checked his reaction and found him continuing to listen without judgment, at least without any that was visible on his face. "I thought that those were the only things that mattered," I added. "Until I met you. I was so wrong about him." I shook my head angrily.

"Well, you weren't the only one," he agreed. "We were friends for years. Decades. I knew he could be pushy if he didn't get what he wanted, but I can't believe I so underestimated someone I considered a good friend until…"

"… until me," I finished.

Pursing his lips thoughtfully, Corey seemed to want to ask a question, but changed his mind. With an easy gesture, he lifted the hand that still clung to the edge of the tub and stroked the back of his fingers across my cheek.

Reflexively, I closed my eyes and leaned into his touch.

"It's all right, Freya, you don't have to go on," he said.

Smiling to myself, I was grateful for the offer. Even more grateful, because I knew that his questions still remained largely unanswered, and he must have been aching for a better justification of my behavior.

"I think," I sighed, bracing myself, "I think it all stems from not feeling loved as I was growing up."

"Freya," he warmly soothed. "You really don't have to do this."

Opening my eyes, I fixed him with a confident expression of resolve. "I want to," I nodded. "I want you to know."

"All right," he accepted slowly.

"I... I was born in Fresno to quite poor parents.... My mom didn't work then, at least I don't think she did. My dad was some kind of salesman." As the words tumbled out, they began to come easier. But it didn't stop me from nervously grasping my thighs with both hands as I spoke.

Feeling the tension in my wrist, Corey continued to gently stroke his fingers back and forth, but it did little to relieve the rigidity in my body.

"I wasn't planned," I mumbled. "My mother told me that almost every day from as far back as I can remember. I don't remember a time when I wasn't aware of the fact I hadn't been wanted."

"Freya," Corey whispered.

"I'm not sure my sister had been, either," I added, barely registering his words. "She... um... was six when she drowned. I was just three, but I remember my parents arguing afterward. I remember my dad blaming my mom and saying that she was supposed to be watching us. It wasn't very long after that they got divorced." Chewing on my bottom lip, I felt oddly numb, as though I were simply recounting something that had happened to someone else. It was strange: it had all been kept inside so long that I was unsure how I felt about it until it was spoken aloud.

"Your dad left?" Corey asked.

"Yeah," I replied absently. "Yeah, he left. And almost as soon as he did, my mom started looking for someone else. Men were coming in and out of the house, and she never seemed to have any time for me. I'd ask her to play with me, or read to me, but she wouldn't. So, I just... sat by myself, watching TV, or just sitting in my room."

"You didn't have anyone?" he asked, concern putting deep creases in his handsome brow.

A seemingly inappropriate smile lifted the corners of my mouth as I recalled the one person I did have. "Mrs. Johansson," I whispered, suddenly aware that while suppressing all the unpleasantness that had surrounded growing up, I'd also pushed memories of her aside. "She lived next door," I said. "She'd talk to me over the fence, and I guess she must have known that I wasn't eating very much, 'cause she'd always offer me a slice of bread or fruit."

"She knew your mom wasn't around, but she didn't do anything?" he asked, his shoulders lifting with tension.

"I don't think she knew exactly what was going on, she just knew that we weren't exactly rich, and so she'd treat me if she had anything spare," I replied. "Anyway, Mom was working as a waitress. Dad, I think, sent some money, but things weren't great for him, either. Most nights, I went to bed hungry."

"Freya, I'm so sorry," Corey mumbled, shaking his head.

"It's not your fault," I responded calmly. "So... um...." I hesitated. "About a year after my sister died, my Mom found out she was pregnant. She'd had a brief fling with a doctor.... I think he must have been married."

Pausing, I cast my mind back to the doctor. I had a very vague picture of him in my mind: middle-aged, not bad looking, but always red-faced and very sweaty. At the time, I didn't understand why he'd always looked like that the few times I'd seen him. It wasn't until much later I realized I'd caught a glimpse of him after his sordid rendezvous with my mom.

"And then my brother came along," I continued. "And things were very different with Scott," I said slowly, feeling familiar resentment burning a hole in my gut. "He was the golden child, the one my mother had been waiting for, the one she'd wanted."

"But..." Corey muttered. "He wasn't planned, either, right?"

"Who knows?" I shrugged. "I used to think that, but I wonder if she deliberately got pregnant, knowing that this doctor could afford child support. And maybe a little extra to keep it all quiet.... I... I don't know."

Releasing a heavy breath, Corey shook his head.

"All I do know," I whispered, peering down at the rippling surface of the water, "is that my mom worshiped the ground he walked on. He was going to have everything; he was going to be everything. And even though we weren't as poor as we had been, I went without so that Scott could have the very best."

Having to force my hand away from my leg, Corey urged me to release my tight grip so that he could lift my fingers to his face. Tenderly, he kissed my knuckles, then urged me to relax my fingers so he could place another kiss on the palm of my hand. The gesture was small, but it reminded me of the tenderness of the man I was with. It gave me the strength to continue recounting the tale I had begun.

"I remember," I replied, watching the top of his head as he brushed his lips across my hand once more. "On my sixth birthday, my dad bought me a teddy bear. It was the first one I'd ever gotten. And when I took it home, my mom grabbed it from me and said I had to give it to my baby brother." With a humorless scoff, I shook my head. "I know it sounds ridiculous to be upset over something like that now..."

"No, it doesn't, Freya," he replied, lifting his face to mine.

"But it wasn't just that, you know. He got everything. All the money Mom had, she spent on him. He had the bigger room, he had all the toys, and I didn't even have any books. When I started school, I still didn't know how to read or write, not even one damn letter. He, on the other hand, was given all the advantages that she could offer him, because she wanted him to grow up and be a successful man."

Moistening my dry lips, my eyes unconsciously moved to the bottle of wine on my left.

It didn't go unnoticed by Corey. "You want something to drink?" he asked, already sweeping back a little and scooping up the bottle.

"I don't want you to think I have to be drunk to get through this," I said wryly.

Offering me a small smile, Corey unscrewed the lid and poured some of the Rioja into the two glasses. "I'm not trying to get you drunk," he promised, setting the bottle down and picking up both glasses.

Handing one to me, he sipped a quick mouthful from his own before placing it on the edge of the Jacuzzi.

I followed his lead, taking a grateful sip of the drink. However, rather than giving up my hold on it, I carefully cupped it between both hands.

"I...." I tentatively uttered. "I didn't get to see very much of my dad, but the two or three times a year I did see him, he was always so different with me. He acted as though he loved me, and I wanted to live with him. I asked him almost every chance I got, but he always told me he couldn't take me with him. He had no permanent home and was always traveling, so...." I finished with a shrug, unsure how much of that I believed anymore. As an adult, I couldn't help but wonder what I would do if a child of mine was in that situation and, traveling or not, I knew there was nothing I wouldn't have done to get her out of that nightmare.

"So?" Corey asked softly.

"So, I stayed where I was and nothing changed. Except, the older I got, and the older Scott got, the more obvious my mother's favoritism became. She used to tell me that it was important for Scott to get a good education, because he was going to become a surgeon. And when I asked if I could be a surgeon, too, she told me that because my dad was a nobody, I was destined to be a nobody as well." Haunted by the sound of those words echoing in my head, I vividly recalled my reaction to them. "I cried for hours after that," I whispered, the thoughts given voice before I'd realized I'd said them.

"Oh, Freya," he cooed, lifting both hands to my face and stroking his thumbs across me cheekbones. "You could never be a nobody."

Attempting to show him that it was all okay now, I forced a small smile, but I suspected it wasn't very convincing. "Around that time, my mom started working more. She got a new job, and she wanted me to take care of Scott."

"How old were you?" he queried.

"Six, maybe seven." I shrugged. "Yeah, something like that. I was falling behind at school, because I didn't have the books to study with and didn't have time to go to the library, 'cause I was babysitting my brother. Eventually, I was so embarrassed about how much smarter all my classmates were I began to skip classes."

I scoffed, letting the not-quite-a-laugh out before I could stop myself. The situation was just silly when I thought it about it.

"Imagine that: an elementary kid skipping class already. Of course, that just made things worse." I sighed, pointing out the obvious. "The more school I missed, the dumber I got, and the more I began to believe my mom when she said I'd never amount to anything."

The warm, soft pad of Corey's thumb slid smoothly across my bottom lip as the creases in his troubled brow deepened. "Don't say that," he whispered. "You weren't dumb, Freya. You aren't dumb."

Resisting the urged to suck his thumb into my mouth, I became mesmerized by the movement of his dark gaze across my face. He was studying me with such care, as if caressing me with those beautiful eyes.

"You were never less than anybody in any respect," he insisted.

His assurance was sweet, but I wanted to tell him that we were quibbling over semantics. Dumb may have sounded harsh – and it was, but it was the truth. By the time I reached fourth and fifth grade, I was falling way behind my peers. I hadn't used the word 'dumb' to be self-deprecating or to elicit reassurance from Corey: I was simply stating a fact.

"Well...." I sighed, determining it would be best to forge ahead. Besides, it felt like I was past the point of no return. Memories and events were pouring out of me, and the flow was beyond my power to stop. The wine helped, but it wasn't the reason I was talking. Corey was somehow able to make it all feel safe.

"The days I went to school, Mom would stay home with Scott, until I got back. Then she'd go straight out to work. I'd cook for him, bathe him, read him a story and put him to bed. After he was down, I'd try to get my homework done."

"You had to grow up so fast," Corey noted, his head shaking slowly. It didn't seem as though he was talking to me specifically. His expression certainly didn't imply that he was waiting for a response. It was just a softly spoken observation.

"I remember," I mumbled, stopping short of finishing the thought.Something had come to me out of the blue;: something I hadn't thought of in years, and was suddenly drifting out of the dark corners of my mind. "I remember one day, I'd stayed home from school, because she had to work an extra shift. Scott was two, maybe just turned three, I guess. After giving him lunch, I'd left him to watch TV while I read one of my school books." Swallowing, my gaze dropped to Corey's chest. "When she got back, she was in a rage about something. She was swearing and she said something about not taking any more of the crap. When I asked her what was wrong, she told me to shut up and mind my own business."

Corey's sure, comforting right hand continued to cup the side of my face, his fingers gently stroking my jaw.

Allowing my eyes to slip shut, I leaned into his palm, desperate to absorb its warmth and succor. "And then," I added quietly, "she wanted to know why Scott was watching TV. 'You're supposed to be taking care of him,' she said.... I told her that I was taking care of him, but I just needed a read a book for school. She... she just flew off the handle. She started screaming and then she practically ran across the room toward me...”

The fingers pressed against the side of my face tensed a little.

"She snatched the book from my hands, and she... she...." I faltered, the same panic I'd felt as a young girl rising up, as if that afternoon was happening all over again. Suddenly, I had to get out. I had to run away, get out of the tub and get as far away from everything as I possibly could. I fought the panic, and forced myself to remain with the man who was being so patient with me: the man whom I loved completely.

"It's okay, Freya," Corey gently said.

"She started hitting me," I stated, eyes wide as they focused on his chest, but they weren't really seeing anything. "My arms, my legs and then my head," I told him. " I was crying and pleading with her to stop, but she didn't."

"Oh, Freya," Corey sighed, his hands suddenly leaving my head as both arms enclosed around my middle, and he pulled me flush against his solid, naked torso.

I let him take me, automatically wrapping my own hands around his back and clinging tightly – as if my life depended on it.

His embrace was strong, a little too constricting to be comfortable, but that was fine by me. I never wanted him to let go.

Squashing my breasts to his hard chest, I leaned my head against his as he tenderly smoothed his hands across my back. "That was the day," I breathed in a rush. "That was the day I decided that I had to prove her wrong. I had to show her that I could be something. I just wanted her to treat me the same way she treated Scott."

"None of it was your fault, Freya," he mumbled, his deep voice rumbling in his chest. "You did nothing wrong. You know that, right?"

"Yeah, I guess," I grudgingly replied. Part of me did know it.

Part of me knew that, despite what I'd believed as a child, the problem didn't lie with me and never had. Part of me knew that a young girl could never do anything so terrible as to deserve what I went through. Nevertheless, a small voice – that little girl's voice – still wondered whether I could have done something differently. If I'd been better, maybe Mom would have loved me like she'd loved Scott. If I'd been smarter, maybe she would have encouraged me to do well in school. However, experience would come to teach me that both of those hopes were misplaced.

"Things, um.... got a little better when Scott was old enough to start school. Then, I wasn't stuck babysitting him and I started to catch up in class," I continued, grateful for the vice-like arms unrelentingly clinging to me. "I didn't get to see much of Mom, because she'd quit her waitressing job and started working strange hours," I commented, recalling how odd it seemed that she would sometimes leave for work long after Scott and I had gone to bed. "But the times I did see her, she wasn't pleased about my good grades or that I was at the top of my class on a test. None of it made any difference to her," I added, bitterness coloring the words with its ugly taint. "She thought I was wasting my time: filling my head with a bunch of stuff I'd never need."

"She was wrong," he drawled softly. "Wrong about you, and wrong about a lot of things."

"I couldn't see it at the time," I mumbled. "I just wanted her to love me, and I thought the reason she didn't was Scott. He took all her time, her attention, and her affection. And I began to hate him for it."

Knowing that admission didn't paint me in a flattering light – after all, it wasn't Scott's fault that he'd been born – I waited for some sign that my childish spitefulness met with Corey's disapproval. But that sign didn't come.

Instead, the man who continued to hold me slightly loosened his bear hug and tipped his head back to meet my eyes. "You still beating yourself up over that?" he asked, as though he could read my thoughts.

"Yes," I nodded weakly. "Because I still hate him for it," I admitted in a whisper. "Even after all these years, and knowing that it wasn't his fault that he was spoiled and had every whim indulged, I still can't even bear to think of him." Entwining my fingers at the back of his neck, in an attempt to prevent him backing away, I shook my head. "I know it's wrong-"

"No," he quickly interjected. "No, it's not wrong."

Blinking, I nibbled on my bottom lip. My thoughts drifted slightly. "I had this friend in middle school. Her name was Monica." I sighed. "She had two younger brothers, and her parents were together. They all seemed so happy, y'know? They were a family. A real family, and

I was so envious of her." With the ghost of a smile at the recollection, I shook my head. "That was all I wanted."

Corey's hands slipped smoothly down my back, stopping when he reached my hips. "You will have that one day," he whispered. "I promise."

I wasn't entirely sure what he meant by that. Was it anything more than a platitude? Was he, in a roundabout way, suggesting that I'd have that family with him?

"And that was why you wanted to marry Tristan?" he asked gently. "You wanted that family."

"Partly," I agreed, tipping my head forward in a half nod. "But, I guess, there was more to it than that."

Carefully, he nodded.

"When I was twelve, my dad moved to Sacramento. He'd..err..." I hesitated, forcing down the fresh lump of emotion that constricted my throat. "He'd met someone, and they got married, had two kids..." I paused, remembering the one letter he'd sent me with a picture of him cradling the twins his wife had just given birth to. He'd had such a broad smile, wider than I'd ever seen. "It's not like I saw him much before that, but he'd been the only one I could really turn to... and then, he just forgot about me."

"How could he forget you?" Corey whispered, his fingers slipping easily over my wet skin and massaging the tops of my thighs.

"He was in love," I shrugged. "And he'd found happiness. I guess I brought back nothing but bad memories for him. It was better to just make a clean break from his past."

His jaw tensing, he shook his head as his right hand stroked slowly around my inner thigh, the tips of his fingers brushing the crease of my groin. I tried to ignore the sensations that he brought to my body so that I could finish the story.

"I just...." I muttered, tears filling my lids as I vividly recounted the pain of waiting for Dad to call or write. "He'd been the only I could count on and I didn't even have him anymore."

"I understand, Freya," Corey assured me.

His soft voice made me want to just crawl into his arms and stay there forever.

"Until recently," I sniffed, willing the emotion back, "I don't think I realized that I've spent the rest of my life trying to get that back. I've been searching for someone to take his place."

Corey was nodding, his fingers sweeping up and down that tender spot at the top of my thigh. "I know," he breathed. "I know exactly what you mean."

He did. It wasn't just a foolish expression, designed to comfort. He really did know. He had lost his mother, and she had been his entire world, just as my father had been the only person I could count on.

"Things at home were getting worse..." I sighed shakily. "I think my mom must have been drinking: she seemed pretty out of it. And she was still working late, leaving sometimes after midnight and not getting back until breakfast." Feeling foolish for not realizing, even at thirteen, what was going on, I clamped my eyes shut. "I didn't find out until later, but she was... er... she was working as a prostitute."

Corey didn't bat an eyelid, maybe because he'd been smart enough to realize that was what had been happening. Or maybe, being a man of the world, he simply wasn't shocked at the buying and selling of sex.

Either way, not wishing to linger on that part of the story, I forged on. "When Mrs. Johansson realized we were being left alone in the house all night, she must have called the authorities, because one night, there was a police officer at the door."

"They got you out of there?" he wondered, the grave rigidness still marring his otherwise beautiful face.

"No," I whispered. "No, Mom came back just as the policeman was walking into the house. And, somehow, she managed to sweet talk him into believing that she'd just slipped out to pick up some medicine for Scott."

"And the cop bought it?"

"She could be charming when she wanted to be," I announced flatly. A lot like someone else I know, I silently told myself. "Anyway, she stopped me from talking to Mrs. Johansson after that, and I was cut off from everybody."

"You're safe now, Freya," he quickly reminded me, methodically molding his fingers into my thigh.

"I know," I spoke through trembling lips as I forced a smile. "I know." Before I could lose myself in the comfort he offered, and therefore lose my nerve, I turned back to my memories and recounted the painful events of my life. "Years passed, and when I was in high school, she forced me to get a job to contribute to the house and Scott's college fund."

"What about you?"

"I wasn't going to college," I replied. "She made that quite clear." Incredulously, when I thought about that period of my life, it brought a small, but genuine, smile to my lips.

Noticing the curious quirk of my lips and almost joyful glint in my eyes, Corey cocked his head to one side. "Freya?" he asked.

"It's weird," I exhaled. "But that was probably the best time in my life up until that point."

"How so?" he asked.

"I got a job in a factory," I smiled. "It was completely mind-numbing work, but that's where I met Daniela."

"Oh," he said softly, his own mouth mirroring the upward curve of mine. "And you guys hit it off right away?" he asked.

"Yeah," I quickly agreed. "Yeah, it was like we were soul mates or something. We just clicked: we got each other. I'd never had a friend like her before, nor have I had one since." Meeting his dark eyes, I

113

felt myself melt beneath the warmth of his gaze. "Well," I chuckled, "until I met you, that is."

Gracing me with an appreciative grin, he leaned forward and kissed me gently.

Tenderly gripping the nape of his neck, I moaned softly into his soft lips before they were all too quickly gone.

"So, you had a confidante?" he asked.

Nodding, I found one wrist sliding down from its perch on his shoulder and allowed my admiring fingers to swirl over the well-defined muscles of his chest. "She understood," I said absently, as my focus followed the lazy motion of my fingers. "She didn't exactly have the most stable of families, and she knew what it was like to grow up without a cell phone, or all the other things that our peers were taking for granted. And we had something else in common, too."

"What?"

"Her mom was bipolar. That's why Dani was working: to help pay for her mother's medical treatment."

Slowly Corey approached his next question with what seemed to be great care. "You think," he began calmly. "You think your mom was bipolar?"

Shaking my head, I drew my tongue along my top lip. "No, my mom's problem was a little different. But....Well, after Dani had heard about some of the things my mom had done, she persuaded me that there was something not quite right and that I should speak to a doctor about what was happening."

"And?" Corey urged.

"After I'd told him a few things, and answered some of his questions, the psychiatrist thought my mom suffered from some kind of antisocial disorder...." I quietly told him. "He thought that my mom was incapable of loving me... incapable of loving anything, even my brother. Scott was just a means to an end. She believed he could become rich through him: that Scott could offer a golden ticket out of the crummy life she'd wound up with. In the end, for her, everything was about her."

The first time I'd heard those words, I hadn't believed them. She didn't love me, of that there was no mistaking, but she seemed to adore my brother. He was her whole world. It just didn't ring true that he was nothing but a meal ticket in her eyes.

"When I got home that night," I continued aloud, "I went to my mom and asked her whether she loved me. She just snapped that it was a stupid question and demanded to know where my paycheck was." With an incredulous shake of my head, I recalled the sting of her words. She might as well have said, 'no, I don't love you,' because her refusal to answer was the equivalent.

"I'm sorry, Freya," the handsome man before me sighed.

"What for?"

"For what you've been through, and for making you relive it all," he offered sincerely. "We don't have to talk about this anymore, you know?"

Contentedly slipping my fingers down to his abdomen, I flashed him a brief smile. "I want to give you everything, Corey," I breathed. "I want you to see everything: the good and the bad. I want to give you all of me."

"You sure?" he wondered carefully.

"Yes." I nodded emphatically, and took a deep breath. "Because I want you to know that this is different, that the way I feel about you is different from anyone else. So I want to take you to those places: even though they're ugly and I'd rather pretend they weren't there. I want you to be where no one else has been."

His dark eyes closed and when they flicked back open, I thought I saw the merest hint of wetness swelling in the lower lids. But he blinked away the possibility of tears and schooled his features. "Thank you," he whispered.

"Thank you," I echoed.

Chuckling softly, he ran his hand down to my knee, circled it with the backs of his fingers and then swept them all the way back up my thigh. "So," he sighed, a faint crack to his voice, "from then on, it was you and Dani against the rest of the world?" he suggested.

"Yeah." I smiled. "Yeah, that's exactly how it felt sometimes. And we believed in each other. We both wanted to get the hell of the crappy lives we were living, and we knew how to do it."

"What did you do?" he asked, with a curious flick of his brow.

"I applied to colleges." I shrugged. "Even though I knew my mom would go crazy if she found out, I was determined to leave."

When I was pensively silent for several moments, and he'd watched the smile slowly fade from my features, his concern rose again. "And?" he probed.

"I was right," I quipped darkly. "She did go crazy when she found out I'd been accepted at Towson University on a scholarship program. But nothing was going to stop me, not once I could see the light at the end of the tunnel...."

With a crooked smile that seemed to reflect a little pride, his index finger stroked the curve at the top of my leg. "So you went?"

"I went." I nodded. "Dani came too. She didn't want to go to college, but she came to Baltimore: we rented a place together...and we've lived together ever since," I acknowledged, realizing as I said it, that it was the longest and closest relationship either of us had ever had. "I was a phys-ed major, and I was going to be a teacher, but one of my professors...." Slowing, I wondered how much of the next portion of the story Corey needed to know right then and there. "His name was John Lytton," I whispered, determining that I'd already revealed the worst. "He took an interest in me, and, in turn, turned me toward yoga."

"You loved him?" Corey perceptively asked, without a hint of accusation or jealousy.

"I-" I'd been about to deny it, but caught the words before they came out of my mouth, because they weren't true. "I suppose," I nodded. "In a way, I did, yeah." Waiting for a comment or a disapproving remark, I was silent for a moment.

But Corey said nothing. Instead, his soft hand simply drew closer to my sex, fingertips tenderly rolling over my inflamed labia. I shuddered with anticipation, but knew I had to stay the course. There would be time for that later.

"He was twenty years older than me," I admitted. "But here was this man, who was attentive and affectionate.... He..." I stumbled. "He was offering me everything I'd never had before. So, when things started to turn from friendship to romance, I... I happily went along with it."

"And..." Corey hesitantly began. "He was a good guy?"

"Yeah," I said, smiling softly. "Yeah, he was. I mean, he was sort of breaking the school's rules by having a relationship with me, but he treated me well. He told me he loved me."

The sound of those words striking my ears caused me to grimace inwardly. Was that all it took, a man saying 'I love you'? The cold hard truth was that was all it had taken for me to go along with it. It was all it had ever taken, because I was so desperate to hear those words that I would have been prepared to do anything for someone who said them.

"I was nineteen," I muttered. "And he was my first."

"You hadn't had a boyfriend before that?" Corey asked, his index and middle fingers tenderly rubbing my folds. "Not in high school?"

"In high school, I was branded a dork and a loser," I replied, only half focused on my reply as the motion of his hand allowed me to forget everything else in the entire world. "None of the boys would have touched me with a ten foot pole."

"Their loss," Corey softly responded, his firm forefinger sweeping up to my hood and rolling in small circles.

"John was gentle with me, and respectful," I continued. "But it was never.... I mean, I never.... Well, y'know," I whispered, my eyelids trembling closed as I began to feel heat beating at the walls of my sex. "And then, once I'd graduated, he... he...." I whimpered. "He helped me set up the studio in New York, and...andthat's how I came to be in Greenwich teaching yoga. It's also how I came to meet Blake, and eventually Tristan. I was attracted to him, because he treated me well... to start with anyway."

"What-?"

"It's not important," I uttered, shaking my head. There was no desire to protect Tristan. But I did want to protect Corey. Giving him the full details of my sexual relationship with Tristan would only place unwanted images in his mind – and, if he knew exactly what Tristan had done to me, it would possibly enrage him enough to do something he'd regret. I'd never seen an angry side to Corey. So, on the face of it, had no reason to assume he was the 'fly off the handle' type. But a voice inside argued that everyone had their tipping point.

"He was sweet, and he was offering me a life that I... I could only have dreamed of as a girl. It wasn't about the money," I quickly insisted. "At least, not really. It was about more than that: it was security. And I never want to go back to the life I had in Fresno," I huffed.

"You won't, Freya," he insisted. "And, you know, you don't need a man to give you security. You've got it. You've made it for yourself."

"I..." I mumbled. "I guess," I agreed. "But I still.... I get scared sometimes."

Smiling gently, he shook his head. "There's no need to be."

Knowing no words could adequately express my gratitude for him... well, for just being him, I leaned into him and claimed his mouth with ferocious need.

He gave a joyful groan and returned the kiss languidly before slowly pulling back. "So, you never went back home?" he asked, the motion of his own fingers continuing.

118

Without the help of my brain, my hand seemed to realize how selfish I was being and quickly swept down to his rigid shaft. Without hesitation, I clasped him ardently and began to stroke him with the same tenderness he used on me.

Peeling my eyes open, I looked into his, loving the erotic swell of his pupils as I rolled my thumb around his soft tip. "No," I whispered, remembering he'd asked me a question. "No, I never went home."

"You never saw your mom or your brother again?"

"No," I replied on a barely audible exhalation. "I did hear from Scott, though. When he was in college, he took a psychology course and wrote to tell me that he thought mom had a psychopathological disorder. A month or so later, when he went home for the summer, he somehow convinced her to go to a doctor and she was finally diagnosed."

"She got help?"

Wondering how he could stay so clear-headed despite my best efforts to reduce him to a gibbering idiot, I shook my head in mild wonderment. "I guess." I shrugged. "But I never replied to his messages. I just wanted to draw a curtain over that part of my life."

"And you still feel that way?" he asked.

"Yeah," I determinedly responded. "Yeah, I can't forget or forgive. I know that doesn't make me a patient or compassionate person, but I just... can't."

Sliding his fingers slowly down to my pleading entrance, he carefully circled that swollen ring of flesh. "Nobody can judge you for the way you feel, Freya," he insisted. "They've got no right to, because they don't know what you've been through."

"But you're a..." I sucked in a breath as his digit slowly entered me. "You're a better person than me." I gasped. "You'd be able to forgive, wouldn't you?" It wasn't really a question, because I was so sure I knew what the answer would be. I'd seen the way Corey was with people: he was the rare kind of person who wanted to help everybody and ensure that he trampled no one in his path.

"I don't know about that," he thoughtfully mumbled, shocking me enough to jolt my mind from the glorious things he was doing to my body. "I... I couldn't forgive everything," he said.

With quaking fingers, I continued to rhythmically work his hard, sleek manhood. "Really?" I asked.

"Yes," he assured me with a nod. "I'll tell you about it some other time," he added, wiping the seriousness from his face and flashing me a steady smile. "Right now, I think we ought to get you out of this tub before you turn into a prune." He chuckled, his free hand taking my left wrist and lifting it so he could study my wrinkling fingers.

Shriveling or not, I didn't really want to leave the warm water... or the intimacy that we'd found. It seemed so much more profound now, even more so than after the first time we'd made love. I felt closer to him, something I had previously thought impossible.

However, I didn't argue as he urged me from the Jacuzzi and I put up no fight as he wrapped a robe around my shoulders and clasped my small hand in his much larger one. I made no complaints as he led me up the stairs, and I certainly did not protest when he laid me down on the bed and proceeded to love me more thoroughly than I ever could have dreamed.

CHAPTER SEVEN

All of You

The night I revealed my past to him, Corey was like a man on a mission. I had been able to tell, from the somber look in his eyes, that he'd been affected by the story of my childhood. His natural capacity for caring and empathy meant he had felt my pain almost as harshly as if it had been his own. I felt sure he would have felt the same way if it had been anyone else, and it was one of the reasons I loved him.

But once he'd got me into bed, I began to realize just how deeply he'd taken the events of my childhood to heart. He said very little as he tenderly, generously and fervently graced my body with the adoration of his hands and mouth. However, there was a different quality to his lovemaking that night. It was as if he was pouring his heart and soul into it: reminding me that I wasn't alone and that all of those nightmares were behind me now.

Perhaps it had all been in my imagination, though. Maybe I was the one imbuing his actions with meaning that wasn't really there. I wanted him to wipe all of those ugly memories away, so I willed it to happen. It wouldn't be the first time I had imagined something that wasn't really there.

Whichever the case may be (and my heart has always wanted it to be the former), the powerful, magnetic, passionate force between us that night crackled with its vibrancy. For a few moments, as he was bringing me to my third or fourth orgasm, I felt as though I left the bed: as though I had left the room, or even left the house. I was somewhere else entirely. I was floating above the world. And he'd been right there with me.

In that strange fantasy, he'd said between passionate kisses, "We'll never be apart again. We are together now, my goddess, and this time, I'll never let you go."

As the rapturous spasms subsided and my breathless pants eased, I found myself back on the bed, sitting on Corey's lap with my legs and arms wrapped tightly around him. He'd been looking up at me, with a dazzling smile.

"What did you say?" I'd asked, unsure at the time what had been my imagination and what was reality.

"Nothin'," he chuckled, with a quick shrug of both shoulders. "You okay?" he'd added, lifting his right hand to my face and smoothing some damp hair from my cheek.

"Yes," I'd whispered, the remnants of my daydream leaving me slightly disorientated.

At the time, I had no concept of the passing hours, but when we both finally collapsed side by side on the mattress, I realized that the rising sun was beginning to edge up between the mountains, and create a warm glow that crept through the large window.

Corey had swiftly pulled me into his arms as he covered us both with the soft, cotton sheet. And just before he'd closed his eyes, he'd mumbled, "I love you."

I was as exhausted as he was, both physically and emotionally. Yet, sleep refused to claim me. I lay there, fascinated by his face, the soft movement of his features as dreams glittered through his brain. I wondered if I was in any of those sleeping thoughts. And I wondered if he knew just how much I loved him.

A few strands of his hair, which had been messed by my clenching hands, flopped forward on his brow and gave him a boyish quality that reminded me he needed protecting. I couldn't be sure whether my drawn-out confession had eased his concern that I was some flighty gold digger, only interested in his money. To be fair, he'd never said those words; he had never even intimated them. He was just worried, I suppose, that I didn't know what I wanted. A month ago, he would have been right. Now, everything I wanted was crystal clear and right in front of me.

"I'm never going to leave you," I whispered, unconsciously stroking those locks of soft hair. "You're the only one, Corey," I added, knowing he was insensible to the words but wanting to say them aloud anyway. "I love you."

I snuggled in his arms for an hour or so, content to bask in his embrace. Eventually, however, I found my attention drawn to the windows and the balcony beyond them.

Carefully disentangling myself from his strong arms, I pulled my surprisingly energetic body from the mattress and sauntered to the doors, feeling sated, satisfied and almost nauseatingly happy. Who would have thought, I wondered as I realized there was a wide grin straining my cheeks, that I was capable of being so happy? No fear, no wanting, no doubts, no question in my mind. I was exactly where I belonged. I was with him.

Casting a quick look over my shoulder, I watched him roll onto his back and mutter something in his sleep before settling once more. Pleased that I hadn't disturbed him, I reached for the doors and quietly slid them open. The fresh morning air was a little chilly, and a soft breeze brought pimples to the surface of my skin, but it wasn't cold enough to be uncomfortable. Instead, it was a wonderfully refreshing sensation. It filled me with a fresh vibrancy and reminded me that I was alive. I loved the cool air on my face, and a took a deep breath of the rich, clean mountain air.

Gazing up at the still soft morning light, I leaned my head to the left, stretching my neck. With a quiet moan as the muscles relaxed and extended. Then, gently, I rolled my chin to my chest and all the way around to my opposite shoulder. It felt good. I felt good, as though the tension I'd been carrying around with me for over twenty years, a sensation that was so familiar it seemed normal, had gone. It had evaporated like the mist that rose off the water on the Jacuzzi's surface.

There was nothing to fear anymore. I no longer needed to dread the day that Corey would discover my past and what his reaction might be. I didn't need to worry about him knowing anything else about me: he knew the worst. He knew that I'd been born to a seriously disturbed woman (and shared those genes), and knew just how much my upbringing had messed with my head. He also knew how much it had messed with my relationships, and that 'healthy' wasn't the best way to describe any of them. Yet, he hadn't bolted, nor had he even flinched. On the contrary, he'd been so incredibly calm, supportive and accepting, I was beginning to wonder if perhaps he was listening to my story at all. But I remembered how he seemed to feel my pain, and I knew in my heart that he had heard, and he had accepted.

Inhaling deeply, I stretched my arms out on either side and closed my eyes as a wispy cloud shifted from the sun, letting its strong rays heat my face. Entirely naked and offering myself to the beauty that lay before me, I had never felt such unmitigated and glorious freedom.

Consuming the warmth and vitality of the sun, tempered with the gentle wafts of crisp air, I released a languid sigh.

A soft cough behind me interrupted those long moments of peace. Lowering my arms, I twisted, already smiling at the man I knew I'd find.

"You know," he said, one hand propped against the door's frame. "I'd thought that the view from here couldn't get any better," he paused long enough to allow his gaze to travel down the length of my body. "I was wrong," he added, grinning.

Cheeks warming slightly, as they always did under those passionate eyes, I chuckled. "Hi," I whispered.

"Hi," he echoed.

"I didn't mean to wake you. I'm sorry," I continued, taking a sliding step backward, until the small of my back was resting against the balcony's thick wooden rail.

"I'm not," he countered, shaking his head. "It is funny though," he offered quietly. "I never used to mind sleeping on my own. But..." Blinking, he hesitated briefly. "But, ever since we shared that bed in Florida, I just haven't felt right without you by my side."

Curious, I reached back and clasped the rail while tilting my head to one side. That night at his Nirvana home, things between us had been completely platonic: frustratingly so. I'd assumed then, and had continued to assume until the ordeal between Tristan and him, that he'd been unaffected by me. He'd slipped off to sleep, carefully keeping himself to his side of the large bed, and had seemed to rest much easier than I had. It struck me as strange that there had been so much going on beneath the surface that he'd kept well hidden.

"Silly, I guess," he chuckled with a shrug.

"No," I instantly replied. "I don't think it's silly at all."

He smiled. "So, do you want some breakfast? Or you feel up for taking a hike in the mountains?"

"Don't you need some sleep?" I suggested in reply.

"The nap was good," he assured me, nodding. "And I certainly don't intend to waste the day unconscious, when I could be with you."

"Okay," I grinned. "Well... er... breakfast first?"

"Sounds good to me!"

I eagerly followed him downstairs where we ate fresh, delicious papaya on the patio.

***

As the days passed, I began to explore more of what had become 'our' home, and one day I stumbled across a room that appeared to be his study. A curved corner desk sat on one side, with a desktop as well as a laptop on its surface. There was a file cabinet that sat beside the door, and rows of bookshelves, each burdened with dozens of tomes, lined the whole of one wall. And, on the opposite wall, there hung a bunch of photographs. Three of the pictures were around eight-by-ten and boarded by cherry wood frames. A fourth frame was a collage, with six different-sized images. In all four of the frames were pictures of Corey and me.

Both touched and inquisitive about the photos, I took a step toward them.

Every single one was a selfie that he'd taken on his cell phone. I remembered well the first image, which he'd snapped the first time he took me to lunch in New York. I'd thought it strange that he wanted to take a picture of the two of us together, and felt slightly uncomfortable about the idea of nestling close to him while he stretched his arm out in front of us. However, those thoughts didn't seem to show on the captured image of my face. I was smiling, and my eyes were not on the camera lens but focused to the right and the man beside me.

The second shot was taken in the helicopter on our way to Florida. The third on the way back from our stroll along the beach.

The collage was all taken during our travels; in front of the Eiffel Tower; in Cannes; on his yacht; and in Rome. Just quick, fun snaps – nothing fancy or artistic about them. In fact, the one in Paris was at an angle that made the Eiffel Tower look more like the Leaning Tower of Pisa. Nevertheless, Corey had enlarged them and framed them, presumably because they meant something to him.

He hadn't done it to prove something to me: he'd kept them in this quiet little corner of the house, and hadn't even told me they existed. The fact that those moments meant so much to him, and the fact I'd always meant something to him, filled me with a rush of tenderness for him.

Hurriedly leaving the room, and not bothering to close the door behind me, I went in search of him.

I scoured around half of the twenty-seven rooms when I finally found him in one of the west-facing bedrooms. He was sitting in a white Van Keppel-Green lounge chair, the reddish hue of the setting sun illuminating his face. With one hand behind his head and the other holding his phone to his ear, he seemed totally relaxed.

"Well, has the media frenzy died down at least?" he asked softly of whoever was on the other end of the line. After a moment's pause, he began to chuckle. "Hmm, that's good. Listen, just keep doing what you're doing," he added. "I really appreciate it, and it won't be forgotten, I promise."

Pausing by the door, and knowing that I shouldn't really be eavesdropping, I nevertheless waited until he'd ended the call before stepping forward.

Realizing no doubt that I had been listening, Corey turned his head and smiled. "Hey, I was wondering where you'd got to." As he spoke, he leaned down and lowered his phone gently to the carpet before offering his hand to me.

Accepting the silent invitation silently, I allowed him to tug me close. When I was standing beside the chair, he wrapped an arm around my waist and coaxed me down until I was sitting across his lap.

"Is everything okay?" I asked, my hand automatically lifting to his hair and stroking through the thick, dark locks above his ear.

"Fine," he assured me. "Rebecca's having to deal with a lot of crap from Tristan. Apparently, he keeps calling and threatening me, her, and the company: basically anything remotely close to me. But she's handling it like a trooper," he continued.

"The papers?" I asked, knowing that the succinct question would be understood.

"Ahh," he crooned, a mischievous wriggle of his brows. "Well, it seems that Tristan's attempt to shine a light on his so-called broken heart has backfired. A handful of his exes have come out of the woodwork suddenly wanting to sell their stories."

"And?"

Smoothing his hand around my hips, he grinned. "Let's just say, Tristan's not coming out well in it all."

"These women just happened to go to the tabloids now?" I wondered, peering at him a little suspiciously.

"Well, they might have been found, and the suggestion may have been planted." He shrugged. "But no one's been made to do anything they didn't want to," he added emphatically. "No coercion and no incentive other than the satisfaction of seeing that smug grin wiped off his face."

My fingers continuing to move through his soft hair, I smiled. Even when going to war, Corey's ethics were at the forefront of his mind. "So, what's he going to throw at us now?" I asked quietly.

"I don't know," he whispered truthfully. "Maybe he'll think twice before trying anything else," he suggested, although there was doubt in his tone. "Whatever he does, we'll be okay," he added, this time with complete certainty.

"And your company?"

"That'll be fine, too," he quickly insisted. "Rebecca's got everything under control." Tugging me closer, he smiled. "Like I said, I don't know what I'd do without her. She's the best."

Trying to offer him a sincere smile in response, I found myself faltering. "Is she?" I asked.

"Hmm?" he hummed, confusion sweeping across his brow.

"The best?" I clarified. "The two of you..." I mumbled. "Y'know, so... what was she like?"

"Freya," he sighed, shaking his head. "That isn't.... It's not important."

"You wanted to know why my relationship Tristan was different from my relationship with you," I argued gently. "And.... Well, she obviously still means something to you... so... I...."

Exhaling, he lifted his upper half from his reclined position. "She does mean something to me," he agreed.

Instantly, I felt a stab of jealousy, but I was still grateful for his honesty. Most men would undoubtedly deny it. They'd pretend that an ex held no place in their heart in order to placate the new girlfriend, and insult her intelligence in the midst of it all. But Corey chose instead to give me honesty, even if that honesty might sting a little.

"She's damn good at her job," he continued. "She's a friend: someone I can rely on. So, yes, she means something to me. But in the same way Travis means something to me," he added, smiling.

"You've slept with Travis?" I quipped.

Chuckling, he shook his head. "No," he conceded. "But that part of my relationship with Rebecca feels like ancient history, for both of us."

"You loved her?" I wondered, hoping he would grant me the same level of openness that I'd given him.

"In a way," he responded thoughtfully, his eyes leaving my face and dropping to my lap. "In the same way I've loved all the women I've made love to," he added. "Except you," he concluded, forcing his eyes back up to me. "With them, it was always like I needed to block something out. They were like a drug." He shrugged. "They... I..."

"It's okay," I told him.

"Every woman before you was fulfilling something in me. Satisfying a need, and soothing a pain that I wasn't even conscious of still carrying with me."

"And I-" I began, cutting myself off when I realized my tone was more abrasive than I intended it to be. Swallowing, I inhaled a deep breath. "And I don't do that for you?" I asked quietly, with a shake to my voice.

"No," he replied simply. "No, Freya, you do so much more than that. You're... well, you're...." he fumbled. "It's like," he added, his brain quickly pouncing on an analogy. "It's a little like, they were just putting a bandage over this wound. And you," he added, smiling. "Well, you heal it. You make me whole again."

"Really?" I asked.

"Yeah," he replied, nodding as his eyes sparkled. "Yeah," he repeated, more quietly. "I guess, I guess I didn't have a particularly healthy relationship with sex," he admitted. "I didn't realize I was using it to numb something."

"Your mom?" I offered softly.

His features stiffening, he gave a grudging tip of his head. "And something else," he softly added. "Anger."

"Anger?" I repeated, confused. I'd known Corey for almost two months by that point, and had become convinced that anger wasn't an emotion that he knew well. After all, even Tristan's promises to ruin him hadn't ruffled Corey's smooth exterior. He was a mild-mannered, peaceful kind of guy.

"Yes," he replied, evidently not proud of whatever it was that had (or maybe was still), eating away at him. "See, I... um..."

"Corey?" I probed, trying to remind him that I was there and, more importantly, that I wasn't going anywhere. Tenderly smoothing my hand around to the back of his head, I leaned forward and kissed his tense forehead.

"After the accident," he began, his focus drifting slowly to my face as he gave me a soft, grateful smile. "I was pretty messed up. I felt guilty because I'd survived and I was angry with my father."

"Why?" I softly breathed.

"He was driving," he explained simply. "I kept thinking that, if it had been my mom behind the wheel, she would have been more careful. She would have slowed down at that intersection, and she might have seen the truck running the red light."

Those were big maybes, and I guess he knew that as well as I did, because he squeezed his eyes shut and shook his head.

"I blamed him." He exhaled before adding somberly, "I hated him. He had lost something too, but I was still so mad at him for taking her away from me that I never thought about how he felt."

"You were still just a kid," I whispered, leaning into him once more and pressing my lips to the thin lines that crinkled his brow. "Of course you were angry. Of course you had to blame someone."

"I guess I was a bit of a handful for my foster parents," he continued, almost as though my words were washing over him unacknowledged, although I sensed they had penetrated on some level. "They sent me to see a therapist," he added. "I didn't want to go, because I didn't want to admit there was anything wrong."

My lips softly lingering on his head, I gently kissed my way across to his temple.

"Eventually, I agreed to go just once... and... there was this woman, who looked a lot like my mom."

Intrigued, I shifted my face back far enough that I could look at his. "She did?"

A smile of nostalgia gracing his face, he drew his arms a little tighter around me. "Yeah," he mumbled. "She had the same long, auburn hair, and the same slender frame. She even dressed a little like her. I don't think that registered with me on a conscious level at the time," he added, shaking his head. "But I'm pretty sure that's why I was attracted to her."

"You were attracted to her?" I asked quietly. I suddenly remembered his reference to Freud after our first trip to Thimphu. My mind jumped back to Psych 101 in college when I learned about the intricacies of the Oedipal Complex. But no, at 16, he would have resolved those conflicts, right? Still...

It was like Corey could read my mind, though. "It wasn't like that," he quickly explained. "Yes, I was attracted to her, but more because of the comfort of what she represented. Her physical attributes reminded me of my mother. It's kind of like smelling some familiar scent from childhood. It brings you back, you know? Just for a minute."

I knew what he meant. Every time I thought of the toast Mrs. Johansson used to make me, with a small helping of applesauce it, it brought me back to my lonely childhood. Applesauce still calls those memories up for me, like a bittersweet bite of nostalgia.

Nodding, I simply teased my fingers along the nape of his neck as I waited for him to continue.

"We talked about the accident and how I felt toward my father," he sighed. "And then, she..." Pausing, his lips parted as though in wonderment. "She suggested that all that rage, all that tightly wound energy, could be channeled in another direction." Swallowing, his hand rubbed gently up and down my side. "She told me that she was also a Tantric therapist."

"What?" I asked, shock causing the word to jump from my mouth before I had a chance to stop it.

"Yeah," he replied, nodding sagely. "I'd never even heard the word before: I had no clue what she was suggesting."

"How old were you?" I wondered, trying to remove some of the wide-eyed astonishment from my features. He didn't need me passing judgment now on his decisions, or even his therapist's actions. Corey needed to talk, to convey this part of his life to me and even though I knew I wasn't going to like what I heard, I was determined to listen without censure.

"Sixteen," he offered calmly. "So, she told me in no uncertain terms, that if I was interested in learning what she had to teach, it had to stay strictly between us."

"And?"

"And when I realized she was talking about sex, I... I couldn't believe my luck," he scoffed. "Here was this older woman, who wanted to show me how to make love."

"So, you said yes?" I asked rhetorically.

Smiling, he unashamedly met my eyes. "I don't think there are many sixteen-year-old guys who would have said no," he responded evenly. "She was attractive, worldly, intelligent, and keen to show me the ropes. She was everything a teenage boy fantasizes about."

"And that's how you learned to make love like you do?" I asked. I was beginning to understand what it was that made him such a different lover from those who'd come before him.

Nodding, he gently swept his right hand up my torso until the edge of his finger touched my breast through the shirt I wore. His hand lingered right there, teasing me but refusing to fully claim my bosom as his.

"The first time... I was so nervous," he mumbled. "I remember, I was shaking and she took my hands and told me that there was nothing to be frightened of. She said she'd take things slowly, and she'd explain everything to me." His eyes taking on a faraway glint, I figured he was reliving that very first experience and couldn't help feeling envious. "She took me to this special room she had. It had a big bed and soft lights, with lots of pillows and cushions. And then she started to take off her clothes. It seemed so natural to her, like it was no big deal."

I felt very similar about being nude before him, and I couldn't help the smile that tugged at the corners of my mouth.

"But to me," he added, eyes widening. "It was a very big deal. I'd never seen a woman undress in front of me like that before. And then she just stood there, letting me look at her. I was getting so flustered, because I had this massive erection that I knew she could see through my jeans. But she didn't laugh at me, didn't even mention my over eagerness: she just smiled and held her out to me."

Stroking his hairline, I let my fingers dip a little lower until they were creeping beneath the edge of his white T-shirt.

"She pulled me closer to her, and she began to tell me what Tantra was. 'It's more than just sex,' she said. 'It's not just two bodies coming together: it's two souls creating an energy force. A force so strong, but it can't be explained by science or medicine. It can't be seen or measured; it can only be felt by the ones engaging in it.' I remember those words so vividly," he mused. "She told me that the word actually meant to extend or expand. It was about expanding the mind, finding a kind of enlightenment that just isn't available to us in any form on Earth."

Curling my arm around him, I pulled him close, allowing his cheek to press against my bosom. Listening to him, I was transported to the times we'd been entwined with one another; I was taken back to the peace and serenity I'd achieved and the way our love had made me so open with him. He'd given me moments of enlightenment.There was no doubt about that.

"She explained that it was important to become totally absorbed in your partner: fascinated with them to the exclusion of all other things. No distractions, no thinking about what you've got to do later that day, and no focusing on your own pleasure," as he continued to speak, his hand inched a little higher and he stroked the outer curve of my breast. "Then, she said that it was nothing like I'd been used to with masturbation. 'When you pleasure yourself, it's all about getting to that orgasm as quickly as possible,' she told me. 'With a partner, if you want to achieve that connection, those moments of pure bliss, the orgasm isn't the goal, it's just a by-product.'"

I hummed a sound of acknowledgment as I began to understand so much more about the first time we'd been together.

"Then," he continued, snuggling his cheek to my bosom, "she kissed me, and started to take my clothes off. Once I was naked – and feeling like I was gonna explode right there and then before she'd even touched my erection – she took me to the bed. We both sat down and looked at each other, and she told me just to breathe.

Deeply and slowly: breathe. So I did, and as we both inhaled and exhaled, we found a rhythm. We were in tune with each other," he commented. "And then she started to touch me, not in any place that was obviously arousing: my arms, my ears, my neck. It was the sexiest thing I'd ever felt, and she must have realized how excited I was getting, because she'd stop, and tell me to breathe."

Partly fascinated by his story and partly uncomfortable about the special place in his heart that would always belong to this woman, I let my hand smooth down his spine.

"We didn't actually make love that day," he said. "She massaged me, and showed me how to massage her and then finally she stroked my lingam: my penis," he explained. "And I climaxed incredibly quickly. It was so intense that it left me trembling all over."

Knowing the feeling, I nodded.

"Over the next few weeks and months, she gradually showed me more. Taught me how to really appreciate a woman's body. She told me that it wasn't just about heading straight for her sex, but it was about paying homage to every single inch of her. It was about becoming as aroused as possible before actually joining together, and it was about much more than just chasing a few seconds of oblivion."

I suppose I should have been grateful to this woman. And, on some level, I think I was. I've certainly made my peace with it since the first time he told me about her. However, in that moment, I wasn't considering the fact that I had her to thank for the lover he was. I was too consumed with the knowledge that she'd shared something with him that I never would.

"She taught me self-control, how to appreciate delayed gratification, and I came to realize how much stronger the pleasure was when it finally did come."

"So," I breathed. "That's why, when we were in Florida, you...?"

Tipping his head back from my torso, he tilted his face upward to mine. "Could stand to keep my hands off you?" he asked with a knowing wriggle of his dark eyebrows. "Yeah," he added, answering the question without needing to have it confirmed. "For what it's worth, though," he whispered, stretching his lips to mine. "I could only just keep my hands off you," he mumbled before claiming my mouth in a sweet kiss.

So much about what had been an enigma over the previous weeks was making sense. He hadn't been disinterested in me; he just had an amazing amount of self-control. When he'd said he wanted to wait until we'd reached the perfect place, he wasn't wrestling with reservations about what we were doing: he was building the anticipation. He was ensuring that we were both as aroused as possible, so that when the final wave of pleasure came crashing down, it would be the most powerful thing I'd experienced. He was doing exactly what he'd been taught.

"Hmm," he murmured as he gently disengaged from my lips. "Beyond learning how to make love," he said, "the therapy worked. At least, I believed it had. Because when I was with her, when I was focused on her; pleasuring her; and finding pleasure in her, I wasn't thinking about anything else. All the rage I felt – that burning pool of energy in my gut that didn't have a home – found a way out of me. I focused that energy on being the best lover I could be." Dropping his head onto my upper arm, he smiled. "And after that, with every woman, each time I brought her to climax, I felt better. Some of the hurt had gone."

"But it didn't last?" I asked quietly, recalling the start of our conversation.

Shaking his head, he lifted his pensive eyes to mine. "It was temporary," he breathed. "It was always only temporary."

"So..." I hesitated. "What's.... I mean, how am I...?"

"I don't know how," he chuckled. "And I don't know why it's different with you. All I know is that it is different. It's not just a quick relief from the pain. When I'm with you, I feel like you're giving me a part of myself back again."

"But I..." I stumbled, feeling sure that couldn't be what he was saying. If the Tantric therapist hadn't been able to heal him, then how could I? I had no experience with the art of Tantra, and, although I'd had a pretty good clue about what was bothering him, I hadn't any real appreciation for what was going on his head. Fumbling around completely in the dark, how could I possibly have offered him what he'd needed?

"It's you, Freya," he grinned, seeming to have read the insecure thoughts that were racing through my mind. "It was nothing youdid, and nothing you said. It's just you." Briefly kissing my arm through the thin fabric of my blouse, he tugged me closer to him. "There's something about you that makes me feel whole. While I've got you by my side, I'm stronger. I'm a better person."

That, I very much doubted. But I didn't argue with him.

"I'm happier, and I know that everything is right with the world," he continued. "And that's why I'm so scared of losing you. Other women... I've had feelings for, I've loved, and I've connected with them on some level. But there's never been dependence with any of them. They didn't feel that way about me, and I didn't feel that way about them. If one woman decided she wanted to move on, it was no big deal. I knew we'd both have pleasant memories of each other, and we'd just part on good terms."

With the exception of my professor, I didn't part on good terms with any of my exes. It was always an awkward, horrible mess. Corey's way seemed infinitely preferable, and damn healthier, and I wondered what that might be like. The situation he described struck me as alien, but I was starting to comprehend how he could retain a professional and amicable relationship with women like Rebecca.

"But I find myself needing you, Freya," he concluded soberly. "I don't know what I'd do without you. I couldn't just kiss you goodbye and move on to the next girl, you know? You've got a piece of me. You own a part of my heart that I've never given anyone else. When we connect, it's more profound than it's ever been. And I think that's because I finally let my guard down." As if the realizations were striking him as he was speaking, the words tumbled easily from his lips. "With you, I'm opening myself completely. Nothing is hidden, nothing is held back. And now, I'm starting to truly appreciate what my teacher told me so long ago. My mind, my heart and my soul are expanding, Freya. And they're so full that I can't ever contemplate going back to the way things were before."

"I don't want to go back, either," I told him tenderly. "I want to stay right here with you," I added. "Here where it's safe, and where I'm loved. Where I love… more fiercely than I've ever loved before."

With a soft sigh, his shoulders dropped. "So, I should stop worrying?" he asked.

"If you're worried that I'm going to suddenly walk away," I soothing said, rolling my palm over his shoulder blades, "then the answer is yes. There is nothing in this world that could persuade me to walk away from you. We're together now, and nothing is ever going to tear us apart again."

"Again?" he smiled.

I hadn't realized I'd said the word. But I knew well enough where it had come from: that strange flash when I'd seemed to have an out of body experience. However, I wasn't about to tell him something that had the potential to sound crazy. So, I simply shrugged it off, and changed the subject. "I love you," I told him emphatically, pressing myself to him and lowering my mouth over his with a passionate moan.

CHAPTER EIGHT

My Love River

The following morning, I awoke to an empty bed. Groaning, my hands reached out and smoothed over the sheets, searching for the body I'd become so familiar with. But it wasn't there. Peeling my eyes open, I gazed down at the wrinkled white cotton covering the mattress.

Unwilling to move just yet, I had to make do with what was available. Stretching out, I grasped his pillow and hugged it to my chest. Allowing my eyes to drift closed, I dipped my face to the soft fabric that still smelled of his shampoo and breathed deeply of the scent. I was addicted to that smell; I craved it when I was around him as well as when he was absent. When we made love, I'd spend long minutes inhaling the clean, soft scent of his hair. Some nights, long after he'd fallen asleep, I'd keep my head nestled close to his so I could continue to breathe him in. It made me feel even closer to him.

I don't think I could have remained that way for more than a few minutes, before his soft voice roused me.

"Freya," he said smoothly.

At first, I wasn't sure whether I was hearing him call my name in reality or in a half dream. However, as my eyes fluttered open and I found him peering at me from the foot of the bed, I got my answer.

"Morning," he greeted, grinning.

"Morning," I replied, lifting my upper body from the bed and not caring that, as the sheet fell away from me, it left my breasts exposed. "You're up early," I noted, eyes glancing quickly behind him and making a quick estimate of the time based on the sun's lazy ascent.

"Yeah," he nodded. "Your surprise was arriving, so..."

"This early?" I queried. "That's a pretty dedicated package delivery company they have here," I chuckled.

"Didn't arrive by package," he replied, shaking his head. "Srista very kindly made the pick-up at the airport and then drove up here."

"Wow," I chuckled. "Well, then she's pretty dedicated."

"Well, he couldn't wait," Corey explained.

"He?" I mumbled, still half asleep and unsure I was following the conversation.

Lips spreading into a broad grin, Corey seemed determined not to say any more. "Follow me," was all he murmured, as he tipped his head toward the open bedroom door.

I remained on the bed, watching as he excitedly swept through the door. Gradually, however, I began to disentangle my legs from the soft cotton and drag my curious body off the mattress. Absent-mindedly, as I wandered around the bottom of the bed, I stooped to pick up a shirt Corey had abandoned the night before. I enjoyed being naked around him, wandering around the house – our love nest – with complete freedom. However, I also enjoyed the sensation of his clothes against my skin. I like having his lingering scent on me, and I got a strange sense of belonging in the simple act of wearing his shirt. A belonging that cut both ways; I belonged to him, and he belonged to me.

Loosely buttoning the long sleeve shirt that was long enough to reach my mid-thigh, I padded gently to the door.

"Come on," I heard him eagerly call.

"I'm coming." I chuckled, entering the hallway and following the path I assumed he'd taken to the stairs.

Sure enough, I found him at the bottom of the staircase, one hand still clinging to the rail as he peered over his shoulder.

I jogged down the steps and nestled by his side. "This is it?" I asked, looking about me and finding nothing that appeared different from the way it had the night before.

"Nope," he smiled, shaking his head before placing his hands on my shoulders and spinning me ninety degrees. He stayed close behind me and leaning into my back, carefully slipped his hands over my eyes.

"What are you doing?" I asked, chuckling.

"Trust me," he whispered, tipping his face to my ear and kissing the skin just beneath it.

"You know I do," I replied softly.

Kissing me once more and then carefully taking my earlobe between his teeth, he urged me forward with a soft push of his hips against the small of my back.

Bare feet moving over the granite tiles of the hall, I shuffled forward, trusting him completely to keep me away from walls and furniture. "You know you don't have to keep surprising and spoiling me," I commented gently, realizing even without my sight that we were heading to the large living room. "I've already been wooed." I smiled.

"I like surprising and spoiling you," he replied, his lips still teasing my ear. "Making you happy makes me happy."

"You make me happy," I countered.

"Hmm," he chuckled, sucking my lobe over his tongue and sensuously licking the soft curve. "Well, hopefully this will make you happy, too."

Stopping when the pressure against my back eased, I felt the thick, coarse fabric of a rug beneath my feet. Then, swiftly, he lifted his hands from my face. Blinking, my eyes moved hurriedly about the room at the level of my head. Eventually, though, my gaze drifted lower. A large, cream-colored rattan pet carrier sat in the middle of the room with its cage door wide open.

"Wh-?" I began to breathe before a soft meow caused my focus to dart to the right.

Celestin stood by the large glass doors; apparently he'd been staring fascinatedly at the view. However, as his head lifted curiously to me, and his almond-shaped, dazzling blue eyes settled on my face, he hurried forward.

"Cel," I cried, delighted. Sinking to my haunches to greet him, I scooped the slender Siamese into my arms and hugged him to my chest.

Purring loudly, Celestin nuzzled my neck and chin with his head.

"How did you get him here?" I blurted, swinging my face to Corey.

Grinning, Corey seemed content to drink in the sight of my reunion. But gently, he reached forward and tickled the bundle in my arms. "Sorry, it took so long," he smiled. "I had to get his passport, and arrange for transportation. But I didn't want him to be stuck in quarantine for months."

"That's so sweet of you," I crooned, melting at the sight of Celestin curiously sniffing Corey's hand. "It's funny," I added. "He doesn't usually take to strangers."

"I guess he doesn't think of me as a stranger," he replied with a shrug.

"Hmm," I agreed. "I guess not."

***

Days turned to weeks and weeks turned to months, and Corey and I fell into a strange kind of domestication in Bhutan. A handful of locals had been employed to help with cleaning and other chores, but a lot of the day-to-day tasks Corey and I would do on our own. For example, I quickly discovered that he was a wonderful cook. With an interest in learning new recipes and experimenting with fresh ingredients, he'd begun serving several Bhutanese dishes, including spicy emadatshi and a noodle soup called thukpa. We'd spend large portions of the day together, but had also begun to develop individual interests in the beautiful country we were living in.

I'd started traveling down to a temple every morning; there I would chant with the locals and even teach yoga to some of the women. It was a strange kind of instruction, because few of them spoke any English, and I'd only managed to master a few words of Dzongkha. The eighteen other languages spoken in the country were still beyond me.

Nevertheless, the local women were wonderfully welcoming. They knew that I was living in the 'palace' in the mountains; I was an outsider, and a very wealthy one at that – although the money wasn't technically mine, that wasn't a distinction they'd made. Yet, not once did they treat me with anything other than kindness and a genuine desire to embrace me into their way of life.

I'd loved every second of my time there. Thanks to Corey opening me sexually, I found that I was much more unburdened in all aspects of my life. I wasn't scared of embracing new things, meeting new people, and exploring the depths – and darkness – of myself.

Mornings at the temple were wonderfully spiritual, liberating hours. And I would always return to our love nest feeling full of joy, and hope and love.

Mornings at the temple were wonderfully spiritual

Typically, while I was down in one of the villages, or sometimes Thimphu, Corey would travel down into the capital's Himalayan valley and play golf at the nine-hole course. He, too, was making friends with locals and with other tourists. Of course, given his easygoing nature, it was no surprise that he found himself greeted warmly wherever he went.

One afternoon, when we'd been at the palace for around six months, I returned from a small temple in the beautiful village of Talo to find Corey lounging in the living room.

Sprawled on his back across the couch, he held a tablet computer in one hand and tapped at the screen with the fingers of the other. He wore an unusual, grave expression, but as I was about to ask him about it, he seemed to notice my presence. The troubled look almost instantly vanished.

"Hey, you're back," he smiled.

"Yeah," I nodded, dropping the small bag I carried with me and approaching the couch. "No golf today?" I asked.

"No," he replied, letting the hand with the tablet sink to the floor. "Didn't really feel like it," he explained.

144

"Something wrong?" I asked, perching my butt on the arm of the couch and allowing my hand to drift unthinkingly to his bare feet.

"No," he responded.

Lifting his foot and beginning to massage the arch with a firm push of my thumb, I looked carefully at his face. "Thought we weren't keeping anything from each other anymore," I commented dryly.

"Mm," he groaned, clearly appreciating the attention his sole was receiving. "We're not," he agreed. "It's nothing to worry about. Just Tristan seems to be shorting the shares in my business."

"What does that mean?" I asked.

"Well, it's...." he sighed, relaxing into the couch cushions as though he didn't have a care in the world. "It's not a good thing," he admitted, with a wry smile. "I'll explain it another time," he added.

Wondering why he'd suddenly started shutting me out, I ceased the movement of me fingers. "Why not now?" I insisted.

Releasing his hold on the computer, he let it gently drop to the floor before pushing himself into a sitting position. Both hands reaching out to my legs, he rolled his palms softly over my thighs, while his eyes settled on my face with that constant steadiness of his that made it impossible to doubt his candor.

Nonetheless, I wanted to know what was going on back in New York. "Corey?" I probed. "What's Tristan doing?"

"Later, I promise," he replied calmly. "There something else I want to focus on right now, something I've been thinking about for a long time. And something I've been laying here waiting for you to get back for."

"What?" I wondered.

Tucking his feet up and folding them before him, he made space on the couch and tugged me into it. "Have you ever heard of amrita?" he asked.

I turned to face him, and tucked my feet in beneath me. The motion seemed entirely automatic. "No, I don't think so."

"In Sanskrit, it literally means immortality. But it can also be used to mean divine nectar," he said, his hands massaging my upper legs with what had become incredibly familiar intimacy. "It's thought to be liquid energy, a higher connection to the sacred," he added softly. "It's a higher level of release, and it's said that when a woman experiences the flowing of amrita, she's also releasing the goddess within herself."

Still not quite sure what he was talking about, I nodded in invitation. I wanted to hear more about this amrita. But I wanted him to know that he wasn't going to get me to forget the other issue. "That other conversation isn't over," I said firmly, clinging stubbornly to the last threads of that other world before they broke. Then, curious, I continued to listen attentively.

"It's the flow of your love river," he added, ignoring my last statement. The man could be as stubborn as me sometimes. "It's a more intense pleasure."

"Love river?" I repeated. Yep. We might as well have exclaimed, Tristan who? Bring on the love river. "You mean..." I inhaled. "Are you talking about female ejaculation?" I wondered.

"Yes," he smiled.

"I always thought that was a myth," I replied dubiously. "You know, something peddled by pornographers."

Chuckling, he gave me a quick tilt of his head. "It's certainly something they like to portray, and not necessarily in an accurate way," he admitted. "But ejaculation is something women have experienced since the dawn of time," he insisted gently.

"Really?" I asked, still doubtful over the whole subject.

Smiling, he nodded assuredly. "Do you want to experience it?" he suggested softly, his hands sliding all the way up to my hips as he continued to massage my legs.

"I..." I mumbled. "I don't think I can," I told him, shaking my head.

"Yes, you can," he countered, without so much as a trace of uncertainty.

"But it's never happened before," I reasoned. "I've had incredibly strong orgasms with you, but my.... What did you call it?"

"Amrita," he supplied.

"My amrita has never flowed."

"It takes time," he quickly responded, unperturbed by my lingering skepticism. "You needed to feel completely comfortable; you needed to know the power of your body; you need to be in touch with that part of yourself."

"What part?"

"The goddess," he answered swiftly. "Because you are a goddess, Freya," he added, his eyes moving over me with that mixture of arousal and awe that kept me feeling perpetually giddy.

"I just.... Wow." I breathed. "I don't think it's possible for me to feel any more than I already do with you. It's so intense, Corey. It's.... I can't even put it into words."

"I know," he replied with a soft half smile. "I know, but trust me, there's more."

Studying his strong, dependable features, I nodded. "I believe you. But what if I can't-"

"Uh uh," he hurriedly interjected, lifting one hand to my face and sliding his finger across my lips to silence them. "You can, Freya. You just have to release the sexual goddess."

"How?" I whispered.

"I'll show you," he responded tenderly, his hand sweeping across my cheek.

Before I had a chance to voice any more of my doubts, he was untangling his feet and getting up from the couch. Both of his large, warm hands grasped mine and he urged me to stand.

With nothing more than a confident smile, he led me from the room. I followed unquestioningly, and we walked hand in hand upstairs. I'd assumed we were heading to the master bedroom, but when we reached that floor, he turned away from the room we shared each night and strolled all the way down the hall to a narrow, wooden spiral staircase. I was curious as to where he was headed, but I simply walked behind him without protest.

Up we climbed, into the attic space that I'd never bothered to investigate before. I think I'd always just assumed it was exactly that: attic space. Oh, how wrong I'd been.

We were in the roof space sure enough, but it was by far your ordinary attic. With a high vaulted ceiling and an antique oak floor, the whole area was open plan. The only exception was an enclosed bathroom in the left corner. But the rest of the space was a massive bedroom on one side and living area on the other.

The king size bed was a simple, low frame with a luxurious deep mattress, and linen that I'd later learn was Charlotte Thomas, with twenty-two karat gold thread woven within the fabric.

A massive c-shaped sectional couch with hardwood frame and white cushions was on the other side of the space. But what was most impressive was the view from every inch of the room. From the very roof of our love nest, we could see the crest of some of the smaller mountains. It was even more breathtaking than the view from one floor below.

"This is it," he said, still clutching my hand as we walked toward the couch and the windows that ran the whole of the east-facing wall. "This is the view that convinced me I had to buy this place. I didn't even need to see it in real life," he added, chuckling. "They were just pictures on a property auction site, but, it was enough, that was all I needed to fall in love with the place."

"It's beautiful," I whispered, mesmerized by the sight of the Himalayan Griffin, which soared serenely above the peaks.

The room's other three walls were covered in brightly colored murals that were reminiscent of paintings I'd seen in temples all around the local area. And the space had also been decorated with sweet-smelling magnolias and the blue poppies that are the national bloom of the country.

"I was going to make love to you here the first time," he added. "But I wanted to save it for this."

"Corey," I exhaled, clinging fiercely to his hand. "Wherever we are, it's always amazing to me."

"I know." He smiled. "For me too, but I wanted this to be our special place; it's the place where you finally discover that you're a goddess."

My eyes closed as his face drifted inexorably down to mine and his lips brushed sweetly across my mouth. His tender tongue softly flicked over my bottom lip and I instantly responded with a moan that granted him access.

Eagerly accepting the invitation, his warm, wet tongue slid erotically between my wanton lips. Wrapping his free arm around me, while the fingers of his other hand remained entwined with mine, Corey pulled me close making his heated erection clear.

Like Pavlov's dogs, my body's response was as fast as it was intuitive. The familiar flush of heat settled in my loins, moisture pooled inside me and my yoni was expanding in readiness – I'd long since stopped calling it my sex or my vagina. Corey had insisted that it was the sacred part of me, and therefore deserved to be referred to with reverence.

"It isn't just another body part," he'd insisted. "And words have power, whether we realize it or not," he'd added. He encouraged me to view my femininity with the same respect he'd shown it from the moment we met.

Eager and ready to feel his hands on me, I began to pull my fingers free and guide his palm to my breast.

With deference, he carefully cupped the soft flesh, leaving my hands free to unbutton his shirt.

I had become obsessed with his chest, a fact that amused and, I think, flattered him. Every time we made love, I needed to explore his naked torso; I had to feel his perfect skin against mine.

Helping me by shrugging off the shirt, Corey's mouth never once disengaged with mine. Once my greedy fingers met his sleek, muscular flesh, I stroked every inch of it, sweeping up to his shoulder, down over the pecs, teasing his nipples in that way I knew made him chuckle, and then playing with the soft line of hair that led beneath his pants. As my fingers lazily met at his belt buckle, I began calmly unclasping it.

Unlike the first few times we'd made love – at this point in our relationship – I'd learned to temper my aching desire. I knew, without question, that the connection would come: as would the immense pleasure. There was no longer any need for me to fretfully seek a climax that I'd previously feared wouldn't come. And in the process of becoming more relaxed, I realized he was right: the longer we allowed the anticipation to build, the much better that final explosive ecstasy was.

He smiled against my mouth, his tongue moving languidly across the roof of my mouth, as I edged his pants and his underwear off his hips.

Letting gravity take them down his thighs, I blindly wrapped my right hand around his swollen manhood, and tenderly massaged him. There was no effort to arouse him further or bring him close to the point of insensible pleasure. It was nothing more than a gentle stimulation, and grateful homage to that part of him that had given me so much pleasure.

As I enjoyed the smooth sensation of his taut skin moving under my loosely clutched hand, I was also aware of the glorious sensation of his hands, claiming my breasts, sliding down my sides, my hips and sweeping over my buttocks.

We continued to tease each other was we undressed. And then, when we were both naked and beaded with sweat, he took my hand and led me to the bed. Smiling, he sat down, and silently urged me to sit in his lap. I straddled his knees, knowing, quite instinctively now, that we still hadn't reached the moment of complete and unyielding arousal. He didn't have to tell me much about Tantra: I grasped most of it just by the way he interacted with me. And I was learning more every day.

Flicking my hair away from my face, I wrapped my hands around his neck, and allowed my head to drop forward until it was resting against his.

For some time, we stayed that way, smiling at each other and breathing as if as one. His hands moved constantly, warming my skin with wordless but profound affection.

My cheeks and the skin on my chest flushed a light shade of pink, and I struggled to keep my breathing calm and deep. My yoni was hot, growing restless, and was fully expanded in waiting for him.

"Are you ready?" he asked rhetorically, his voice taking on that deep huskier quality that he always got when we were making love. His tone was so erotic it alone was close to bringing me to orgasm.

"Yes," I whimpered.

"Okay." He chuckled, gripping me around the middle and rolling us both over until I was beneath him.

Through habit, I wrapped my legs around his waist and kept a tight grasp on him as he nestled me against the luxuriously soft sheets.

However, he didn't enter me. Instead, he began to kiss his way down my cheek, along my collarbone, down my sternum. Forcing my legs to relinquish their hold, he shuffled downward, licking my belly and finally placing his lips on my mound.

Arching my back, I thrust my hips gently upward. "Corey, I'm ready for you."

"I know you are," he whispered.

"Inside me," I gasped, my lower half undulating gently with need.

Lifting his head, his chin brushed my mound as he looked up at me. "The easiest way to encourage the release of your amrita is to stimulate your G-spot," he smiled. "And the easiest way to do that is with my fingers," he added.

He had stroked my G-spot on several occasions. He had found it the very first time we'd made love, and had even stimulated it with his lingam when he entered me from behind. However, he was right: his fingers had always been more accurate in gauging the exact amount of pressure I needed.

"Just relax," he mumbled, face tipping back down to my skin and kissing a gloriously sensual path to my folds. "Relax," he whispered, his soft breath stroking over the damp entrance of my yoni.

Clutching at the sheets, I let my body sink into the bed as he began to kiss that most sacred part of me with a tenderness that only he had ever shown me. Slowly, and with deliberate movements, he licked my folds and teased the bud until my hips were jerking beneath him. Reaching the height of need, both hands darted down to his head, tangling in his hair.

"Please, Corey," I mewled, my entire body ablaze with desire.

"I know," he soothed, placing one strong palm over my mound and ceasing the feverish motion of my lower body. "I know," he repeated, peering up as he slipped one finger softly between my labia. "I need your G-spot to be as large as it'll get," he explained.

Desperately trying to keep control of my breathing, I sucked in shaky lungs full of airwhile my eyes flickered, and tried to focus on him. "Now, Corey," I wheezed. "I need you now."

"I'm here," he calmly assured, his finger slowly sliding inside me.

"Ahh," I moaned in relief, tossing my head back on the pillows. It was only one finger, and it didn't stimulate me anywhere close to satisfaction, but it was a blissful sensation nonetheless. My hips bucking, I tried to encourage him to thrust his digit. However, he was a man with a plan and he wasn't going to be swayed from it.

As my hips lifted from the mattress, he gently but firmly, pushed me back down with the palm that continued to rest on my lower abdomen. The finger within me, meanwhile, was slowly rubbing my front wall. He found my G-spot almost instantly, and as his pad brushed over it, I realized just how aroused it had become. Flushed with blood, it was at least twice the size and sensitivity than it had ever been before.

As I closed my eyes, lights flashed before my lids, and I felt waves of pleasure run through my body as he carefully rolled just the pad of one finger gently over that rough spot. "Oh, God," I mewled, spreading my legs wider and pulling my knees closer to my chest.

"You are a goddess, Freya," Corey smoothly said, slipping another finger into my wet, willing yoni. "You're a beautiful goddess," he continued, both fingers gliding forward until they met that glorious spot.

"Argh," I moaned in delight.

"You're powerful," he added. "So very powerful. You have all of this glorious sexual energy." As he spoke, slowly and calmly, he began to move his fingers in firm circles.

Every moment created a spasm that shook all the way through the rest of my body. Each touch caused my pinned hips to shudder and quake. I was already on the verge of an immense climax: that much was clear to me.

"Let it out, Freya," Corey urged, pressing his fingers more firmly to that spongy flesh and eliciting a strangled sob of pleasure from me.

Tears were pooling in the corners of my clenched eyes. My entire body was expectantly poised for something that it had never known before.

"Breathe, my darling," he instructed.

Realizing I'd inadvertently held my breath – an old habit I thought I'd managed to break free of – I struggled to focus on the simple movement of air in and out of my lungs. At first, I though it would be impossible: the pleasure was so great I couldn't focus on my breathing. But eventually I did, and I took a long, slow inhalation through my nose and released it calmly through an open mouth. The exhale accompanied by a groan of, "Oh, Corey. More!"

His strong fingers pressed a little harder, and the pleasure was so intense it was almost painful.

"Release your goddess, Freya," he steadily uttered. "Find yourself."

The white lights that had been flashing in front of my closed lids were shifting to a multicolored kaleidoscope that began to form shapes and images. I saw Corey as a god, a fearless warrior, who loved me like no other man had before. I was the goddess he'd spoken of, and while I'd known many lovers, none of them had been in comparison: I had never felt that strong connection with anyone but Corey. Something, I couldn't quite discern what, had parted us, and I'd gone in search of him, vowing to never stop until he was once again in my arms.

The dreamlike thoughts were abruptly torn from my mind, though, when the burning, swelling sensation in my yoni finally hit fever pitch. My eyes snapping open, I clutched at my own thighs, desperate to cling onto something, My nails digging themselves deep into the flesh, I locked eyes with Corey's and found his dark gaze brimming with heat, passion and love.

"You are a goddess," he breathed in a gentle whisper.

For a suspended moment, I was frozen, my mouth partly open, my eyes unable to break free of his. And then, the ecstasy crashed over me.

It was a feeling of complete surrender. Unlike any orgasm I'd had before, it felt like I was sharing the sensation with Corey. And as our gaze continued to meet each other and his eyes began to sparkle with delight, I felt sure it was not all in my head.

Gasping, my body began to tremble violently and then the gushing began. Warm, clear fluid flowed from my yoni, drenching his fingers, the bed clothes beneath me, and even splattering his chest.

"Oh, Cor-" I panted, mesmerized by both the feeling of freedom that came with the release and the sight of so much amrita violently leaving my body. It seemed to go on and on, wave after wave of pleasure, continuing to quake me. "Oh, Corey!" I eventually screamed, as my brain drifted into that sweet oblivion. I found myself getting lost in darkness, the pleasure dragging me deeper and deeper.

It was several moments later before I managed to open my eyes. When I did, I was flopped listlessly back on the bed, my arms spread wide either side of me, and my quivering legs still jerking with the aftershocks.

Feeling the tip of Corey's tongue on my thigh, I tipped my chin forward and watched as he lapped at the translucent nectar.

Noticing the weight of my stare, he lifted his face and with a wriggle of his brows, he grinned. "It's immortality," he said.

"Corey," I mewled, trying to lift one arm, but finding it too leaden to get more than an inch off the bed. "Come here," I begged.

Without hesitation, he placed his hands either side of my waist and pulled himself up until his body was completely covering mine. Our faces mere millimeters away, and he nuzzled my cheek with the tip of his nose. "I told you, you were a goddess," he chuckled. "How did it feel?"

"Like..." I puffed, unsure whether there were any words in the English language to accurately describe the sensations I'd experienced. "Like heaven," I eventually sighed. "Paradise, where there was only you and me."

"Hmm," he hummed, clearly approving of that thought. "You were beautiful," he added. "So incredibly beautiful. In fact... I think you've become even more beautiful... changed even more, just this minute."

"Changed?"

I was curious to see if he sensed what I felt. Indeed, I was so unbelievably satisfied, I could easily start purring like a cat with a dish of cream, but I was invigorated at the same time. Something was changing inside me, and it had everything to do with Corey and his Tantric teachings.

Corey nodded, as if he could see my musings. "You are you, but a million times more, Freya, my goddess. Finally you, in your truest form."

I pursed my lips together. "I think I know what you mean. For the first time ever, I feel like I'm starting to fall in love with myself. I'm no longer that doormat my mother made me, I'm not some victim of some screwed up relationship. I feel beautiful – truly beautiful – and it's because you have made me feel that way."

He pushed himself onto his elbows and looked sternly into my eyes. "This is not because of me. Well... maybe I helped you a little by helping you discover your Amrita. And," he mused happily, "now that it has begun, your G-spot is going to be stimulated every time we make love. Your love river will continue to flow freely and you can always look forward to feeling so delicious and pleasured."

Now, I began to purr. "I feel so special now. But powerful too. I feel this new source of potential in me. When I felt my Amrita flowing – felt that intense source of pleasure – I felt as powerful as when I was the Goddess Freya. And even though it's over, I still feel that way. Powerful. Beautiful. Invincible. Nothing can bring me down again."

Corey nodded, silently pressing his lips to mine. I felt a different level of respect and admiration that I never thought possible. Suddenly, I wanted him to come to climax as well: and, a little selfishly, I wanted him inside of me. I wanted that physical connection.

"Make love to me, Corey," I whimpered. "I need to feel you inside me."

Happy to oblige, Corey slipped his right hand between our bodies and guided his lingam to my yoni. He made slow, tender – but no less passionate – love to my fatigued body.

Left so sensitive from the release, every subtle movement he made within me caused a tingle of pleasure that set off dozens of miniature orgasms. And then, finally, he climaxed, releasing himself to me and creating another intense series of spasms in every muscle I possessed.

Long after we were both spent physically, he remained within me. Tangled in that gloriously intimate embrace, neither one of us was keen to move.

"So..." I sighed, my hands moving in small circles over his shoulder blades and lower back. I had regained a little strength into my limbs once again. I was slightly reluctant to break the comfortable silence, and it was a few seconds before I finished the thought. "What is shorting stock?"

Laughing, he lifted his head from the crook of my shoulder and stared deep into my eyes. "I'm not talking about it now, Freya," he said firmly, covering my mouth and swallowing any protest I might have offered.

CHAPTER NINE

Massage for Corey

I sat in my space near the temple, stretching my muscles. The setting was tropical, beautiful. A natural clearing, surrounded by rhododendrons and magnolias. The clearing was open, full of light; a bit of a trek to get to, but it was the perfect place for the spiritual connection that could be found in yoga. The noises that surrounded us were the songs of hawks, cuckoos, and crows. It wasn't quiet, or even serene, but it was the most natural place I could imagine to hold a class.

No students had shown up for today's class. Life works differently in Bhutan. Time is slower, even, and there was no offense if someone didn't show up for something like this. Things needed to be taken care of. I might see the usual group next week, or even next month, if things are busy right now.

Still, I enjoyed the chance to stimulate my muscles. Both poses of Lord of the Dance, then the Crane and Pigeon poses helped me calm and center myself, as well as working my muscles. It felt good and natural to move this way. At my studio, I might teach four or five classes in a day, here it was a few a week. When I had the opportunity, I worked myself through poses, even without a class. It helped keep me relaxed.

After a few more minutes of tranquil bliss, I decided to head back to the love nest. I would be early, but the idea of surprising Corey with lunch excited me. I stopped at the market to pick up strawberries that had been picked that morning, mangos, and cheese.

Pulling up to the house, I noticed a car she hadn't seen before. I didn't give it much thought; the love nest was a work in progress, and sometimes extra staff came to work on the gardens or other areas of the palace that needed attention. I parked, pulled out the groceries, and made my way into the kitchen.

I sliced and arranged our impromptu lunch. I enjoyed taking the time to make things special for Corey. It was one of the ways that I really showed him that I care for him. I know how important little things like that can be in a relationship. Our cook was just coming in to begin dinner preparations, and we easily worked in the large kitchen, staying out of each other's way.

Walking through the palace,I thought I heard noises coming from upstairs. Expecting to find him in his office, I was surprised to find him moaning under the hands of a gorgeous woman, who was massaging his lower back, right above his bare buttocks. Her sheer top left little to the imagination, her large, full breasts and hard nipples were fully on display. Her tiny skirt was little more than a thin band of silk wrapped around her hips; I could see the entire length of her long legs, which were the color of a perfectly made cup of mocha. The stark white of her clothing was a sharp contrast to the perfectly sun-kissed tone of her skin and her long dark hair. She walked around the massage table on six inch heels. She was older than I was, and had an air of confidence I could only hope to achieve one day. She was sexy, self-assured, and voluptuous; everything I would never be. Suddenly, I understood what Tristan had meant when he said I wasn't Corey's type. It had nothing to do with hair color or the clothes I wore. I could see an empty bottle of champagne, neck down in an ice bucket. I felt the plates of fruit slipping out of my fingers as I stood there, slack-jawed, unable to accept what I was seeing.

Corey jumped at the sound of the plates crashing onto the floor. He looked around, and his face fell as he realized that I was standing there. Sitting up, he made no attempt to cover himself in front of the woman. She stood at the side of the massage table, her hands extended, unsure of what to do next. He jumped off the table and turned towards me; I was even more horrified to realize that his lingam was fully erect.

"Freya," he called, stumbling as he came toward me.

How much had he had to drink?

"Freya, let me explain." he said, his voice almost pleading.

"Get out," I said, my attention on the woman. "Don't bother coming back. Send your bill to Corey's office." The woman turned, started gathering her things.

"Get out now! Your things will be returned to you. I want you out of this house, now."

The masseuse stood up straight, her shoulders back, not at all ashamed of her nearly nude appearance, and obviously fully aware of how provocative she appeared as she walked past me. She walked out of the room slowly, deliberately. An anger I didn't know I possessed reared its ugly head as she walked by. I wanted to hit her. I was surprised by this visceral reaction to Corey's betrayal and the haughty attitude of the masseuse.

"Freya," Corey said, putting his hand on my arm.

I didn't want to hear his explanation. I couldn't believe what I had just witnessed. I turned on my heel and began running down the hallway. I ran down the back stairs, into the kitchen. Our cook, an older married woman of about forty-five, was getting ready to do some baking. I pushed past her, and found both maids in the dining room, cleaning the windows. I hadn't realized before how beautiful they were, their light brown skin perfectly complementing their long dark hair. How many sexy women did Corey need to have working for him?

"You, both of you! Get out! You're fired. Do not ever come back here again."

Both maids looked at me, and then at each other, a puzzled look on their faces.

"I'm the boss here! This is my home! Get out! Now!" I screamed.

Corey walked up behind me, grabbed my arm again. I pulled away from him, more angry than hurt now.

"You can't fire the entire staff," Corey said.

"I can and I will, if I want. Since I apparently can't trust you around them, I need to make sure that you're not going to be letting them rub your naked body when I'm not home."

I walked toward the stairs, with Corey following on my heels.

"It wasn't what it looked like."

At the bottom of the stairs, I turned to face him. "Funny, that's exactly what Tristan said to me when he had his dick in his secretary's mouth."

I turned and ran up the stairs, into the bedroom. I slammed the door, hoping that would keep Corey out. I couldn't imagine that he would have an explanation for this, and, even if he did, I didn't want to hear it. I just wanted to run away. Why did every man in my life make it his mission to hurt me?

Corey was at the closed door; I could hear him knocking, saying my name softly from the other side, as I found a bag and threw some clothes inside. I changed out of my yoga clothes and into some comfortable jeans. Corey was begging by now.

"Freya, please. Let me talk to you."

"I'm not interested in anything you have to say. You're no different. Tristan told me you would play me. I have been such a fool."

"I'm not playing you. Please, Freya. Just open the door. I really want to talk to you. I need to explain."

I was tired of yelling through the door. I opened it, giving him just enough room to walk inside. Corey was carrying the bottle of twenty year old Scotch that sat on the bar downstairs. He sat down hard on the bed and took a long swig out of the bottle. I couldn't believe what I was seeing.

"Freya, I never slept with her. I swear."

"Why was she even here?"

"Because I wanted a massage. You know how much stress I've been under lately. Tristan is doing his damndest to ruin my business, Freya. Before I even knew you, I was building that business to provide for you and our family. I don't want you to ever want for anything."

He took another drink.

"So I hired a masseuse. Truthfully, I'm not even sure why you're mad." Corey's words were beginning to slur now. A bottle of champagne and several long pulls off that bottle of Scotch were doing him in.

"You were naked! Erect. Another woman touched you, and you enjoyed it so much that it gave you an erection. You know, Corey, I really want to tell myself that you're saying that because you're drunk. That you can rationalize the fact that you called a masseuse who dresses like a prostitute to rub your body while you're naked and I'm not here because you were drinking, and that it won't happen again. But I thought the same thing of Tristan, the first time he was an ass when he was drinking. Do you do this every time I go to class? How long has this been going on?"

"No. Not every time. But almost."

"So this has been going on for the entire eight months we've been here? You can't see how hiding this from me, makes me mad?"

"That's not what I meant."

"Then you should tell me what you did mean."

"I would. But I'm not sure what I meant. Freya, I'm drunk."

"Yes, you are. I've never seen you this drunk. Do you always drink this much when you're getting a massage?"

"No. I'm never this drunk. Ever. I've been drinking since I was fourteen. I think that by now I know how to control it. In fact, you could even say that I'm a professional at it."

"A professional? You're drinking Scotch out of the decanter. You look sloppy, not professional."

"Look, I never binge drink like this. I don't even drink that often. It's just that I'm kind of messed up right now, Freya, because you showed up. You fired my masseuse. Why would you do that? Do you know how long it took me to find her?"

I turned and walked out of the room, heading downstairs, to the kitchen. I found the cook, muttering loudly to herself as she wiped down the counters. Word of our argument had passed very quickly through the house.

"How often do you buy champagne?" I asked her.

Khawae, the cook, was not used to being in this position. Corey had recruited her out of the best five-star restaurant in Bhutan, offering her double the salary to come cook for us. She specialized in the vegetarian dishes that Corey preferred. Freya could see the surprise in her face when she asked Khawae about the alcohol. Freya wondered if she would answer honestly, or if she would be loyal to the man who paid her extravagant salary.

Hesitantly, Khawae chose the truth.

"I'm sorry, Madam. It's not exactly like that."

I learned that there is no alcohol in Bhutan. She told me Corey imported a case of champagne each month, and a case of Scotch once every few months. I had been so stupid. I never even realized he was drinking, much less that much. I went back up to the bedroom, my feet dragging. After my peaceful morning, connecting with my body and the nature around me, this was the last thing I expected to be doing today. What in the hell had brought us here? I went back upstairs.

"Corey," I said, softly, standing in the doorway. He was sitting on the edge of the bed, his head in his hand, crying. It was sad, almost pathetic. Either this was another ploy to try to manipulate me, or he had just disintegrated into a sad shell of the man he was. I had never imagined that I would see Corey this way.

He looked up at me, tears in his eyes. It broke my heart. I walked into the bedroom, grabbed my bag.

"Wait," he pleaded.

I turned to look at him. I wanted to take him in my arms, to comfort him, but I couldn't. The pain was too raw.

"I trusted you," I whispered.

"Part of me knew I really didn't love Tristan. Everything just moved so fast. But you? I love you to my core. In my soul, there's no longer just me there. It's you and me. I fell in love with you, I trusted you, I let you inside. I believed you when you said you loved me. Was it always just a competition for you?"

"No, Freya, never."

I was good and mad again. "Is that all I was? Some status symbol? Did Tristan piss you off, so you wanted to take what was his? You reeled me in, made me fall in love with you, and then, what? Just decided one day that it was okay to hire a sexy masseuse to get drunk with, and hide it from me? You ruined my love story."

"I don't drink that much, Freya."

"You go through two cases of champagne and two liters of Scotch a month, Corey! How is that 'not that much'? So you're going to rationalize that you're not drinking too much, and that it's okay that you had a sexy, almost naked masseuse come up to the house twice a week. You're going to tell me that it's okay that you lied to me, and that I don't have a right to be mad. Sounds like someone we know."

"What are you even talking about?" At this point, Corey had probably been drinking for hours. His eyes were starting to droop

"Tristan. First, he said he didn't drink that much. Then, he said he only acted the way he did because he was drinking. Then he tried to tell me that blowjobs weren't cheating. Then he tried to tell me that I was over-reacting."

"I know everything about me seems perfect. I guess it's just not. It just gets to me sometimes. Freya, I need to explain this to you."

"No, Corey. I don't want to hear it. Whatever you have to say to me is just going to be you not taking responsibility for your behavior."

"It was nothing. I didn't sleep with her. It was just a massage. Every time she was here, all that happened was the massage. I swear. It was only you. It's only been you since the first moment that I saw you. I have her come when you're not here because I know that I have a few hours to enjoy myself. The massage relaxes me. It's just a chance for me to unwind. With everything that's been going on, I need that.

"I can't stand appearing weak in front of you. You've needed me to be strong to help you get past what Tristan did to you. I don't hide my drinking from you. I just don't like to drink around you. I would rather enjoy you sober. But things are so hard right now."

"So, you have so little faith in me, in how I feel for you, that you would rather let some sexy stranger come in here, dressed in little more than a strip of silk, and help you relax, than to tell me about your problems? I feel like I don't even know you right now."

I turned and began walking towards the bedroom door.

"Freya, you can't leave!" Corey jumped up off the bed, his long legs closing the gap between us. I hurried down the stairs, toward the front door.

"Freya, please," I could hear him yelling, over and over, as I opened the door and went to my car.

"You have a problem," I said as he finally caught up to me.

"Maybe I do. I started drinking after my parents died, you know. I just couldn't deal with everything. The therapist helped a lot. I honestly don't think that I would have gotten through this without her. But even she couldn't take away all the pain. I was 6'2", everyone looked at me as a man, but I was still just a little boy who had lost both of his parents. No one ever knew I was drunk. Even you didn't suspect that I was drinking."

166

"No, Corey, I didn't. And don't you understand, that is part of the problem? We've been so intertwined these last several months and I didn't have a clue that you were drinking. I think you need professional help."

"I'll be fine. I can stop. It just helps me relax. I promise, I'll stop."

"You've been drinking like this since you were a teenager, and you think you can just stop on a whim?"

"Yes, I can. Because I have always been able to do what I wanted or needed to do when it came down to it."

"Corey, your issue is deeper than that. Our issues are deeper than that, now. You hid this from me. Deliberately. You need to go to rehab."

"No, I don't. I can control this. I can stop whenever I want to."

"You're saying the same things that every alcoholic who isn't ready to stop has always said. You need to figure this out. And I need to figure out how I feel about all of this. I can't be here right now."

"I'm sorry. Please, don't leave. I need you so much. I can't live without you!"

"Right now, I can't live with you.

Corey reached out to me, but I put my bags in the car and climbed in the driver's seat.

"Oh, God, Freya no. Please don't leave. You're my goddess."

I shut my car door and pulled out, leaving Corey standing, still naked, in the driveway. I could see him standing there, as I looked in my rear view mirror. Still holding the bottle of Scotch, watching my car, looking sad and pathetic. Part of me wanted to go back and comfort him, but he had hurt me too badly. As much as I loved him, I couldn't be with him.

I drove quickly down to the airport. I was afraid that Corey would call his driver and come after me, and I intended to be gone before that happened. Pulling into the parking lot, I was surprised to find it mostly deserted. I got out of my car and walked to the man who was locking up.

"Sir, is it possible to book a flight tonight?"

"I'm sorry, ma'am. You can't fly out of this airport at night. We're in a valley, and night flight is very dangerous here because of the wind shear off the mountains. You can try in the morning."

I should have known. The airport is a single landing strip, surrounded by mountains. When Americans think of the word "airport" we associate it with the big, modern, city-sized travel centers like JFK or LAX. The airport in Thimphu looked much like a lot of the buildings in Bhutan. Older, sprawling, with a colorful green roof. But it had only four check in desks in its one passenger terminal. In a year, it handled as many passengers as LAX handled in a day. Sometimes, Corey had come to meet his pilot here for various things, and I had watched planes land here. I wondered if the pilots got hazard pay. Sometimes they had to bank suddenly or come in from a steep angle to deal with the wind coming off the mountains during their descent.

I got back in the car and sat there in the parking lot for awhile. I wasn't sure where to go from here. I didn't want Corey to find me. As I sat there, thinking of the afternoon's events, I almost started crying again. I shook my head to clear it. There would be time to break down later.

I drove to Thimphu, wanting to get lost in the crowds. The city of 80,000 beckoned to me, so very modern, yet so very irretrievably stuck in the past. Ancient temples and palaces stood near modern hotels designed to mimic the older buildings, on streets traveled by the newest cars. It was a beautiful and rich city, and I would be sorry to be leaving.

I drove around the streets for hours. I drove into residential neighborhoods that I had never known existed, and studied the architecture of local schools and shops. I stopped at a small vendor for tea, and then drove some more. I drove until I was exhausted. I was certain by now that Corey was looking for me, but I couldn't go back to the love nest. I decided I needed to find a hotel.

I pulled into the Hotel Norbuling. It was a family owned hotel, and I had heard wonderful things about their service. I booked an Executive Suite, and was greeted by warmth and elegance as I went into my room. The floors were rich hardwoods, and the view was breathtaking, even at night. The hotel offered less than thirty rooms, so I knew that I wouldn't be disturbed. I had attended a yoga class here when Corey and I first came, and had been dazzled by its elegance. The suite did not disappoint.

I settled into my suite, and pulled my cell phone out of my purse. I found fourteen text messages from Corey, and two from Daniela. I was sure that Corey had called her. Normally, she was the first one I would have run to when I needed help. I called her back to confirm my suspicions, and let her know I was okay.

We talked for a few minutes. Corey had called her three times in the last four hours. I told her she could tell him that I was fine, but not to say where I was. I wanted to tell her everything, but I was just too tired. I promised I would call her in the morning, and hung up.

I read through Corey's text messages.

I'm so sorry Freya. Please come back. I need you.

Freya, where are you? I need to talk to you.

I'm sending my chauffer to look for you. Please let him bring you home.

He's checked all the hotels and you're not at any of them. Where are you?

Please, I want to fix this. Please come home and talk to me. It's okay that you fired the masseuse. I'll just do massage with you from now on.

I need you Freya. I'll do anything if you come home.

Please come back. I'll go to rehab like you said. I'll do anything.

The rest were more of the same. They were tempting. But would he actually go to rehab? I was unsure. I wanted to believe him, but part of me felt like he was only saying this to get me back. I was afraid that he wouldn't follow through. I knew that for rehab to be successful, the addict has to be ready to break free of their addiction. Was Corey really ready for that, or was he just saying the words I wanted so desperately to hear?

I laid down on my bed, and, finally, let the tears come. Earlier, I had been so mad I was shaking. Now, I was gutted. I felt like Corey had ripped my heart out. I was confused about everything. I went back to the beginning of our relationship, looking for clues about Corey's drinking, and found none. How had he been able to consume that much alcohol on a regular basis without me knowing?

Had Tristan been right? Was Corey playing me, from the beginning, because he was jealous? Was I just some toy, some play thing for him to possess until Tristan moved on? Did I believe Corey when he said he hadn't slept with the masseuse? Massage had often been a component of our Tantric love making sessions; I knew what an effect it could have on him, and I could not come up with another reasonable answer as to why she would have been dressed the way she was. Women who aren't expecting sex generally don't dress in see through tops and skirts that barely covered their rear ends.

I had left the love nest without a real plan. Now, through my tears, I tried to come up with one. I still had Corey's AmEx. I could use it long enough to get back to New York. Daniela had been running the yoga studio without me; it would be easy for me to pick up a few classes and get myself slowly back into the day-to-day of my life. It would take me awhile to pay him back, but I could do it.

Despite my pain and anger, I couldn't imagine what life was going to be like without Corey. We'd been inseparable the last several months. Even the thought of waking up without him in the morning made me sob. While, realistically, I knew I needed to move forward with my life, the thought of doing so made the pain fresh all over again.

Resolve is a funny thing. It's because of Corey that I have the resolve to stand on my own two feet, but it's also because of Corey that I am forced to do so. I had few lovers before him, and while I had given myself freely to each of them, emotionally I had only fully given myself to Corey. From the first time he touched me, I think I knew, even if I didn't admit it to myself, that we belonged to each other. The realization that he had so thoroughly broken the trust that he had taught me how to give, threatened to crush me.

He had taught me how to be the woman to be strong enough to get through this. But the thought of having to do it without him was terrifying. But I had made my decision. I knew that my only choice was to leave Bhutan on the earliest flight I could find. I would get up early, and wait at the airport until I could catch a flight to anywhere, and then go on to New York from there.

The decision ended up being easier than I thought it would, once I got around to actually making it. Just like when I left home, I knew I wouldn't look back. I loved Corey too much to watch him kill himself. With as much alcohol as he had been importing, he was, as he said, very good at hiding the fact that he had been drinking since he was fourteen. He'd built an empire while drinking. He could probably go on hiding it for years. But the damage that it would do to his body would surely lead to a premature death, and I could not sit around and wait for that to happen.

My heart ached, but I was focused on what I knew I must do. I wanted Corey to get better, but I felt like he was not going to as long as I was here. I was worried that if I went back to him, he would view that as permission to go on as he had been. He could be better than that. I deserved better than that.

I lay in the bed, trying to sleep. I stared at the ceiling for what seemed like hours. I turned the television on, mainly as a distraction. I hadn't really watched television in months. I found an old movie, translated into Dzhonkha, just to occupy my mind. Finally, around 4 am I drifted off to a sleep, my last thoughts of lounging with Corey on his yacht.

I woke around 9 am. I felt like I had been run over by a giant truck. I took a shower, and then wandered down to the dining room for breakfast. The dining room was bright and well lit, and even it was breathtakingly gorgeous like the rest of the hotel. Red panels decorated one wall, and the rich beamed ceilings and sheer white curtains gave the impression of elegance. I found one of the few tables set for two and sat down.

She was looking over the menu to choose her breakfast when a voice behind her said "Good morning, Freya." She did not want to believe what she was hearing. She must be mistaken. She was still upset over the events of last night, and that must be disturbing her thinking. Surely, she was wrong.

She turned around...

CHAPTER TEN

An Unexpected Visitor

Couldn't could not believe my eyes. Tristan was standing there, smiling broadly, as if they were old friends who hadn't seen each other in ages instead of former lovers who had ended on a very bad note.

"It's so good to see you! I've been looking for you. May I sit down?"

I sat there, looking at him, unsure of what to say. Taking my silence for permission, he took the vacant seat across from me. He gestured toward the waiter, and then ordered breakfast for both of us.

"Tristan, I don't know what to say. I had no idea you were here."

"I'm surprised that you hadn't heard. I've been here for a few days, and I've made it no secret that I was looking for you. Apparently there aren't many secrets in Bhutan."

"What do you mean?" I asked, confused.

"Everyone knows about the rich American couple living in the palace up the hill."

Tristan smiled as the waiter brought a full pot of coffee and two substantial mugs. Coffee was not a regular part of Bhutanese cuisine, and generally only served to tourists, and they thought we all had huge appetites for it.

"Everyone seems to love you. I had hoped to catch you at your yoga class yesterday, but by the time I got to where the locals told me you usually had class, no one was there. I didn't want to go up to the palace and disturb you and Corey, but I'm really happy to see you. What brings you down to the capital so early?"

I couldn't believe what I was hearing. Truthfully, I couldn't believe that I was sitting across from Tristan at a table in a hotel in Bhutan.

The last time we had spoken, his voice had been anger filled and full of venom. His last messages to me had been slightly threatening. He had been running a campaign to destroy Corey's business. Now, he was sitting here, the picture of charm.

"I'm sorry, you must be really confused. Let me start from the beginning. Freya, I've been acting like a child. When you told me that you had fallen in love with Corey, I was angry. I felt betrayed, and, to be completely honest with you, you broke my heart. I've never loved a woman like I love you. I went off the deep end."

I cleared my throat, trying to will myself to speak. 'Went off the deep end' was putting it mildly.

"I was grieving you, the loss of you, and, clearly, I didn't handle it well. I was highly stressed because of that stupid trial, and even after it was over, you asked me those questions about justice, and guilt, well it got me thinking. So here I was, having a crisis of confidence, of not being sure of myself, and then you come and tell me that you've fallen in love with my best friend. It was everything at once, Freya. I'm generally a very reasonable man, but it was too much to take all at once. I'm really sorry for everything that I said to you."

I was stunned. By his own proclamation, Tristan never apologized. Ever. He also never conceded a loss. He didn't lose. Being a winner was very high on his priority list.

"Tristan, I'm shocked. I don't know what to say."

"I know, Freya. I still remember how arrogant I sounded that day when I told you that I never apologized for anything. But it was like I crawled out of this deep, dark hole a few days ago, and saw the light. You never meant to hurt me. You were being honest with me, which is something I didn't even have the decency to give you in return. I've acted like an asshole, and I've come to ask your forgiveness. I'm not here to try to win you back or talk you into anything. I just want you and Corey to hear me out and give me the chance to explain and properly apologize."

At the mention of Corey's name, I felt tears begin to well up.

"Freya, what's wrong?" I felt Tristan's hand on mine, rubbing my skin lightly.

"It's nothing. I don't want to talk about it right now. I'm sure everything will be cleared up." Tristan pulled his hand away from mine as the waiter brought our food.

Tristan had ordered a much more extravagant breakfast than I was used to having with Corey. At the palace, our diet had consisted primarily of traditional Bhutanese food. But in the nicer hotels in the capital, meals were different, usually structured to the tastes of the tourists. The waiter sat down plate after plate of sausage, eggs, fruits, and breads, served family style. I helped myself to a little fruit and some eggs.

"Well, I certainly won't push you, Freya. But I'm here if you need to talk." Tristan piled his plate high with food and started eating. I pushed my food around my plate. I knew I needed to eat, but I had no appetite. I pushed my plate away just as a giant thunderclap sounded. Tristan reached out to grab my hand again when I jumped from the noise.

"Dammit," I hissed, looking for a window. I had hoped to be able to leave today. There were no windows in the dining room. I could feel a headache starting, at the base of my skull. I was afraid if I stayed longer that Corey would find me, and I was not ready to talk to him. When the waiter came to check up on us, I asked if it was possible to get some aspirin. He nodded and hurried off.

"I'm sorry, Freya, I know I said I wouldn't push you, but I can tell that something is wrong. Can I help with something?"

I shook my head as the waiter returned with a bottle of aspirin. I took two with my coffee.

"No, Tristan, I just don't feel well. I just want to go home." I almost broke down then, but managed to remain calm.

"I'm going to go back to my room." I stood up, and then Tristan was at my side, helping to move my chair, his arm around my waist, guiding me through the restaurant. As we walked, his hand moved so

175

that it was discreetly at the small of my back, guiding rather than holding me, and much more appropriate, I thought.

I thought. Truthfully, I didn't know what to think. I was confused by Tristan's sudden arrival, and his apology seemed genuine, but I wasn't sure if I could trust him. Tristan opened the door to my room for me and stood aside so I could walk in. He followed me, and grabbed the phone on the sidetable. I could hear him issuing instructions in his businesslike manner. I sat down on the bed.

Tristan finished his phone call, then pulled one of the chairs over next to the bed. He sat down, and crossed his legs, looking very elegant in his tailored suit. It was hard to believe that this was the same man who had challenged Corey to a race with me as the prize.

"I've instructed the front desk to switch your tab over to my credit card. If anyone comes looking for you, they're to say that you've checked out already. I'm kind of assuming here, Freya, that by home you don't mean that gorgeous palace on the mountain, or you would be on your way already. Have you left him?"

I couldn't answer Tristan, because I didn't know the answer. When I had left the palace last night, I didn't really plan on it being forever, but I knew when I went to bed last night that I couldn't go back if things didn't change drastically. I love Corey, but I can't trust him right now. I shrugged my shoulders. It was the only honest answer I had.

Tristan leaned forward, took my hands in his.

"God, Freya, I'm so sorry. If I hadn't have been so childish, so stupid, this never would have happened. Even if you had still fallen in love with him, if I could have spoken to you about things logically, instead of yelling and screaming, then maybe I could have saved you this pain. Are you sure you don't want to talk about it?"

I stood up and walked to the window, my arms crossed against my chest. The visibility was terrible, with thick rain rolling in waves down the glass. I was certain this room had a beautiful view, but not today. I was fairly certain that unless it stopped raining soon, I wouldn't be able to fly out today. I took a deep breath, and started talking.

I'm not sure why I started talking. Part of me just needed someone to talk to. Knowing that someone was face-to-face, ready to hear what I had to say. I just needed to get it all off my chest.

I didn't tell him everything. I glossed over a lot of the parts of our love story because I didn't want to rub it in his face. He and I had been engaged, after all. I didn't want to be cruel. I did tell him that Corey and I had a special connection, one that couldn't be easily explained. It was the truth.

I continued looking out the window as I told Tristan about how Corey betrayed me with the masseuse. I couldn't look him in the eye. I was embarrassed, and found it hard not to cry. I told him about Corey's drinking, and about how he had hidden it from me for months. By the time I had finished talking, it was after noon.

"I'm so sorry, Freya. I wouldn't have had you hurt for all the world."

I nodded my head and stared at the rain. Finally, I couldn't hold in the tears any longer. Tristan was a gentleman, bringing me a box of tissues and then a glass of water when I was done. By the time I was done, I was exhausted, every last ounce of energy was spent. Tristan helped me into bed, and then I was blissfully unaware of the next several hours.

I awoke to the sound of someone knocking on the door. I sat up, trying to get my bearings. I heard Tristan's voice, and saw two valets bringing in trays with covered dishes. Tristan had ordered dinner delivered to the room. I couldn't help but think that maybe he had changed.

I moved over to the table and started eating. I hadn't realized how hungry I was until I started eating. I hadn't had anything sizable to eat since breakfast yesterday, and now that I had finally gotten some rest, the rest of my body had apparently decided it was time to get back on track. I ate fruit and a scrumptious beef and rice dish while Tristan talked.

"So, I've done some asking around, and Corey has been looking for you. His driver was here once last night, before you checked in, and then again today, just a few minutes after I made my earlier call to the front desk. From the sounds of things, he's checked every hotel in the region."

I nodded my head as I ate. I didn't want to sound rude, but I was starving. Tristan continued.

"I've called my pilot. The rain stopped around six, but by then it was dark. There are several flights that have been delayed, but we've been able to have my plane moved to the front of the line. We can leave as soon as the sun is up if we leave the hotel before sunrise in the morning. I can have you home pretty quickly, if that's what you want."

I sat and thought for a moment. I was a little surprised at the suddenness. I had wanted to get out of Bhutan, and away from Corey, but did I really want to put myself into Tristan's hands? Of course, since he had found me here in Bhutan, he had been nothing but charm and grace. Had he really changed, or was he just telling me what he thought I wanted to hear? In the end, I didn't feel like I had much choice. If flights had been cancelled for the last few days, what chance did I have of getting out of Bhutan before Corey found me? It was a matter of time before he found someone willing to talk. I decided that I would go with Tristan, but on my terms.

"Alright, Tristan. I appreciate your offer, and I'm going to accept it, on the condition that you understand that my acceptance doesn't mean that I want to be with you. I'm accepting your help, not making a trade."

"Freya, I'm sorry that you feel you have to phrase things that way. I genuinely want to help you. I know that I have behaved like an asshole in the past, but I promise you, I want nothing in return. I've done most of what I came here to do, which was mainly to apologize to you. I would like to have a word with Corey, too, but after what you've told me, I think that's going to have to wait. We need to get you somewhere quiet and familiar, and we need to get Corey some help. I promise, that's all I want right now."

I looked in his eyes. He seemed genuine. I wasn't sure if a tiger could change its stripes, but Tristan seemed to be moving in the right direction.

"Thank you, Tristan. What time do we need to leave tomorrow?"

We agreed on a time, and Tristan left me to make his last minute arrangements. I laid in my bed, my thoughts whirring around in my head. After the last few days, I just wanted to shut down for a little while. I was hoping that when I got home, Dani would be available to cheer me up.

I drifted off to sleep, my last thoughts of Corey, again. When I closed my eyes, his face was there, smiling. His eyes, twinkling when he laughed. I knew it was going to take me a long time to get him out of my mind. It didn't hurt as bad, really, if I only thought about the good times.

I woke up to a banging on my door. I was afraid it might be Corey, but then I heard Tristan's voice from the other side. It was time to head out to the airport. I gathered the few things I had brought with me to the hotel, and walked downstairs. Tristan's car was parked outside, ready to go. To the east, the sky was just beginning to lighten.

I was beginning to get nervous. The drive to the airport seemed to take forever. I just wanted to be home already. What no one explains to you, when they tell you what it feels like to have a broken heart, is the physical pain that goes with it. That feeling you have in your chest, like there's a giant weight there. Or how your arms and legs feel like lead, and lifting them is torture. The thought of being in my own bed was the only thing keeping me going this morning.

At the airport, there was already a line. People had been waiting for days to fly out, but had been delayed due to the same weather that had kept me stuck here. Fortunately, Tristan's last minute arrangements last night included having a valet meet us as we walked in, taking us to an office to get us checked in and onto Tristan's plane. The whole process took less than fifteen minutes, and I was grateful to Tristan for planning ahead.

Once we made it onto the plane, the flight attendant welcomed us with a tray of fresh fruits including strawberries and mangoes, and huge mugs of coffee. I sat and enjoyed the coffee, watching the sunrise. Tristan paced on the other side of the plane, watching the goings-on at the airport. I could hear the plane's engines getting louder as the pilot worked in the cockpit.

"Damn," Tristan muttered under his breath. The whine of the engines decreased and Tristan walked to the door. As the engine shut down, Tristan opened the door. I stood up and walked to stand near Tristan, hoping to see what the commotion was. I was afraid another storm was coming in. I was blown away when I saw Corey standing on the ground near the plane.

"Corey, move your car, now," Tristan yelled.

"I'm not going anywhere until I have the chance to talk to Freya."

"She doesn't want to speak to you right now, Corey. You should go home, to your champagne and your masseuse." Tristan's tone was ugly; the one I remembered from that night in New York, when I told him I had fallen in love with Corey.

"Tristan, wait. You said you wanted to help him. Maybe we should talk to him, get him to come back with us, so that we can get him into rehab."

"Do you have any idea how long the flight back to the states is? Do you really want to sit here for hours and listen to him beg and plead after the way he hurt you?"

Tristan had a point. I started to walk past him, intending to go talk to Corey, but then Corey was at the top of the stairs, inside the plane.

"Freya, I just want to talk to you. I'm sorry. I have so much to say, but that's the biggest part of it. I never meant to hurt you."

Tristan took a deep breath.

"Corey, get out of my plane. I'm taking Freya home, away from you. You hurt her, and she's going home, with me."

The feeling of deja vu hit me like a freight train. I took a step back, intending to move back from both of them, feeling very trapped. Tristan grabbed my arm. I tried to pull away from him.

"Freya, just take a step away from Tristan," Corey was saying, slowly, softly. I suddenly realized that Tristan's face was red. He did, indeed, seem like a ticking time bomb, and Corey was trying to defuse the situation. I tried to take that step, and Tristan held me tighter.

"Corey, you son of a bitch, get the hell off my plane!"

Tristan lost it completely. He began yelling at Corey, telling him that he needed to get off the plane and move his car so that he could take me back to New York. I could see people on the ground looking in our direction. Was is possible that they could hear Tristan's yelling over the other sounds of the airport?

Corey remained calm. "Tristan, I'll get off the plane when you let Freya go. You're hurting her."

Tristan took a step back, dragging me with him, effectively putting me between himself and Corey.

"She's coming with me. She belongs with me. She's finally found out the truth about who you are. She knows that you played her, that you lied. She knows you're an alcoholic. You betrayed her, Corey."

Corey was looking straight at me.

"Yes, Freya knows all of those things. She knows I lied, that I hid my drinking problem. And I'm certain that my actions led to her feeling betrayed. I need to have a long talk with Freya, but you need to put the gun away."

Gun? I froze. I didn't know what else to do. I hadn't seen a gun.

"I won, Corey. Freya is leaving with me. You know I don't lose. She belongs to me!"

He was waving his hand around wildly as he talked. I could see the gun, large and black, in his hand. I was terrified. I didn't know what to do. Suddenly, Corey's foot shot out, connected with Tristan's hand. The gun flew through the plane. Corey grabbed me, pushed me down the stairs ahead of him. I jumped into his jeep. He got behind the wheel and pulled out from in front of the train. The engines started immediately.

Corey drove off of the airstrip and into the parking lot. There were airport personnel all around us. Corey explained that Tristan had a gun and they immediately turned their attention toward the plane, but it was already taxiing down the runway. Corey drove for about a mile before pulling off the road.

"Corey, I'm..."

"Freya, I'm..."

It brought a smile to both of our faces.

"I'm sorry, Freya. For everything. I want to talk, not fight. I'm sorry that I made you feel like you had to leave your home. I'm sorry that you wanted to go back to New York so badly that Tristan got involved."

"How did you know he was here?"

"I have a friend, I'll take you to meet him soon. He knows everyone and everything that happens in Bhutan. He knew that Tristan had been here looking for you, and that he had found you, and that he was planning to leave at sunrise this morning. Nothing happens in Bhutan without Karma knowing about it."

"So he's like the Godfather?"

Corey looked relieved to hear the humor in my voice.

"Well, only if the Godfather is a Buddhist monk. No, Karma is just Karma. He was born here, and he'll likely die here. He knows everyone here, and he's the wisest man I know. When I couldn't find you, I went to him, hoping he had some idea where you were. But he's smarter than I am. He didn't tell me where you were. Somehow, he knew you weren't ready to talk to me yet."

"Karma is pretty smart. I didn't know I was ready to talk to you until I saw you in the plane. It's not that I wanted to leave you, Corey. It's that I needed to be away from you while I figured things out. It was really weird that I ran into Tristan at the hotel. But once I did, he said everything I needed to hear. He must have a radar for vulnerability, because he knew just how to reach me. I'm sorry I almost left with him."

"I think I understand. Karma told me that he was being utterly charming with you, supportive, like a friend, not like a lover, or even an ex lover. And, truthfully, when I brought you to Bhutan, I never thought about how I would be isolating you from your friends. At a time when you most needed a friend, you had no one to turn to. I don't like it, but it's kind of natural that you turned to him."

Corey was being calm and rational. I was still angry at him, but I had at least calmed down enough to listen to him.

"I want to go to rehab and therapy. I think I have a lot of unresolved issues about my parent's death. I don't ever want to fight with you again. You mean to much for me to risk losing. If you still want to leave, I'll call the airport now. I'm not assuming you'll stay with me. But I'm begging you to let me try to fix this."

"I want to fix this, too. But I think we're going to need some time. As long as we're both working together, I think we can do it. Tristan and I even talked about finding a way to get you help. I know it sounds stupid, but he was so...nice. He even apologized. I feel so stupid, being taken in by him. I can't believe he had a gun!"

"You shouldn't feel stupid. Tristan's entire life has been spent manipulating people. Juries, girlfriends, his parents. He manipulates everyone. It's who he is. He knew just how to appeal to you because you're kind, and caring. He saw an opportunity, and he took it. You mustn't feel stupid."

Part of me, most of me, knew Corey was right. But I knew it would take me awhile to move past everything that had happened in the last few days.

"I think we should go to therapy together. I love you, Corey. I can't live without you. But I'm going to have to learn how to trust you again. You really hurt me."

"God, Freya, I'm so sorry. I don't know how I managed to lose control like that. How I could justify that behavior. I'm sorry. I could say it one thousand times and it would barely be a small amount of the sorrow that I have. If I could take back every stupid thing I've ever done, I would."

I stared straight ahead. I wasn't sure what to say.

"I haven't made any assumptions. I had the maids make up a spare bedroom for you, or I can take you to a hotel. Whatever you want to do."

"I want to go home. We'll sort the rest out as we go."

We drove the rest of the way to the love nest in silence. I wasn't sure what to say. I knew that we had a lot of work to do on our relationship, but when I saw Corey standing on the ground next to the airplane, it reminded me of just how much I love him. I want to fix things, not run away.

We walked into the love nest and Corey took my bag and carried it upstairs. He turned in the opposite direction of our bedroom, and opened the door to one of the spare rooms. The bed was freshly made, and scented candles had been lit. It was very welcoming and inviting. Corey sat my bag down near the bed and turned to me.

"I didn't have all of your things moved in here, but it can be done if you want. Whatever you want, Freya. Whatever it takes."

"Thank you."

I moved toward him. I needed to touch him, to start to heal this breach between us. I rested my head on his chest and wrapped my arms around his waist. His arms came around me, and I felt the comfort that I always felt in his arms. His hands were rubbing my back, and feeling his loving caresses made me feel much better about the last few days.

"Freya, I would like to try something with you. Karma told me about a Tantric massage method called Karezza. It's an opportunity for both partners to touch each other in a non-sexual way. It's about intimacy, not sex, and the touch can be very healing. He suggests it for after an argument such as ours, where we both need to be around each other but one or both partners don't want to have intercourse. Would you like to try?"

I nodded my head. Corey pulled away from me and took my hand and led me to the bed, where we sat down next to each other. He began with my hand, rubbing it gently, as he talked to me in a quiet tone of voice.

"The point of Karezza is to bring the partners closer together. There is no genital touching, although nudity is encouraged. But we can get there on our own time. We can lay next to each other or remain seated. I can touch you, you can touch me, we can do whatever feels good to both of us, as long as there's no genital touch."

His massage moved up my arm. He was rubbing my skin over my shirt, and I wanted to feel him directly touching me. I tried to push my sleeve up, but my shirt wasn't really made for that. I unbuttoned it and slipped it off, sitting next to Corey in my bra. He turned on the bed, using both hands to massage up and down my arm. It felt really good to have him touching me.

After a few minutes, I decided to lay face down on the bed. This gave Corey greater access to me, and he could massage my back. I relaxed as he rubbed my shoulders and worked his way down my back. I couldn't resist a little giggle as he massaged near my ribs. I wasn't super ticklish, but he caught me just right.

"Corey, I want to massage you now." I sat up on the bed and watched Corey take off his shirt. I sat behind him and rubbed his shoulders and back, much as he had rubbed mine. I encouraged him to lay down, and then began rubbing his upper chest, being careful not to touch his nipples. After I had spent about twenty minutes on his chest and abs, Corey took my arms again.

"Will you lay down next to me?"

Corey and I adjusted ourselves in spoon position, with me laying on one of his arms while he used the other to touch various parts of my body. I could feel his chest against my back and it felt soothing, comforting. I realized that I was becoming aroused from his touch and I wondered if he was feeling the same.

I closed my eyes, relaxing into him. As had always been the case, feeling his arms around me was comforting, reassuring. It was almost like I could physically feel the bond growing between us. It was nice to have this experience, even though I was becoming sexually aroused, and know that there was no expectation of sex at the end of it. It gave me the chance to remember how being touched by Corey made me feel.

I turned so that I was facing him, wanting to touch him, too. I draped my arm over him, letting my fingertips run lightly up and down his back. He gasped the first time I touched him. His tempo slowed as he closed his eyes to enjoy the feeling of my fingers on his skin. I could feel his chest moving as he took deep breaths, getting lost in the sensations. I, too, found myself feeling remarkably relaxed. I had been pretty stressed out the last few days and the wonderful sensations that our touching was bringing to the surface made me feel incredible. It was nice to be able to connect with Corey on this level. We both desperately needed it.

186

As his breathing deepened, I snuggled in closer to him. While the goal of our massage hadn't been to fall asleep, the thought of being able to fall asleep in his arms brought me more comfort. He held me tightly, and I felt loved and needed. I knew it was a step in the right direction.

CHAPTER ELEVEN

Known You Forever

It took several weeks for Corey and I to work through our issues. Because there's no alcohol in Bhutan, there's no rehab, but we were able to find Corey and I a therapist who understood Tantric methods and was available to work with us. Corey opened up a lot about his past, and shared some emotions about his parent's deaths. I had been able to forgive him for betraying me, and we were moving forward. We made it a point to go out together at least one night a week.

The morning after one such night, as we both relaxed in the large bathtub in the attic's en suite, eating fresh apricots that he'd bought at the market, he gradually began to explain what was happening all those miles away in New York. I had been able to tell that he was stressed about something, but he hadn't sat down and told me the specifics yet.

He sighed and stretched one arm along the edge of the tub while the other hand took the vibrantly colored fruit to his lips.

My focus sat intently on his mouth, and I enjoyed the sensual movement of his lips as he bit down on the fruit. As his tongue quickly lapped at his lips, stopping the flow of juice. I found myself unconsciously mirroring his action as I imagined my own tongue removing that sweetness from his mouth.

"Basically, Tristan is short selling the stocks of the business," he continued, oblivious to my libidinous thoughts.

Tearing my hypnotized gaze from his lips, I met his eyes and attempted to focus on what he was saying.

"I don't know what that means," I mumbled, shrugging as I brought my own fruit to my mouth.

"Well," he began. He swallowed his mouthful. "It's a little complicated, but, essentially, it's borrowing shares from a broker, then waiting for the price to go down. Once their price has fallen, you buy shares and the borrowed ones get returned at their original price, enabling you to pocket a profit."

Eyebrows crinkling, I shook my head. "I don't get it," I told him.

"Think of it like this," he calmly explained. "I show you a new gadget that I bought and tell you it cost me... three thousand," he said. "The next day, you find out that's in available from the same store for only two thousand. So, you grab my receipt and you take the receipt to the store, complain and they refund you the thousand dollars. Tuck the receipt back where you found it, never say a word to me, and that money's yours."

"Okay," I mumbled slowly. "But for that to work, your stock has to be falling, right?"

"Right," he confirmed with a nod.

"Why is that happening?"

With a philosophical shrug, he continued to nibble on his fruit. "Partly, it's just the ebb and flow of the market," he dismissively sighed. "But, Rebecca suspects that Tristan's mudslinging has had something to do with it."

"So, he's slowly destroying your business and making money out of it into the bargain?"

Pursing his lips, Corey offered an acknowledging tip of his head. "That's what he's trying to do anyway. But he's got to buy the shares, and if he can't get rid of them again and the price continues to drop, he's going to lose money, too."

"Somehow, I don't think that will bother him," I muttered darkly.

"No," he agreed softly. "No, I don't suppose it would."

"So, what can you do about it?" I wondered. "Shouldn't you already be on a plane?"

The question was asked reluctantly because if he decided he had to return there was no question that I'd go with him. But I didn't want to head back to New York: We still needed to see our therapist regularly, and I was enjoying reconnecting with Corey.. We were, for the most part, separate from the rest of the world. And I loved that feeling. I guessed at some point, I'd be ready to rejoin hectic western civilization, but, right then and there, I wanted to stay exactly where I was.

"Things aren't too bad at the moment," he breathed. "There's a good chance this will blow over."

"What if it doesn't?" I probed.

"Then we'll fix it when we finally do go back." He smiled. "But I'm not cutting out time together short for him, I'm not letting him win over that, Freya."

Grinning at him, I leaned my head back against the rolled up towel that he'd thoughtfully placed in the corner of the tub when drew the water. I loved the way he thought of the little things like that.

"He can't possibly come between us anymore," I assured him. "We're..." I added, inhaling slowly. "We're bound together somehow, and there's nothing that could ever untie that."

"Good," he said, gracefully pushing away from the edge of the tub and gliding through the water toward me. "I told you before," he chuckled warmly as my arms automatically grasped him and tugged his chest flush with mine. "This," he said firmly, kissing me so there could be no doubt over what he was referring to, "is all that matters to me right now," he hummed. "The money, the company, and everything else can wait."

***

Corey and I had begun making love again about three weeks after we started seeing the therapist. The strange waking dreams I had whenever we made love had continued, and were becoming more frequent and vivid as time passed. They were also whole body experiences. As much as I wanted to think they were just in my head, I found them to be much more than just the wanderings of my imagination.

Almost all of these visions – which is not exactly the right word for them – began the same way: I was laying on a bed of brightly colored petals. I was in some kind of cave or cavern, surrounded by glittering blue rocks. Sometimes, I wore a cloak of falcon feathers, but more often than not, I was completely naked, except for a necklace. At first, the necklace seemed unimportant, but it began to stick in my mind: in reality I very rarely wore one, and hadn't worn one at all the entire time I'd been living with Corey.

Wearing only that necklace, I would lay sprawled among the petals. One of the more bizarre facets of the vision was a wild boar with red fur that sat near the entrance of the cave. I didn't fear the creature. I seemed to know that he was no threat to me. And there I would wait: wait for him.

And, sure enough, he'd come to me, appearing before me as bright as the summer sunshine. His strong chest was usually clad in a thick plate of armor, which didn't seem in the slightest bit strange to me at the time. He'd smile as he gazed down at me, his heated gaze lingering over every bare inch of me.

Without uttering a word, he would remove his clothing and join me on the bed of petals. We would kiss and caress each other, and gradually our limbs would entwine. When he entered me, however, he would always speak.

"My love," he'd whisper. "My goddess. My soul."

"Do not leave me again," I'd groan as the rhythm of passion began to overwhelm us.

"You know I must," he'd gently reply.

"I cannot live without you," I'd plead.

Sweaty and breathless, he continued to move within me with steady, even thrusts. "I must go, Freya," he'd grunt.

"No, Od," I'd reply. "I will not let you."

He'd then silence my arguments with a deep and passionate kisses while we both spiraled into an abyss of pure pleasure.

One night, in the complete stillness and with a blanket of darkness surrounding us, I worked up enough courage to mention these out of body experiences to Corey.

"I know this is going to sound sort of strange," I said, my cheek resting against his chest and fingers, drawing lazy patterns over his abdomen. "But do you ever see things when we're making love?"

"Flashing lights," Corey chuckled. "You," he added, his voice dropping to a more serious tone before he pressed his lips to the top of my head.

"I keep having these...." I paused, unsure what to call them. Every word that flitted through my head seemed either inaccurate or inadequate. "I don't know exactly how to describe them," I admitted quietly. "But I see you and me, but it's not you and me...."

"Hmm," he hummed, mild amusement giving his rumbling hum a soft lilt.

"If I tell you this, you've got to promise not to laugh at me," I warned, picking my head off his chest and fixing him with a steady glare.

Lifting his palms in innocence, he smiled. "I promise, I won't laugh."

"It's always the two of us together, connected and... it's wonderful, but we're not here, and you're wearing like this armor and... and I call you Od."

"Od?" he echoed curiously, the smile still teasing his lips.

Sure he was mocking me, I arched an eyebrow. "You promised!"

"I'm not laughing," he insisted. "I'm just asking a question," he chuckled gently. "So, where are we?"

Continuing to eye him suspiciously as I waited for more obvious signs of ridicule, I slowly answered him. "I'm not sure," I mumbled. "Sometimes it feels like we're outside, in a forest or something. Other times, it's as if we're above the whole world, in a place that only exists for the two of us."

"And while you're calling me 'Od', what am I calling you?" he probed, smoothly.

In reply, I offered him a shrug. "Freya."

The soft smile left his face and his brow furrowed in deep thought. "Od..." he whispered. "Something about that name rings a bell, but I can't quite put my finger on it," he mumbled softly, his eyes leaving mine and drifting up to the ceiling.

"You don't experience these visions when we make love?" I asked.

For a long moment he was silent, until slowly, his gaze moved back to my face. "Well...." he began. "I didn't like to mention it, because I thought it would sound too weird, but I do... feel things that aren't quite... of this earth, I guess," he finished sheepishly.

"That's exactly how I feel, too," I jabbered excitedly. "It's a strange, mystical kind of sensation. At first, I thought it was just being with you, but it's become more intense and the things I see are becoming clearer."

Taking his lower lip between his teeth, he hummed pensively.

Laying my cheek back against his firm, reliable chest, I lazily stroked the side of his torso with the backs of my fingers. "What do you think it means?" I asked.

"I don't know," he replied quietly.

"Not some Tantra thing?" I wondered.

"No," he sighed. "No, nothing that I've ever come across or heard about anyway."

194

A little disappointed with that answer, I sighed softly. "It's good to know I'm not going crazy anyway," I added with a smile, twisting my face and kissing the skin just above his right nipple.

He squirmed a bit as the tease of my lips tickled. "No." He chuckled. "You're definitely not crazy."

Feeling fractionally more content than when I'd brought the subject up, I allowed the steady beat of his heart to lull me into a deep sleep.

And, for the time being at least, I thought that we'd just forget about the issue. But the next morning, we both got a surprise that posed even more questions than it answered.

I woke up before Corey and headed straight to the bathroom. However, I hadn't been in the shower more than a few minutes when I heard the door slide open and the firm step as he climbed in behind me.

I didn't turn as he wrapped his arms around me and pressed his naked form against my back. And my eyes fluttered shut as his lips and tongue began to sample the skin of my neck.

"Hmm," I groaned, leaning back into him and learning that his lingam was already rigid. "You feel good," I mumbled dreamily.

"You feel good," he echoed. "And you taste good," he added before the tip of his tongue began chasing the beads of water that flowed from my chin to my shoulder.

My yoni pulsed white hot in response, quickly reminding me of the emptiness that existed whenever he wasn't within me.

"Oh, Corey," I cried, letting my head flop back on his shoulder as his hands clutched my buttocks and began to massage them with firm strokes.

"You teaching today?" he asked, almost conversationally, while his powerful fingers molded my flesh with deep sweeping motions that followed the curves.

I released an affirmative groan as I lifted my left hand and curled it around the back of his neck. "But not until this afternoon," I added.

"Good," he replied, smiling against my throat. His loving hands slid smoothly over my hips, caressing them before moving up my torso.

Sensing his destination and keen to encourage it, I grasped his right hand with mine and placed it firmly on my breast.

Corey chuckled as he cupped the mounds of slippery, wet skin and gently loved them with reverent strokes.

"You're not playing golf this morning?" I asked, pressing by butt against him and relishing the feel of his swollen organ against the small of my back.

"No," he replied. "I've got a conference call just before midday."

"How long does that give us?" I asked, unsure what the time was when I'd got out of bed, let alone how long I'd spent in the shower.

"Plenty of time," he replied simply, his hands grasping my breasts a little tighter as arousal blushed my chest and hardened my nipples.

Everything else in the world seeming entirely inconsequential as I eased his hands away from me so I could turn in his arms. Once facing him, I realized he'd left the shower door open, but the fact that a thin mist of water was creeping out onto the tiled floor didn't bother either one of us.

"May I touch you?" I asked, smiling up at him, as my fingers slipped over his torso and paused at his hips.

Since the night that we had experienced Karezza together, it had become habitual for us both to seek permission to touch the sacred parts of the other's body. It was a formality really, because not only had the requests never been denied, but we were also both so in tune with each other that it would have been clear if contact was not desired. Nevertheless, it was a mark of respect: a demonstration that, while on one level we belonged to each other, our most private parts were still our own.

"Yes," he responded, before leaning forward and covering my mouth with his.

As our lips teased, merged and parted to allow greater exploration, the fingers of my right hand carefully took his lingam in its grasp. Gradually, I begin to increase the pressure of my grip. Then, I began to steadily draw my hand from the thick, heavy base all the way to the tip. Almost as soon as my right hand left his body, my left took over, mirroring the action from base to bulbous head.

While I continued my grateful and erotic worship of him, I pressed my naked breasts fully to his chest.

With his arms wrapped snugly around me, Corey appreciatively massaged my shoulders, my spine, my lower back, and, eventually, resumed his sensuous manipulation of my buttocks. Throughout the mutual massage, our tongues darted playfully and our breathing came in a synchronized, deep rhythm.

"Hmm, Corey," I murmured, tearing my lips from his long enough to anxiously pant his name.

"Freya," he whispered in reply, palms sliding over my hips and moving in small circles over the rigid bone.

"I want you," I told him, my hands still moving up the length of his shaft one after the other.

"Ugh," he groaned, his excitement mounting. "I want you," he added. "I want to feel the warmth of you around me."

"I'm ready," I panted. "I'm ready for you, Corey."

The steady massage of his palms ceased, and he gently grasped my hips and turned me a hundred and eighty degrees, until my back was pressed flat against the glass panel at the back of the cubicle.

"Would you be more comfortable in bed?" he asked, pressing his chest to me and pinning me to the wall.

"No," I chuckled throatily. "This feels pretty comfortable," I continued, lifting my leg and looping it around his hip.

As they always did, our bodies seemed to fit perfectly. His solid lingam slipped easily between my open legs and nudged at my yoni. He stopped short of completing our connection, choosing instead to pause as his eyes met mine. A soft, generous smile of pure joy stretched his mouth.

"I love you, Freya," he whispered.

"I love you," I echoed, stroking the back of his neck, which was now being hit by the full jet from the shower.

"May I?" he asked, with a subtle wriggle of his eyebrows.

Stifling a longing moan by gripping my lower lip between my teeth, I nodded. "Please," I whimpered.

Keeping his hands on my hips, Corey slowly thrust forward, entering me with the same gradual glide that always caused a spike of need in me.

I felt myself opening to him, not just physically, but emotionally and spiritually: my heart and soul were just as bare as my body.

"Oh, Freya," he groaned, as his hips finally nestled against mine and he was safely tucked within my warmth where he belonged.

His solidness, his masculine power, filled me with the sensation of rightness and completion. I was home, and everything was right with the world. My lower half shuddered and quaked against him as my bud of pleasure demanded attention.

Corey remained still, his eyes still unwaveringly focused on me, as I rubbed myself against the hard bone above his manhood.

It was mere seconds before a climax shook me, causing me to draw in a few gasped breaths and cling tightly to his slippery shoulders. That was, we both knew, just a small preview of what was to come.

In many ways, it was unbelievable to me that a few months earlier, before I'd known the complete, pure pleasure of making love with Corey, and orgasm like that one would have seemed like the greatest gift any man had given me. After weeks and months of learning what my body was truly capable of in the company of Corey, I knew that these small thrills of physical pleasure were just a tiny preview of what was ahead.

"Your muscles are getting stronger," he commented, dark eyes still searing into mine with an intensity and lust that almost pushed me over into another orgasm.

"They are?" I whispered.

"Hmm," he nodded. "The more work your pelvic floor muscles get, the stronger they'll be. They grip me harder now," he chuckled. "And the stronger they are, the more powerful the pleasure, especially when you release your amrita." As he spoke, in a low, soft voice, his hips began a gentle rhythm of shallow thrusts.

"You mean," I mumbled, eyelids fluttering as I tried to remain focused on him rather than what he was doing, "it's.... There's more?"

"Yes," he nodded, thrusting even deeper.

"But..." I replied, inhaling deep into my belly as he'd taught me. "There was so much."

His smile widening caused crinkles to mar the corners of his eyes. "I know it might have seemed that way to you, but you'll see." he whispered. "That divine nectar can be limitless."

As his steady drives pushed me to the heights of pleasure, I tightened my grip around him. I'm not entirely sure what made me break from his gaze, but suddenly my face twisted to the right and I realized that through the open shower door I had a direct line of sight to the full-length mirror on the opposite wall.

Almost instantly I became fixated with the sight of our bodies tangled, the gentle undulation and the glimpse of his slick lingam as he withdrew, only for a moment, before my body to swallow him greedily once more.

I was struck by the vivid difference between the way I felt in that moment and the way I'd felt all those times in Tristan's bed with that huge, gaudy mirror on his ceiling. I'd hated that thing. I'd hated watching him rutting above me. I'd hated seeing the disconcerted and discomforted look on my face. And probably most of all, I'd hated that almost haunted look in my eyes. The eyes of a woman who would take whatever she could get, knowing that she wasn't worth any of it. She had been weak: I was powerful.

In the bathroom of our love nest, the view was so very different. Nothing was being taken from me. My body wasn't being used like a faceless, soulless hole. I was being loved and I was loving him right back. I was being worshipped and I was worshiping him in return.

My eyes were bright and joyful. My face was a picture of contentment and pleasure.

Both men had shown me exactly how they felt about me in the way they treated my body, and I had just been too blind, or too stupid, to heed the warnings with Tristan.

I was captivated by the reflection in the mirror that was now being slightly fogged. I could not take my eyes from the erotic sight of the man within me, enjoying me and giving me pleasure in return.

"Corey," I whispered.

"Hmm?" he said, placing his lips on my cheek and teasing it with feather-light kisses.

"Look," I urged, still unable to take my own gaze from the mirror.

I watched as the reflection of his face slowly twisted until his eyes landed on the image of the two of us. His dark focus devoured every inch of the mirror, enjoying, I suspect, all of the things I'd seen. At no point, did the steady movement of his lower half falter or gain speed.

Once he'd taken in the entire scene, he lifted his attention, meeting my eyes in the mirror.

"You're beautiful," he stated, smiling.

"So are you," I replied, grinning back at him.

For a second I let my attention be grasped by a rivulet of water that ran down his back and then over the firm curve of his deliciously rounded buttocks. By the time my eyes moved back upward, the woman in the mirror no longer looked exactly like me. She resembled me, sure.She had the same bright eyes and long hair: she could have been mistaken for my sister perhaps, yet her features were most definitely not mine. And there it was around her soft, pale neck: the necklace.

Quickly flicking my bewildered gaze to the man in the mirror, I learned that he, too, looked like Corey, but was no longer Corey. Nevertheless, his was a face I recognized: the man from my visions.

"Corey?" I murmured. As I did, I realized that the lips of the woman in the mirror did not move. Instead, she was turning her face toward her lover and the two began sharing a sensuous, passionate kiss.

"What the...?" Corey whispered, his hips suddenly freezing as he followed my gaze.

"Don't stop," I desperately panted. I needed him now more than ever as our alter egos began moving in a deeper, more primal rhythm.

Thankfully, he heeded my request his cheek pressed against mine, his entire body rubbing against mine as he loved the deepest parts of me.

I was close to release, and so was she.

Tossing her head in complete, wild abandon, she seemed to be silently urging her lover on. He, in turn, was giving her is all with energetic and powerful drives. As she grasped the back of his head and clutched onto his hair, I did the same with Corey's.

As her lips parted and offered a soundless scream, my mouth fell open and I cried out a sob of heated pleasure.

"Oh, God!" I wailed, my lower half jerking and bucking against Corey.

Her body, too, was flailing and quivering beyond her control, arching into him and wringing out every last morsel of the sensation that rocked her to the core.

I knew exactly how she felt.

"Yes, yes," I continued to breathe, moving in time with Corey's uninterrupted thrusts. "I love you," I mewled. "I love you. You're my god!"

"Freya," he groaned, a tension creeping into his arms and back. "I have to stop, it's too strong...." Always keen to extend the experience for as long as possible, Corey seemed to make it his mission to help me to multiple orgasms before reaching his own climax. Usually, he exhibited consummate control, but this was one of the rare occasions in which his sexual energy was brimming over.

I had no interest, however, in him stopping. Even if that meant our lovemaking would be cut a little shorter than usual. "Let go, Corey," I urged. "Pour your love into me," I panted, my hands sliding down from the back of his head and all the way to his buttocks. Gripping them tightly, I pulled him into me, encouraging the ceaseless gliding of his rock hard lingam.

The man in the mirror, Od, was continuing to pump his lower body. His face had taken on a look of concentration and determination, while the muscles in his taught backside were clenching.

His eruption of pleasure coincided with Corey's, his head tossing back and a mute shout being issued to the ether.

"Freya!" Corey exclaimed, hips trembling as the muscles in his buttocks spasmed. The warmth of his essence burst forth from him with violent ferocity. "Freya," he repeated, as the heat pulsed into my center, filling me with his love,

I clung fiercely to him, my arms and legs clamped tightly enough that I might have been making it difficult for him to breathe. However, I couldn't stop myself. I need to squeeze him: my body demanded it. I felt full as he released himself into me: his soul and his very essence spreading into me.

Gradually, though, that sensation subsided and my limbs felt drained of all energy.

The woman in the mirror suffered a similar fate, slipping downward until her lover's strong arms caught her and held her close to him. Content, the lovers smiled at each other before their mouths met and merged.

"Corey?" I mumbled, my voice sounding distant to my own ears.

"Yes," he mumbled. He rested his head on mine and I saw that his eyes focused in the same direction as my own gaze.

"Do you see that?" I asked, blinking. When my lids opened once more, the lovers in the mirror had disappeared and once again, I was staring back at myself.

"I saw it," Corey sighed, arms wrapping tightly around my waist and pulling my body flush to his. "I don't understand it, but I saw it."

Blinking again, I half expected the image to change, but it didn't. I was still gazing at Corey and myself with the shower's water flowing over us. Eventually giving up any hope that I might see the two lovers from my visions again, I twisted my face to Corey's.

"That's them," I told him. "Those are the people I see. I'm her and you're him. I can't explain it either, but I know that it's true."

Our bodies still completely as one, Corey massaged my lower back. "They do look a little like us, don't they?" he commented curiously.

"It's a little weird, don't you think?" I asked cautiously.

"I don't know," he shrugged. "I don't really know what's going on, but..."

Realizing my fingers were still clamped quite firmly to his buttocks, I begin to relax the vice-like hold. "But?" I probed, eager for him to continue.

"I think, maybe, I know someone we could ask," he suggested softly. His head dropped to my shoulder and his lips began nibbling at my neck exactly as they had when he'd first stepped into the shower with me.

"You mean..." I began hesitantly. "Tell someone about this: about what I see when we making love?Tell someone about we both just saw? Isn't that likely to get us thrown into a padded cell?" I wondered, with a self-deprecating chuckle.

Lifting his face fractionally, he continued to kiss his way up my throat to the base of my ear. "We don't have to tell him everything if you don't want to," he assured. "But I don't think he'll laugh at us."

"Well..." I mumbled, feeling him begin to harden once more within me and finding my lips quirking at the prospect of another round. I couldn't get enough of him. And the fact he felt the same way was both gratifying and exciting all at the same time.

"Do you remember when I told you about Karma?" he asked. He assumed, I suppose, that my pause had more to do with doubt than with straying from the topic at hand. "I think it's time for you to meet the Godfather. Then you can see what you think of him and get a feel for whether you trust him to share this with."

"Okay," I agreed, nodding as best I could with his head obstructing my chin. "And in the meantime?" I asked, chuckling.

"In the meantime, I think owe you at least one more."

Smiling broadly, I curled my hand around his neck and held him close. "What about your conference call?" I wondered gently.

"It can wait," he whispered offhandedly. "It can wait," he repeated, his hands sliding up my sides. "Everything but this can wait."

CHAPTER TWELVE

A Goddess Reincarnated

Karma was an elderly monk with a bright smile and an almost mischievous twinkle in his eyes, which seemed incredulous to me the first time I met him. His skin was lined and weathered by years of living with, and in, the mountains. Like the first time I'd met Corey, Karma had an almost instantly soothing effect upon me. Any nervousness or embarrassment I'd felt about sharing our experiences quickly faded as the old man – and his kindly aura – put me at ease.

Two days after that bizarre incident in the mirror, we traveled from our lofty palace to the monastery that sat upon a ridge about a hundred yards down. It became clear that Corey had already spoken to the monks and arranged a meeting. We both greeted the man at the door and were instantly taken to Karma's chambers.

Buddhist Monk Preparing Food

I say chambers, but it felt more like a cave. It was, in fact, an almost completely bare room. He had a small stove in the corner, mats to sit on, spiritual decorations around the walls, and religious statues in each corner. Other than that, the room was empty.

"Ahh," he grinned as the door opened and we were gestured forward. "It's good to see you again, Corey," he said in perfect, unfaltering English, "and to finally meet you, Miss Moreton."

Corey and I simultaneously placed her hands together, inclined our heads and offered him the culturally acceptable greeting.

"Namaste."

"Namaste," Karma replied, bowing to us.

"Please call me Freya," I said.

"Very well." The monk smiled almost knowingly as he adjusted his maroon robes, sinking to the floor and sitting cross-legged. "Please," he offered, gesturing for us to do likewise. "I am Karma," he announced gently, "What can I do to be of assistance?"

Unsure where to even begin, I looked plaintively to Corey: he always seemed to know what to do.

With one of his winning smiles, he carefully took my hand, entwining our fingers and giving my palm a brief squeeze. "As you may know, we've been living up in the palace for several months now, and we've been having these... experiences... when we're physically intimate."

"When you become one?" Karma supplied. "Body and soul?"

"Yes," Corey confirmed with a nod. "And these experiences have been becoming vivid."

"Frightening experiences?" the old monk probed.

"No," Corey quickly responded. "No, not at all. On the contrary, they are very pleasant: it just doesn't make any sense to us."

Smiling Karma nodded and turned his focus from Corey to me. "Why don't you tell me about it?" he suggested brightly.

Clearly it was my turn and swallowing a slightly anxious lump in my throat, I inhaled deeply. "Well..." I mumbled. "It's a sort of out of body experience. I feel like I'm someone else. I'm somewhere else. It often feels like I'm in a completely different time and place." Even though I felt no real anxiety around Karma, I still felt gauche speaking the words. What if he laughed at me? What if he thought I was just some nutty westerner who starts hallucinating the moment she's in a beautiful, spiritual part of the world?

"Visions?" he asked with no trace of incredulity to the question.

"That's how they started, yes," I agreed, nodding. "I felt like I was leaving my body, floating above somehow. And then, the other morning-" I stopped short of revealing what I'd seen in the shower, unsure whether it was embarrassment about discussing the intimate details of my relationship with Corey or whether I still feared Karma was humoring me.

The monk simply smiled and closed his eyes and with surprising ease, pushed himself to his feet. "Can I offer you some tea?" he asked, moving to his small stove and lifting the lid on an old iron kettle. Checking to make sure there was water, he placed it over the hotplate and reached for a small box of matches on a nearby shelf.

"Thank you," Corey replied.

"Thank you," I echoed.

"Tea helps to calm the nerves," Karma murmured, striking the match and offering it to the gas stove. His hands shook a little, showing his advanced age, but other than that his movements could have been mistaken for that of a man much younger.

While we waited for the kettle to boil, Corey kept a firm hold of my hand and rubbed his thumb reassuringly over my knuckles. Karma made small talk, asking us questions about drive down the valley and how we found the weather in the high altitude.

Much too soon for my comfort, though, the tea was brought to us in two small cups. Karma resumed his seat with a cup of his own clutched between his lined hands.

Blowing carefully on the hot liquid, Corey and I took a few tentative sips before the conversation moved back to the awkward matter of our visions.

"Keep in mind," the monk smiled. "I may be a man of the mountain, but there is nothing you can tell me that I have not heard before." With a soft twinkle in his eye, he winked at us. "So," he added, taking a small sip of tea. "You were saying..."

Seeming to sense my reluctance, Corey took over. "These visions had originally been in our heads, but two mornings ago, we saw the vision in a mirror."

"And you were connected both physically and spiritually at the time?" Karma asked.

I felt my cheeks immediately flush at the question, although I would be unable to say exactly why the query caused me to blush.

"Oh, there is no need to be embarrassed," he chuckled. "Unlike in the west, here we do not view sexual love as something shameful or dirty. It is a celebration of life, beauty, and passion. It is one of the highest states of spiritualism that can be reached." As he spoke enthusiastically, his eyes moved from Corey to me, and back again. "It is through physical love that we connect with ourselves, with our lovers, and with whatever higher power you believe in, be it a god or just nature herself. But, I think, you do not need to be told this," he finished a slight upward twist to the statement, making it sound a little like a question.

With a small smile, Corey looked at me. What the monk had said about sex rang true for both of us.

"So...?" the monk grinned.

"Yes," I said, swallowing. "We were making love at the time. At first, it was our own reflections in the mirror, but then the image changed and I saw the woman I become when I leave my body. She was with the man who is my lover in those visions."

"Who is she?" Karma asked.

"I… I don't know," I stuttered.

"How do you feel when you're her?" he continued, unfazed by my reply.

Glancing down into the green tea, I allowed that question to roll around my head for a moment. How did I feel when I was her? "Good," I shrugged. "I feel confident, and powerful, and loved. I feel as though I could do anything, almost as though I'm some sort of warrior. But, at the same time..." I knew that what I was about to say was probably the weirdest part of the whole story, and I hesitated to divulge the thoughts running around in my head.

"Go on," the grinning old man coaxed. "You have nothing to fear."

"I don't know," I said softly. "It's as if, I'm not really human."

"Uh huh," he responded, nodding pensively. "That is interesting. And is it the same for you, Corey?"

"Um, yeah," the man beside me nodded. "I guess," he slowly added. "I feel...invincible," he mumbled with a shrug. "At first, I thought that was just being in love and being with Freya, but I'm beginning to wonder if there's more to it than that."

"Hmm," Karma hummed, his head tilting with intrigue. "Tell me more," he urged. "Do you remember what these versions of yourselves looked like?"

"She's beautiful," I automatically responded. "I mean, really beautiful: otherworldly beautiful. And he's beautiful, too. He has this…this warmth surrounding him. It's like a bright light, that's heat and love and... I don't know how else to describe it."

The words coming out of my mouth weren't even coming close.

"Like the summer sun?" Karma offered quietly.

"Yes," I blurted. "Yes, that's exactly how it felt."

"Is there anything else that stands out to you in these visions?"

Taking a quick glance at Corey, I began to quietly explain the most repeated images that I'd seen: the cavern, the boar, and the armor. "And I remember once that I cried out the name Od," I mentioned.

Beginning to chuckle softly, Karma rocked back a little.

"That means something to you?" Corey asked.

"Yes, my son," he mumbled between light laughter. "Yes, it means something to me." Inhaling deeply, he schooled his mirth and took another sip of his tea. "How much do you know of Norse mythology?" he asked.

"Nothing," Corey shrugged.

"You Freya?"

"Um," I hesitated. "Well, my name is from Norse mythology, I think."

Karma nodded, his eyes brimming with kindness and something that looked a little like joy, although I did not understand what had made him so happy. "You already know that these people are you, don't you?" he asked. "I mean, you know that the two of you have loved each other for millennia?"

"Well..." Corey grinned, a slight rose tinge to his cheeks this time. "I felt that way," he admitted, "but it seemed... I don't know... far fetched."

"Not far fetched if you believe that your soul is immortal," Karma said simply. "If you believe that your soul is connected to hers in a way that keeps you bound together for all eternity."

The romantic notion sounded similar to the way I'd felt, and was reminiscent of the words I'd heard during my out of body experiences. The possibility that I was bound to Corey for the rest of time made my stomach flip and filled me with a swell of affection for him. Removing one hand from my teacup, I placed my palm on his knee and rubbed it gently. This caused him to turn his face to me and, as our eyes met, I saw that he felt it, too.

For a long moment, we held each other's gaze, nobody saying a word as we absorbed not only the truth of Karma's statement, but what that really meant: we were destined for each other, and my whole life had been leading me to him. I'd been waiting for him to find me. That certainly explained the instant and fierce connection and felt to him. It explained why I was so sexually connected to a stranger, and it explained why I had been willing to trust a man I thought I'd known for a matter of weeks.

It hadn't been weeks.

It had been years, decades, centuries, millennia – I'd known him forever.

"So," I whispered, slowly taking my eyes from his and turning my focus back to Karma. "What does this all have to do with Norse mythology?"

"You said you didn't feel quite human during this experiences," the man replied. "I suspect that is because, at one time, when you first came to this earth, you weren't human."

"Excuse me?" I mumbled.

"I think you were Freya," he chuckled.

"But... I..."

"The Freya," he added. "The goddess Freya."

My jaw going slack, I simply stared at him. Corey had used the word 'goddess' often during our time together, but suddenly we were talking actual goddess. Perhaps given what I'd already accepted as truth, that one extra step shouldn't have seemed such a reach. But it was, nevertheless, something I wrestled with. I couldn't wrap my head around it.

"I... I..." I stumbled weakly.

Karma was still smiling warmly, and seemed to be taking the whole matter in remarkable stride. "She was a Valkyrie," he explained, "and the goddess of many things: beauty, love, sexuality, war, death, gold, fertility and sorcery." His eyes steadily moving to the left, where Corey sat listening attentively by my side, Karma continued, "And Freya was married to the god Od."

"But..." I breathed.

"I suspect the boar you see in your visions is Hildisvini, a beast she would ride into battle," Karma forged on calmly as though he imparted news like that every day.

"I don't understand," I muttered. "So, I was Freya?"

"No," he replied, beaming broadly. "You are Freya."

"How is that possible?" Corey breathlessly asked, slipping his hand over the one I continued to rest on his knee.

Draining the rest of his tea nonchalantly, Karma shrugged. "Rebirth," he offered as if it were the most obvious thing in the world. "Reincarnation," he added. "The great divine story in which we must all play our parts. You are the god Od returned to us in human form. Likewise, your beloved wife, Freya, is here to play her part. It is destiny, Corey," he added. "It is fate; everything is written, including your return."

"Our return?" I echoed.

"Yes," Karma replied without flinching. "We knew that you would come again to this earth. It was foretold that the goddess would be carried back to us in a giant bird."

"A giant bird?" I repeated, beginning to feel like a parrot. "You mean... the plane?" I wondered, twitting my face to Corey, I continued, "Your falcon?"

With a slight quirk of his head, he smiled back at me in a mixture of shock and awe that I felt sure was mimicked on my own features.

"Ahh," Karma laughed. "Well, you see, our ancient ancestors could not have known such a thing would exist. To them, the plane must have been a giant bird." Shaking his head, he placed his empty cup on the floor before him and laced his hands in his lap. "The important thing is, we knew you would return. We have waited for over a thousand years for you to return to us, Freya."

Head spinning, I took my wide eyes off Corey and twisted my face back to the monk.

"Every half century or so, a god or goddess is reincarnated. So, it is not completely unique," he smiled. "In fact, we have our own goddess down in the valley here. She is the goddess of the seasons, but in her current human form she is just eighteen years old and still has much to learn. And, unlike you, she has not yet found her soul mate."

"He's out there?" I asked, concerned for this girl even though I knew almost nothing about her.

"Yes," he nodded. "Yes, and she will find him when the time is right."

I turned to Corey. "You're taking this all rather well," I commented. "Do you think you are Od reincarnated?"

He nodded without hesitation. "I don't know why exactly. Maybe my therapist helped set the stage to welcome spirituality a little easier than it would otherwise be," he said. "But it all makes sense... the visions we saw... your name...."

"But while I'm already Freya, you certainly aren't named Od, or anything even close."

"Well." He grinned. "I don't have an actual middle name, per se. But my parents gave me a middle initial: O. I bet if we did some digging, we might find more of a connection than we may see on the surface."

Karma clapped his hands gleefully before he settled back into a contemplative posture.

"So," Corey quietly began, "what's next for us?"

213

"You will marry, of course," Karma responded, as if the wedding was a done deal.

The truth was, to me, it was a done deal. If Corey asked me, my answer would be as instinctive as it would be quick. And, even if he didn't want to go through the actual act of a legal marriage, in my eyes, we were already husband and wife. In every way that mattered, we were joined and that could never be altered.

Both men unaware of my thoughts, Karma continued to explain what had been foretold of our future. "You will return to your native land, and you will teach the men and women of your country about true sexuality, beauty and love. You must do this, because much of the world has forgotten, Freya. They no longer worship love, nor do they worship their own sexual beings."

"But I can't change that," I argued.

Karma turned his benign eyes to me and nodded. "Yes, you can. And you will." Smiling with complete confidence, he chuckled again. "And you will bear your husband two daughters girls who will become forces to be reckoned with."

Smoothing his fingers over mine, Corey grinned at the thought. "I bet they will be, too," he stated.

"I'm not sure I can do all that," I whispered, suddenly aware of a great weight on my shoulders. Was I ready for the responsibilities that were about to come rushing my way.

"Trust in the power of your immortal soul," Karma encouraged. "And don't forget, as strong as you are, you have always had him by your side to reinforce that immense strength."

Curling his hand around mine, Corey lifted my fingers from his knee and brought them to his face. Tenderly, he kissed the back of my hand, his eyes flicking to mine as he did so. "I'm right here," he reminded me. "And I'm not going anywhere."

"You have already been through a great deal," Karma added.

Unsure whether his predictions included my childhood, I chose not to ask him to elaborate and simply remained quiet.

"You are mightier than you give yourself credit for," he continued. "And there is nothing standing between you and your destiny now. The worst is behind you, Freya."

"Really?" I asked. My voice sounded like a small child's as I sought reassurance that my life had finally turned a corner.

Karma's gaze moved from me to Corey. "You have him," he explained, tipping his head a little. "You know, don't you? You feel it. While the two of you are together, nothing can defeat either of you. I cannot promise the road will always be easy," he added cautiously. "But I can tell you that, together, you are unstoppable."

Giving me a light nudge of his elbow, Corey chuckled. "I keep telling you," he said.

Turning to face him, I raised my eyebrows in question.

"As long as we're together," he smiled. "That's all that matters."

"Believe in yourselves," Karma urged. "There is darkness in this world, and there always has been, but do not let it drag you into its shadow."

Aware of the darkness I'd seen in my own lifetime, and realizing that I had been pulled into its shadow on numerous occasions, I wondered how I could ensure it never overcame me again.

As if reading my mind, Karma spoke again. "He is the light," he offered, tipping his head toward Corey. "Od is the god of summer, the bringer of life-giving light."

Turning to Corey I smiled. That description of him sounded very accurate. From the very moment I met him, he'd brought light and warmth into my life.

"All will be well if you trust in your love for each other," Karma concluded.

Staring deeply into my eyes, Corey grinned. "I think we can manage that," he murmured gently.

"Good," Karma chuckled. "Well, that is all I can tell you for now," he added, smiling. "But I'd like to invite you to a festival that we're holding in Thimphu in eight days' time."

"We'd love to attend," Corey instantly replied, his eyes quickly moving over my face to ensure I was comfortable with his decision.

Nodding, I added my enthusiasm. "That would be wonderful," I told the old monk. "Thank you... for everything."

"It is my pleasure," he insisted.

***

There was a lot to digest over the next eight days. Every time I caught myself staring at Corey, I reminded myself that I'd known this man, or at least the soul that dwelt within that stunning body, for eternity.

And I would continue to know him: we'd meet and love, again and again, for as long as life existed on earth. Part of me wished I'd known that years before, because the promise of something brighter in my future would no doubt have helped me through some of the dark days and might have even prevented me from making some huge mistakes: Tristan for one. Yet, the path, as unpleasant as it had sometimes been, had led me straight to him – it was destiny, and who was I to try to alter it?

I didn't think it possible, but our lovemaking had become even more beautiful and intense as a result, too. It seemed, knowing about our pasts, recognizing who we were and what we were, had pulled us even closer. Each orgasm was even stronger than before, and, as Corey had predicted, my amrita flowed more fervently. My love river seemed completely unhindered, and the goddess poured out of me in glorious rapture.

Similarly, Corey's releases were stronger, more passionate and more copious. His strong masculine pulses overwhelming my core with his abundance.

And, of course, I was also grappling with the destiny Karma had spoken of: that I was supposed to become some kind of role model for sexuality and empowerment. It seemed so far removed from anything I'd ever imagined or believed myself capable of. However, I trusted Karma. Something inside me, despite my doubts, knew that what he'd said was the truth. And while Corey was with me, I had nothing to fear.

We opted to continue therapy, if only to make sure that Corey stayed sober. With such a monumental task ahead of us, as well as the stresses from Tristan's attempts to sabotage Corey's business, we knew we needed to prioritize Corey's recovery.

On the day of the festival, we drove to down through the striking mountains, on a route we'd both come to know well, but never tired of. The scenery was breathtaking, but beyond that I knew that the company of each other would make even the least desirable scenes enjoyable.

"Do you know where the festival is?" I asked, Corey quietly.

"Hmm," he responded, nodding. "The Dechencholing Palace," he added. "It's a little north of the city center."

I didn't ask any more questions as we drove in that direction. The palace itself quickly made itself known: with its bright white walls, gold spires, and flared roof, it could be seen from miles around.

A broad grassy courtyard sat in front of the building, and the space was teeming with locals.Some of them were dancing, some playing music, and some were simply picnicking on the lawn.

"I guess this is the festival," Corey chuckled with a boyish grin as he pulled the car to a stop and took the keys from the engine.

We both jumped down for the Jeep, Corey moving quickly around to my side and taking my hand in his before we walked in step toward the crowd. A portion of the party scene had been set aside for stalls, selling food as well as fabrics, beautiful clothes, and even some stunning artwork.

The soft strains of traditional music filled the air with relaxed, easiness. Politely, Corey and I moved through the crowds, smiling and greeting the locals as we passed.

Eventually, among a small group of monks, we found Karma.

"Welcome!" he cried delightedly. "I am so glad that you could come. This festival is in your honor. Your return to us will usher in a new era of peace and light."

My eyes glanced up to the palace and the brightly colored flags that hung from the windows. "What are those?" I asked, pointing to the bunting.

"Prayer flags," he supplied with a smile. "They promote peace, wisdom, compassion and strength." His eyes traveled from the palace's facade to me. "All attributes personified by the goddess Freya," he added. "You see," he continued. "Each one has a prayer or mantra written on it."

Taking a few steps closer, I noticed the markings he spoke of and nodded.

"Those are prayers that will be carried on the wind, but they won't go to the gods. Instead, they are messages of goodwill that spread across the land to our human families."

Corey's hand smoothly disengaged from mine and he draped his arm around my shoulder.

"The words will fade," Karma grinned. "And when they do, new flags will be raised up in their place. It symbolizes the ever-changing nature of the world, and shows that our hearts and spirits are open to this cycle of life, death and rebirth."

Prayer flags

Tiger Nest Temple

Pulling me close against him, Corey placed a kiss on my temple.

"And now, my goddess," Karma continued, "it is time for you to continue on the path of your destiny.Greatness awaits you. And we have a gift to celebrate."

"A gift?" I mumbled, turning to face the kindly old monk.

"Come with me," were his only words of reply. Carefully, he took my head and pulled me forward. Corey's arms slipped off me and he remained behind.

As Karma led me to the center of the courtyard, all eyes turned to me and I felt my cheeks heat with self-consciousness. With discomfort plain on my features, I hurriedly twisted my head over my shoulder to catch a glimpse of Corey.

221

He was smiling warmly and confidently, his hands sliding casually into his pockets as he mouthed, 'I love you.'

Reminded of Karma's words the week before, I allowed myself to briefly bathe in the light that radiated from the love of my life. Feeling that warmth bleed into me, like the midday sun, I smiled back at him. It made everything easier to handle, and suddenly the stares didn't bother me at all.

As Karma and I reached the middle of the courtyard, we came alongside a group of gracefully dancing monks, their long, colorful robes sweeping around them. I became captivated by the movementof the men, and as Karma finally released his hold on me, I felt powerless to resist the call to move my own body to the gentle rhythm.

Dancing in public had never been one of my favorite things to do, but this time I felt no shame. In fact, I felt no self-awareness at all. I simply let my soul dictate the movement of my limbs.

Closing my eyes, I tossed my face to the sky, and when my lids fluttered open again, I realized I was no longer in the courtyard. Instead, I was alone on a mountaintop dancing to music only I could hear.

Everything around me was beauty and light.

But suddenly heavy clouds came from nowhere, blocking out the sun. Blinking, I stared up into them and found Tristan's face emerging through the gloom. He smirked, and then began to laugh as I continued to sway gently.

"And now," a voice said, pulling me from the vision.

Breathing deeply, I shook my head, and found myself back in the courtyard. I found myself surrounded by Karma and the other monks and by the Thimphu locals and those who had traveled from further afield to come to this festival. And, directly in front of me, beaming with pride and a hint of arousal in his dark eyesstood Corey. Everything was right: Tristan wasn't here, and I was safe.

"Now it is time to return what is rightfully yours," Karma continued.

Perplexed, my body became still and I shook my head. "I don't..." I weakly muttered.

From within the folds of his long robes, he drew a square box, covered in black velvet. Gently, he opened the lid and turned it to me. Inside was the most stunning necklace I'd ever seen. Made of gold and diamonds, it was also adorned with bird's feathers and it shone almost blindingly in the sun's glare.

"It's... it's breathtaking," I told him sincerely.

"This is yours," he urged.

As he said those words, I realized I'd seen the jewelry before: it had been in my visions. It was the necklace that the woman...no, I... had always worn.

"The Brisings," he added. "It was stolen from you by Loki, and he hid it away in these mountains. We found it, and kept it safe, waiting for your return." He smiled as he carefully removed the necklace from the box. "It is powerful: some say the most powerful of all the gods' artifacts. And now that you have it again, you have nothing to fear. Nothing can harm you while you have this." Passing the empty box to one of his young assistants, Karma took the necklace with both hands and lifted it toward my face.

It seemed far too beautiful for me to accept, but there was something about it that felt familiar. I fetl a sense of ownership. I gratefully inclined my head as the elderly monk slipped the necklace around my neck.

"Now, you are mighty once more, Goddess," he whispered, blessing me with a gentle touch of his hand to my head. In a rush, I felt a strange power course through me as if part of me was reborn... or reawakened. I brushed my fingers against the precious metal and could swear I felt the strength pulsing through it into my very core.

"Thank you," I replied, a sudden and unexpected swell of emotion bringing tears to my eyes. "Thank you very much."

"It is my pleasure, Freya," he grinned, bowing.

I bowed in return before my eyes desperately sought out Corey once more.

He had already moved forward through the crowd and was now only a couple of steps away. At the offer of my open hand, he hurriedly closed the gap and wrapped his fingers around mine.

I found myself staring into his eyes: those pools of light that had always captivated and fascinated me. There was something else in them now. I could see a quiet strength in those eyes, and a glimmer of amber that was more like the eyes of the man in my fantasies than the human standing before me.

"You are my god," I whispered, tilting my head forward in reverent respect of him.

Quickly slipping his free hand beneath my chin, he coaxed my face back to his. "You are my goddess," he stated firmly. Uncaring about the cluster of people around us, he leaned forward and kissed me passionately.

As I curled my arms around his neck and returned his kiss with equal fervor, a cheer rose up from the crowd and I heard the distinctly melodious sound of Karma's joyful laughter.

When our mouths finally parted, I realized our bodies had started to move in time with the music. And the rest of the party was dancing around us.

Smiling, Corey held me close. "I don't think I've ever seen you look so beautiful as you did when you were dancing a moment ago," he said warmly. "You were so...." he inhaled, as he tried to select the right word. "Free," he sighed. "Confident and sexy," he continued, his grin widening. "You sometimes get a look on your face like that when we're making love, but just now it was... complete," he softly uttered. "It was as if you finally felt at home in your skin."

"I think I do feel at home," I replied, tears of happiness spilling onto my cheeks. "I feel at home in my skin, and I feel at home in your arms. But I think it's even more than that. You complete me, but I think I was missing this necklace somehow. I can't really explain it," I said, fingering my necklace again. "It belongs on me."

He nodded solemnly. "I can see that. Freya, you look like you're almost a whole new person."

"But I'm you're whole new person... and as much as this necklace belongs on me, I belong right beside you."

"Good," he chuckled. "Because that's right where I want you."

CHAPTER THIRTEEN

The Darkness that Awaits

The festivities continued late into the night, and by the time we finally got back to our love nest high in the mountains, it seemed like the whole day had been one small part of an incredible dream. I was physically exhausted from the festivities, but emotionally, I was soaring.

I must have driven Corey crazy during the ride home, asking over and over again that he pinch me. Good-naturedly, he laughed and point blank refused to do so.

"It was all real," he assured me. "I know it feels it so strange, but it was real."

Even though I knew it would sound completely insane, I had to share the news with somebody and, the moment I got through the door, I raced into Corey's office where I'd left my cell phone. Unlike New York, I didn't make a habit of carrying the phone around with me in Bhutan. In fact, as I scooped it off his desk, I realized that it had been at least three weeks since I'd even touched the thing.

'I have the most amazing news,' I typed. 'Corey and I have just come back from a festival in the capital, which was given in our honor. The local monks gave me a beautiful necklace, and told me that I am a goddess reincarnated. I know that sounds crazy, but will explain more when we get back.'

"Hey," Corey softly nudged from the doorway. "What you doing?"

He smiled at me, and I felt my feelings for him erupt once more.

"I just... I had to tell Dani about what happened," I babbled excitedly. "I know she'll probably think I've lost my mind, but I just have to tell someone about this!"

"I was hoping to make love to my goddess," he replied with a subtle arch of one eyebrow.

"Well," I grinned, placing the phone back on his desk and perching myself on its edge. "I think your goddess is going to insist upon it."

Grinning, he stepped forward, stopping when he was no more than a foot in front of me. He leaned forward, placing his hands on the desk either side of my hips and effectively trapping me between his arms. It was a cage I was only too happy to find myself in.

Giggling, I parted my chino-covered legs and wrapped them around his waist. "I'm never going to let you go," I whispered. "You do realize that? You're mine, and I'm not going to lose you again."

"I'm not going anywhere," he insisted seriously, as his face drifted to mine, and his mouth lightly teased my lips. "Not this time, Freya," he added. "I know, in the past, in those other lives, I've left you... but nothing's going to keep us apart now."

"Hmm," I hummed joyfully. "That's music to my ears."

As those words left my mouth another sound filled the room: an electronic buzzing.

Sighing, Corey lifted his head. "This is why we have never made love in this room," he chuckled, his eyes roaming over the surface of his desk until he found his cell phone. Picking it up, he gave me an apologetic smile. "Hello," he said as he placed the cell to his ear.

I could hear the soft hum of a woman's voice on the other end of the line, and felt sure I recognized it as Rebecca's.

"Uh huh," Corey nodded, his right hand sliding off the table as he stood straight.

However, I was not ready to release him from the circle of my thighs, and prevented him from moving any further away from me.

"But they haven't found anything, obviously," he stated, a crease of concern forming on his brow. "So, that'll put it all to bed."

I heard the murmur of her reply, but couldn't make out any of the words. What I did understand, from the increasingly perturbed look on Corey's face, was that her reply wasn't what he wanted to hear.

Releasing a heavy sigh, he shook his head. "Are you sure it's going to come to that?" he asked wearily. Her answer must have been brief, because there was no more than a beat before he huffed an, "Okay."

"What is it?" I asked gently placing my hand on his chest to remind him that I was right there with him.

He lifted his hand and his right hand, slipping his fingers over mine as he graced me with a bright smile. "Thank you, Rebecca," he said, continuing to speak into the phone. "I'll be in touch in the morning when I've decided on a plan of action." With that, he gradually lowered the phone, tapped the screen and tossed it down onto the desk.

"What?" I asked. "What's wrong?"

With a subtle purse of his lips, he cocked his head to one side. "I'll give you three guesses."

"Tristan," I mumbled.

"Got it in one," he replied.

Twisting the hand that he held, so I could lace my fingers with his, I slowly released a deep breath. "What is it this time?"

"You remember I said he was spreading rumors to damage the company's stock?"

I nodded.

"Well, those rumors involved lies about unethical business practices," he continued. "None of them are true, so I figured it was no big deal: an investigation would clear me of any suggestion of wrongdoing."

"But?" I urged, knowing there had to be more to the story.

"Thanks to his money and big profile, Tristan's got a lot of political sway," Corey explained quietly and calmly. "Despite the stock-broking commission finding nothing untoward, Tristan's managed to stir up a hornet's nest at the Senate and they want to meet with me."

"So we have to go back to New York?" I finished for him, the question really a rhetorical one. Nevertheless, he answered it as if it weren't.

"Not necessarily," he argued. "You can certainly stay here... and if you want me to stay, I will. Rebecca is more than capable of handling it-"

"No," I interjected quickly. "No, it wouldn't be fair to make her face that alone," I said. "Besides, this is something we have to do."

"We?" he echoed, grinning.

"Yeah," I nodded. "Karma said we're strongest when we're together, right?"

"Right," he affirmed.

"So, we're in this together," I continued, smiling as I rubbed my inner thigh over his hip. As I gazed into his smiling eyes, I recalled the strange image of Tristan I'd seen during my dance in the courtyard. "Corey," I whispered, my own grin falling.

"What is it?" he wondered, concern evident in his tone.

"I saw him," I uttered.

"Saw who? Tristan?"

Nodding, I slowly explained the out of body experience I'd had earlier that afternoon. "It wasn't just the darkness," I added. "There was something about his eyes; they were evil, you know? And an odd desperation filled his face. He terrified me with that frantic desperation. It was more than just losing me, I think."

"It's okay, Freya," Corey insisted, sweeping his arms around me and pulling me to his chest. "He's not going to hurt either one of us, and he's certainly not going to come between us."

"I know," I responded sincerely. "But he's not going to stop. He's clearly willing to do anything, lie to anyone, including me."

Unwilling to give me false reassurances, he quietly stroked his hands down the length of my spine.

"We have to go back, Corey," I added gently. "We have to put a stop to this once and for all."

"Are you sure you don't mind?" he asked.

"I'd love to stay here forever," I told him, smiling softly. "But I know we can't. And I think it's time, don't you?"

"Yeah," he agreed, nodding. "Yeah, I feel it, too," he added, with an almost sad smile. "It's probably better that I return and help stop the bleeding with the stocks. Tristan has done a number on things. I honestly think he's poured his fortune into ruining me. I don't want to see him go down, but at this point, if my company manages to survive this, he may be ruined."

I shivered, understanding the desperation now. I didn't want to go back: not really. I knew we had to return but I missed the serenity we found in Bhutan. "Promise me we'll come back soon, though," I quickly begged.

Chuckling, he kissed my mouth. "We'll come back very soon."

"Not that it matters where we are," I added thoughtfully. "All that matters is we're together."

***

The next morning, as we drove back to the valley and the small airstrip, Karma and a few of the other monks accompanied us to the plane. It was a bittersweet goodbye, and I held back tears as I embraced the people who had quickly become like a second family to me.

"Thank you for everything," I said to Karma as I slowly released the bear hug I'd given the elderly man.

"You have nothing to fear," he replied. "The time is right for you to return, and although you face obstacles, nothing can stand in your way."

"Come on," Corey urged, leading me toward the Falcon.

"We will keep a watch on your palace while you are away," Karma called as Corey and I reached the steps of the plane and began to mount them.

"We appreciate that," Corey waved in reply.

Nothing was said for a long time while Corey and I settled into the plane and the large craft took to the skies. I gazed out of the window, feeling as though I was leaving every good thing I'd ever known behind. Of course, I knew that wasn't true. The really good thing – the best thing – was the man by my side. Still, leaving a place that contains such happy memories is always painful, and I felt a longing inside of me as I watched the country disappear below.

"You okay?" he asked, noticing a single teardrop that spilled onto my cheek. He reached out and stopped its path with the warm pad of his thumb.

"Yeah," I replied, struggling to smile at him. "I'll miss it."

"We'll come back soon, I promise," he smiled quietly.

"I know," I sighed. "And I know that we're doing the right thing... it's just..."

"Sad," he finished, his hand still caressing my face.

"Hmm," I agreed, nodding.

Very little was spoken during the long flight back to New York. Corey left me to sleep in the bedroom, while he took over from his pilot for a few hours. When I awoke, he told me we were over the Atlantic.

Thanks to the luxury aboard the plane, Corey and I were both able to shower and change before we landed in New York to a throng of waiting photographers. As we climbed down the steps to a cacophony of shouts and flashes, I realized the journalists weren't the only ones waiting for us. A few yards up the strip, standing beside his white Mercedes S-class was Blake. And right next to him was Dani.

"Mr. Wallace, have you got anything to say about Tristan Lucas' accusations?" one of the photographers hollered.

"I have no comment to make at this time," Corey firmly, but kindly, replied.

"Where have you and Miss Moreton been for the last several months?" another shouted.

Choosing not to answer, Corey pushed his way through the crowd, keeping a tight hold of my hand.

"Miss Moreton," one female voice piped up above the rest. "Is it true that Tristan Lucas is a dud in the sack?"

If you count getting off within a couple minutes and never getting me started, let alone finished, a dud, I thought to myself. It was funny really. Tristan had been so selfish, and I could see it as clear as the day now. It had taken the god of sunlight to illuminate it all, but I saw it now.

Refusing to turn my head, I kept my thoughts to myself and continued toward Blake, who was already opening the rear door of his car.

"Please," Corey called as we reached the car and he gently coaxed me inside, "Miss. Moreton and I are more than happy to talk to the media, but I have some pressing business to attend to. Once the Senate has cleared my name, and the name of my company, I'll be happy to answer any of your questions."

"Including the ones about when you started fucking your best friend's fiancee?" a middle-aged man with a potbelly asked. The question caused a few chuckles to rise up among the crowd, but Blake wasn't laughing.

"You'll want to watch your mouth," Blake said, beginning to lunge for the man. However, Dani placed one hand on his arm and Corey calmly put a palm to his chest.

"That's disrespectful to both Miss Moreton and me," Corey said, directing his steady gaze toward the crass journalist. "But as these questions are going to keep circling, let me just be clear: the relationship between Freya and Tristan ended before my own relationship with her began. I did not betray anyone, nor did Freya. Any suggestion to the contrary is a lie."

"Yeah," Blake insisted. "So shove that in your stinking tabloid!"

"Come on," Corey mumbled, steering his young friend to the driver's seat. "Are you guys coming with us to Washington?" he asked quietly as Blake lowered himself into the driver's seat and Dani eagerly trotted around to the passenger side.

"Absolutely," Blake replied. I never doubted him: by the determination in his voice, it would have taken an army to keep him from going with us. "I figure I can put in a word for you if you need me to."

As Corey dropped into the seat next to me and firmly closed the door, I instinctively lopped a hand through his arm and leaned my head against his shoulder.

He tipped his face to mine and pressed his lips to the top of my head. "I'm sorry," he whispered.

"I knew it wasn't going to be pleasant," I replied simply. "Blake," I called. "You meant what you said? You'd speak up against your own brother?"

"If I need to," he replied unhesitatingly as he dragged a hand through his blonde hair, which had grown longer in the time we'd been away. It was thick and touching his collar: it was no coincidence that it was the kind of style Dani loved.

Meanwhile, my best friend was glowing, too.Her bronzed skin clear and healthy. Something inside her seemed to shine, as she slipped her feet from her sandals and propped her bare feet on the dashboard. I wondered if I looked similarly fresh-faced, contented by the previous six months.

"Celestin's still on the plane?" she asked, twisting her face over her shoulder.

"Travis is going to take him back to my apartment," Corey automatically replied, before second-guessing himself. "I mean, as long as that's okay? Would you rather he went to yours?"

"It's fine," I agreed softly. "Your place is fine." Glad to feel the car finally moving and see the photographers and journalists disappear from view I sank back into the seat.

"So..." Corey hummed, leaning his head against mine as his eyes moved from Dani to Blake and back again. "Has Tristan been badgering you two?"

"Not so much," Dani shrugged. "For the first couple of weeks, he kept insisting that we tell him where you were, but he soon got bored with that and got into his other tricks."

"I tried to talk sense into him, Core," Blake added. "But he just wouldn't listen. Now, if he continues to try and accuse you of something you haven't done, I won't hesitate to tell the Senate the truth."

"Thanks, buddy," Corey hummed. "I appreciate that."

Twisting her upper body as far as she could, Dani's eyes seemed to take me in for the first time since we'd seen each other. "You look wonderful," she beamed.

"So do you," I countered quickly.

She raised her hands to stave off any other comments I might have been tempted to make. "I mean it," she said with a grin. "You look like you... but not like you, if that makes sense. It's like someone planted a light inside you. You have never, ever looked this amazing, not even after that spa treatment we treated ourselves to last year. Remember how great you looked?"

I nodded, a little embarrassed at her attention, but curious to hear her impressions.

"Compared to the what you look right now, that spa day didn't change you at all. Your time in Bhutan really brought you into your own, Freya."

I was speechless and searched her eyes for any signs of teasing. There were none. All I saw was a warm appreciation as she reached and squeezed my hand.

"And that necklace," she added, tipping her face to the chain that I now wore all the time. "It really is as stunning as you described. I don't pretend to understand everything you say goes along with it," she continued chuckling. "But it is truly stunning."

"I'll explain it… at least, as much of it as is explicable when we've got this whole thing out of the way. Right now, the priority is saving Corey's business from ruin."

We shared some small talk on the long drive to Washington, but none of us were really in the mood. All minds were elsewhere, it seemed. I could feel an unusually and worryingly pensive Corey by my side, which caused me to wonder whether he was quite as confident about the Senate meeting as he'd implied.

However, as I lifted my head from his shoulder and asked him straight out if he was worried, he shook his head confidently.

"I've got you with me," he offered. "How can anything go wrong?"

If I'd thought there was a large crowd of reporters at the airport, it was nothing compared with the mass of people waiting outside the bright, white Senate Office.

"Jesus," Dani mumbled. "Is this really that big of a deal?" she asked.

"Tristan is making it into that big of a deal," Blake informed her. "He's stirred up as much media frenzy as he can over this thing.

Think about it: two of the richest men in New York doing battle over a woman and over business. It's the kind of stuff the papers love."

"We're not doing battle over a woman," Corey stated matter-of-factly.

"No," I chimed in. "That battle was won a long time ago." As the words slipped from my mouth, I turned my face to Corey and smiled impishly at him. Only he could possibly understand the true meaning of those words.

And he did. Grinning back at me, he placed a hand on my stocking covered knee and gently squeezed.

"I know, I know," Blake said, dismissively waving his hand as he drove through the gates and directly to the office doors. "You know what I mean. That's exactly how the press is spinning it. And it suits Tristan just fine."

Getting out of the car and into the building was a similar ordeal to the one we had getting at the airport. And the same old questions were fired at us. This time, all four of us remained in dignified silence as we quickly hustled ourselves behind the quiet doors.

A smartly suited aide quickly met us and led us to a large, high-ceilinged room, where a dozen members of the Senate were waiting for our arrival. Also waiting was Rebecca, looking pleased to see us. She gave Corey a brief but warm hug before greeting me in the same way.

"Good to see you both," she smiled, handing a thick file to Corey. "This should be everything you need," she added.

"Thanks for holding down the fort while we were gone," Corey offered quietly.

"I don't feel like I held it down very well," she grumbled.

"You did a fabulous job," Corey insisted. "None of this is your fault, understand? Besides, it's going to be fine."

"Mr. Wallace," a bald-headed senator, who was apparently chairing the meeting. "Are you ready to proceed?"

"Yes," Corey emphatically replied. "Absolutely."

He stepped forward, taking a seat at a thin, rectangular table that sat before the large semi-circular one the senators sat around.

Not letting him get far from me, I followed Corey and took a seat next to him. Rebecca, Blake and Dani, meanwhile, remained behind us where lines of chairs had been set out for journalists and a few members of the public. Casting my head over my shoulder, I hurriedly looked around for Tristan, but he didn't seem to be present. I was glad of that: I had no interest in laying eyes on him ever again.

"Mr. Wallace, I understand you cut short a vacation to attend and for that, we're grateful," the chair said, his gravelly, reedy voice rasping from one too many cigarettes. "You didn't seem concerned by these accusations when they first came to light, though," he probed passive aggressively.

Whether aware of the attempt to bait him or not, Corey responded calmly. "No," he simply replied. "No, I wasn't concerned, because I knew there was no foundation for them. I also knew that my staff was more than capable of furnishing the review boards with any information necessary, which is exactly what they did." Unhurried, Corey glanced down at the file and flicked it open. Browsing a couple of pages, he removed a small sheaf and held it aloft for the assembly to see. "This is the report an independent investigation," he said. "It has found absolutely no proof of any unethical practices in my company."

"Mr. Lucas," I chimed in, unaware of the desire within me to speak up but unwilling to prevent it, "was hell-bent on destroying Mr. Wallace's company, and has been seeking to do so for the last six months. When he failed to accomplish his goal, he turned to his contacts here in Washington and applied the necessary pressure to bring about this hearing."

"And you are?" the chair asked.

"My name is Freya Moreton," I confidently announced.

"And your place in all of this, Miss?" he asked.

"Mr. Lucas was angry with me," I asserted simply. "He was angry with me for calling off our engagement, and angry with me for falling in love with another man. This whole thing has been about making Mr. Wallace pay for that. But any taxpayers interested should know that they're paying for it, too. This whole investigation is being funded by tax dollars, and is a complete waste of time and money. There was no basis to launch it in the first place: just the word of a man whose financial records will show that he has been shorting stock in Mr. Wallace's company for at least three months."

I didn't exactly know where it was all coming from, nor did I know how I was managing to speak with such poise and confidence, but it flowed from me as easily as my love for Corey did.

"Influence and money are what has enabled Mr. Lucas' claims to get this far. Evidence has seemed completely inconsequential," I added.

Corey's left hand slipped under the desk, and he gently stroked my knee. "I would ask that the senate stop wasting its and the people's time," he continued, picking up seamlessly from me as if we'd rehearsed it. "All you need is to spend a few moments looking over these records to see that all that lies behind these accusations is the bitterness of one man."

The other eleven members of the assembly looked a little uneasy as they glanced from one to the other, a few whispers were exchanged: then all eyes moved to the chair.

With a discomforted adjustment of his tie, he coughed. "Right," he mumbled. "Well, we'll certainly look at those documents Mr. Wallace. In the meantime, we'll take a brief recess."

As the sound of scraping chairs filled the expansive room and the Senators rose from their seats, Corey turned to look at me with a beaming smile.

"You were brilliant," he whispered, his soft hand slipping up beneath my skirt and the tips of his fingers meeting the edge of my stocking.

"I'm sure you didn't need my help," I replied quietly. "But... I...."

"You were great," he insisted, his hand stopping at the top of my thigh and rubbing gently at the bare flesh he found there. "You were so great!"

Chuckling, I reached down and stopped the motion of his hand by grasping his wrist. "Don't tease me," I encouraged. "You know I'll only want you."

"Sorry," he sheepishly replied, removing his hand slowly.

The recess lasted ten minutes, and by the time the senators returned, a new person had taken the chair: this time it was a woman, with short, curled locks of red hair and wearing a sharp, pinstriped pantsuit.

"There certainly seems to be some evidence," she began when the room fell into expectant silence, "that this investigation was brought to us unnecessarily," she stated. "We apologize to you, Mr. Wallace, and we must also apologize to the taxpayers. Please rest assured that the process by which this was brought to us will be thoroughly analyzed, and any person found guilty of abusing their position will be held accountable for that."

"So, that's it?" a loud female voice from the back of the room hollered. I didn't need to turn around to know that it was Dani's.

The senator's eyes flicked in that direction before drifting back to Corey and me. "I think this whole incident has caused us enough embarrassment," she said. "So we would like to draw the line under it as quickly as possible."

"I feel the same way," Corey agreed, nodding. "I have no interest in making any effort to retaliate against you or Mr. Lucas," he assured her. "I simply want to continue running my business."

"Of course." She smiled gratefully. "We will ensure that there is a clear statement that confirms these allegations were entirely without merit."

"That's all I need," Corey smiled. "Thank you."

"Then, we'll call this meeting to a close. Thank you, Mr. Wallace."

With a broad smile, Corey got up from his seat and reached for my hand. I rose with him, but ignored his effort to take my fingers in his. Instead, I threw my arms around his neck and pulled him in for a hug.

He chuckled as he snaked his arms around my waist. "Well, that was all pretty simple," he laughed. "Thanks to you," he added, pulling his head back far enough that he could look into my face.

"I didn't do anything, really," I mumbled.

"Yes, you did," he insisted, nodding. "You were commanding, and persuasive, and assertive and... you made them listen you, Freya. They were captivated. Tell you the truth," he mumbled cheerfully, "so was I."

I hadn't noticed Blake and Dani striding up the aisle toward us until Blake clapped Corey smartly on the shoulder. At the same time, Dani swept an arm around my back.

"That was phenomenal," Daniela enthused. "Girl, you had them eating out of the palm of your hand."

"Yeah, you were great, Freya," Blake added.

"So, what's say we got out and celebrate, huh?" Dani asked, giggling. "We've got a lot to catch up on, and we've got a lot to be thankful for!"

"Sounds good to me," I replied, smiling as I looked questioningly at Corey.

"Me too," he nodded. "But there is something I want to do first."

"What?" I asked.

"Put an end to the rest of it," he said, disentangling his arms from me, but taking my hand before he headed back to the doors. As we walked from the room and through the building, several people smiled and congratulated us. Both Corey and I responded politely and gratefully, pleased that there had been people who were genuinely on our side.

Grinning at Rebecca, Corey thanked her for her help and she joined us in the walk to the main doors. News from inside the meeting had, obviously, already made it out to the waiting reporters, because as soon as Corey and I emerged on the steps of the building questions were fired at us at a ferocious speed.

"Are you sure you have no interest in making a formal complaint against the Senate, Mr. Wallace?"

"What's next for you, Corey?"

"Any way you'll ever be able to patch this up with your old friend, Tristan?"

Lifting the hand that wasn't clinging to mine, Corey silently called for a hush, which obediently fell. "I'd like to just say a few words if I may," he announced. "After which, I might take a few questions, if you still have any."

Any kind of recording devices, including cell phones, were hurriedly snatched from pockets and held up to catch Corey's statement.

He waited patiently for that shuffle to die down before flashing me a smile, then returning his focus to the large crowd. "I want to make three things completely clear," he began. "First, my company was founded on the ideals instilled in me by my parents and my foster parents: I don't believe in stepping on anybody to get ahead, I don't believe in lying to reach the top, and I have never believed in money for money's sake. I know that might make me seem naïve, but it's worked out pretty well for me."

His joke elicited a ripple of laughter.

"All of the accusations made against me are false, and have been found to be false not only by an independent investigation, but also by the Senate. So, I want to reassure our investors and anyone who has ever attended one of my seminars that nothing you've heard over the last few months is true. Business is once again back to normal." As he spoke those words, I sensed the pleasure he had in speaking them and I squeezed his hand.

"Second," he continued, "my relationship with Miss Moreton has never been sullied by infidelity or betrayal. Yes, we met while she was engaged to Tristan Lucas. Now it would be a pretty transparent lie if I were to say I felt nothing for her then, but I would never have acted upon those feelings had they remained together. It was only after their relationship ended that I told Miss Moreton how I felt about her."

During his eloquent speech, I could feel myself looking up at him with proud and adoring eyes.

"Lastly," he sighed, smiling, "I'd like to halt the rumors that this is just some fling," he continued, gesturing with his free hand to me and then to himself. "I know people are going to continue to believe what they want to believe. And I know that my past has given some people a perception about my life, and my love life in particular. But, for the record, Freya and I are both very serious about this relationship. We're also both happier than we've ever been." With an uncontrolled smile quirking the corners of his mouth, he turned to me. For a long moment, he held my gaze and I joyfully basked in his attention. He gave me a look so full of love and affection that it made me tremble with desire for him.

Eventually, though, his eyes broke free from mine and he twisted his head back to the crowd. "That's all I wanted to say," he told them clearly.

"How about you, Freya?" a young, blonde journalist with heavily made up eyes asked. "Would you like to make a statement?"

Swallowing, I found myself nodding. "There are some things that I want to say," I stated calmly. "But I won't be doing it here."

A collective groan rose up among the throng.

"I would just like to reiterate Corey's words, though," I continued. "There has never been anything illicit about my relationship with him, and I was never interested in his – or Tristan Lucas' – money. Mr. Lucas has had every gift he ever gave me returned to him, by the way," I mentioned offhandedly. "I fell in love, that's all. I found the man that I'm meant to be with."

"When can we expect to hear more from you Freya?" the same woman in the front row asked.

"I'm not sure, yet," I admitted. "But soon, I promise."

CHAPTER FOURTEEN

Telling the World

It was only an hour or two later, as the five of us, Dani, Blake, Rebecca, Corey and I, sat in a quiet corner of the 1789 Restaurant in Georgetown. As we sat there, Rebecca gleefully announced the share price of Corey's business had already jumped up by five percent.

"That's great!" Blake declared, reaching into the inside pocket of his jacket with one hand. Corey had encouraged us to order champagne to celebrate, but we decided to stick with sparkling water. Blake took a drink, and grimaced, then turned to Corey and smiled good naturedly.

Turning to face Corey, who was sitting on my left, I slipped my hand over his forearm and gently stroked the soft wool blend of his tailored jacket. "That's good?" I asked. "I mean, five percent doesn't sound like a lot." I absently pushed aside my dinner plate – the heavy sauced dishes I used to love no longer appealed to me – and reached for my fruit and cheese plate. I missed the simple dishes we shared in our beloved Bhutan palace.

Lifting his left arm, he took a look at his watch. "An hour and forty five minutes after the hearing? It's great," he chuckled.

"That's fast," Rebecca added, still consulting the screen of her iPhone.

Corey's smile was a mixture of relief and acute elation. "It's better than fast. It shows that while stockholders might have been concerned with the garbage that Tristan tried, in the end, they not only believed me, but it looks like our success at the hearing has brought their confidence to an even higher level than ever!" He squeezed my hand, meeting my eyes with an adorable wink before an incoming text on his phone caught his attention. His smile widened.

I couldn't control my curiosity. "What is it?"

"'Fantastic job today,'" he read. "'I've already asked my broker to double my shares in your company. You're only going up!' And here's another: 'Corey, never had a doubt. That yahoo might have tried to sling some mud, but it looks like he got that mud in his own eye.' And he sent me a link. Hold on, it's loading….'"

We all watched as his excitement evaporated. My stomach heaved. Could Tristan have swayed the opinion again? We were all silent until Blake spoke up. "What's going on?"

"Oh, God," Blake murmured in disbelief. He was looking at his phone with a perturbed crease in his brow.

"What's wrong?" Dani quickly asked of him, snaking an arm around his shoulders and peering over his arm to catch a glimpse of whatever it was that had troubled him.

"Tristan," he groaned, content to hand the phone to her.

Dani took the cell from his fingers with comfort and familiarity. As her eyes moved over the screen, she seemed to struggle to suppress a smile. "Well... I don't think that's going to do his career any good."

"What is it?" Corey gently asked.

All heads turned toward her, except Rebecca's. The assistant still diligently monitored all of her incoming messages, while keeping an eye on the ever-fluctuating stock market. Any twinges of jealousy I may have harbored toward her were put to rest as I observed how dedicated she was to Corey's company.

"What's going on?" Corey urged when his first question went unanswered.

Dani lifted her face to his and smoothly offered him the phone. Corey peered curiously at the object before taking it from her. As he brought it to him, I leaned closer and caught my own glimpse of the cell phone screen.

The image it displayed was a shot of Tristan on the steps of the Manhattan Supreme Court, his face a brilliant shade of red and screwed up as he shouted something. The brief article beneath the image explained that he'd been approached for comment regarding the hearing, and had promptly lost his temper in rather spectacular fashion.

"Have you seen this?" Corey asked, his face turning to Rebecca.

She flicked her eyes up from her iPhone and nodded. "It's on YouTube in all its glory," she added, smiling.

"Oh fuck," Blake muttered, propping his elbow on the table and resting his chin in the palm of if hand.

Meanwhile, Corey's thumb skipped across the cell in his hand and he called up the video Rebecca had been talking about. In a short clip, which had obviously been taken on someone's iPhone, Tristan angrily addressed the small clutch of journalists that were huddled around the courthouse steps.

"The Senate is full of fucking idiots!" he raged. "They've been fooled by a smooth-talking, glorified realtor, for Christ's sake. And as for that slut: he's welcome to her."

As we listened to the tinny sound of Tristan's enraged shouts, Corey slipped his hand from the table and seemed to wrap it protectively around my back. It seemed to me that he wanted to keep me safe from the man on the screen, even though he was nowhere near either of us. Then again, it may have been in my head. What I do know for certain is that it felt good. Whether conscious on his part or not, he had become my protector: my champion. I suppose that was the Od in him.

"My parents are embarrassed enough as it is about all this: they're gonna hit the roof when they find out he's making scenes outside the courthouse," Blake grumbled as Corey handed him back the phone.

Dani swiftly snaked her hand around his shoulders and rubbed the base of his neck. "I feel bad for you, and for your folks, but I can't find it in myself to feel sorry for your brother," she said. "He had this comin': you know what I mean?"

"I guess," Blake shrugged. "I hate what he tried to do to Corey and Freya, but... I don't know, a part of me still feels that I should have some sense of responsibility. I should have stopped it all before it got to this."

"He was out of control," Corey reasoned quietly. "There was nothing you could have done, Blake."

"Corey's right, honey," Dani uttered softly, tipping her head until her forehead was resting against Blake's temple.

Corey's hand moved gently over my shoulder blade before stroking down to the base of my spine. "And I'm not sure there is any stopping his self-destruction now," he mumbled with a hint of sadness.

I glanced over at him with a quizzical crinkle of my brow. Even after everything Tristan had put us through, even though Tristan would have destroyed Corey's business and life without any tinge of conscience, Corey seemed to feel some empathy with the guy. That fact baffled me slightly, but it also made me fall in love with him that tiny bit more – he was a good man, a genuinely decent human being, who couldn't bear to wish ill on anyone.

"You okay?" I asked, still looking at his tense face as he stared unseeing at the surface of the table.

"Yeah," he replied, turning his face to mine. "Yeah. I know he's not getting anything he doesn't richly deserve. But I can't help thinking about the young guy I first met."

"You're too soft: that's your problem," Rebecca quipped.

"Maybe," Corey shrugged.

"Come on," Dani declared, picking up her sparkling water glass and holding it aloft as if it held champagne. "I think we've still got a lot to celebrate."

"That's true," Blake agreed. "Let's try to forget about Tris for a while, huh?"

"Music to my ears," I smiled, picking up the glass in front of me.

"You're right," Corey nodded. "We're among good friends, and that's what's important."

***

We got back to New York late that evening, and I spent my very first night in Corey's apartment. Both feeling exhausted, we didn't make love. But we did fall asleep cuddled up, feeling safe as though, finally, we could put everything else behind us.

The next morning, Corey went off to work. I showered and dressed, ready to return to my own business. What I discovered, when Dani met me at a cafe on the corner of Corey's street, was that there had been a huge upsurge in interest in my classes since Tristan had taken to the papers regarding our split.

"I figure," Dani muttered, as she bit into a croissant she held in one hand, while balancing her cell phone and a to-go coffee cup in the other, "a lot of them just want the gossip, or to be able to tell their friends they take lessons from you."

"Hmm," I agreed, keeping step with her.

"But that's okay, right? I mean, I realize they won't be clients for long, but at least they'll be paying customers for a while. I guess it's true what they say: there's no such thing as bad publicity."

I listened to her intently as I stared at the grubby sidewalk. I couldn't make up my mind whether I agreed with her or not. Interested clients were certainly a plus, especially after having been closed for over six months. But I wanted people to come to me, because they're interested in yoga, not because I was being thrust into a limelight I never asked for. And, I suppose, I was coming to the realization that the longer I held my silence, the longer this whole circus would go on.

When a car suddenly squealed to a halt, only for a man with a camera to rush out and start taking pictures of Daniand me, my decision was made. However, I didn't have the first clue about how to get my story out there, or even how much of it I should tell. I believed Karma when he'd told me that I had to open people's eyes, but would they even listen to me? If I told them I was a reincarnated goddess, would they think I was nothing more than a whack job? The people of Bhutan were spiritual; they were in touch with things that are not always understandably on our earthly plane. The people of America (and New York in particular) were much more focused on what they could see, hear and comprehend with their senses.

Taking the plunge, I figured the test would be telling Dani. She was a pragmatic rationalist, and she didn't mince her words. If she thought I was fit for an asylum, she'd say so... in a loving way, for sure. But she'd certainly say so.

So, over a cup of coffee in my office at the studio, I told her everything: from the visions I'd experienced when Corey and I had made love, to what Karma subsequently said, and the festival that had been thrown.

For a long moment, she sat in silence. "So..." she then eventually mumbled, drawing out the vowel. "You're an actual goddess."

Concerned that she was about to break into derisive laughter, I slowly nodded.

"Yeah," she whispered, a tiny smile turning up the corners of her mouth. "Yeah, I can totally see that."

"You don't think I'm crazy?" I probed.

"No," she responded quickly. "No, I admit it sounds a little fanciful, but if you tell me it's true, then I believe you. Honestly, it really isn't a stretch to believe at all." Dani pursed her lips together in contemplation. "You have really changed since you were in Bhutan.

I don't know if it's that necklace, or finding out you were a goddess... or...." She wiggled her eyebrows suggestively.

I barked out a laugh. "Oh Dani, I know exactly what you want to say. Really great sex, right?" She nodded. "Well, there is definitely that, but-"

She reached out and ran a finger over my necklace. "I know, Freya. Really great sex aside, you have totally changed. This necklace definitely has something to do with your change, but it's more. You have truly come into your own."

"The problem is: how do I get this message that Karma seemed to think was so important, out there? Not everybody is going to be as open-minded about this as you."

"No," she agreed simply, "but that's okay, isn't it? I mean, you can't speak to all the people. It's asking too much to expect the whole world to listen. But there will be those who do, and it will start a... like..." her eyes snapped to the ceiling as she tried to find the right words. "... a ripple effect."

"You really think they'll be people who'll listen?" I asked cautiously.

"Definitely," she stated emphatically, her eyes widening. "And right now, you have the opportunity to really make yourself heard."

"How so?"

"The media is all over you," she exhaled, as if I were being slow to not see what she saw. "Now, you could release a statement in one of the papers, sure. But you could also take your story to the talk shows."

"Oh, I don't know about that," I muttered, shaking my head.

"Think about it," Dani insisted. "You get to put all of the Tristan crap to bed once and for all, and you get to spread your message to a huge audience!"

"But talk shows?" I mumbled, still unable to picture myself sitting on a couch next to the latest movie starlet or rock star. "It's not exactly... spiritual," I grumbled.

"It doesn't have to be," Dani argued quickly, her eyes blazing. She was invested in the idea now, and getting more excited about it with each passing second. "All that matters is that you're reaching people."

I couldn't dispute the obvious reach television would have. Although, I was still concerned about the way a show could spin my interview to make me look like a lunatic.

"You'd have to be picky about which you choose," she conceded, as if reading my concerns without my having to give them voice. "And maybe even get some kind of contractual agreement, so the interview can't be edited in a way alters that your message. But they'll be clamoring to have you, so there's no question they'd agree to something like that."

The longer she talked, the more I began to be sold on the idea. However, I didn't feel that it was a decision I should be making alone. After all, it wasn't just my story I'd be telling: it wasn't just me that would be affected. Corey and I were in this together: partners.

So, as I slowly nodded my head in agreement, I uttered one proviso. "I'll have to run it by Corey first."

"Sure." Dani nodded. "In the meantime, I'll start making some calls." She bolted out of her chair like greased lightening.

"Wait, wait," I muttered. "Where are you going? What calls?"

"Don't worry," she grinned, not stopping as she lunged for the door and opened it. "I'm just going to put out some feelers. I won't commit you to anything until we've talked again, I promise." The last couple of words were spoken from the corridor and came floating back to me.

Trusting her completely, despite her overzealous attitude, I leaned back in my chair as I picked up my cell to call Corey.

"Hello," he answered swiftly, his bright tone soft and intimate. "I'm missing you already."

"Hey," I replied, feeling a shiver of arousal move through me as the timbre of his voice echoed in my head. "I'm missing you, too. How's it all going there?"

"Good," he responded gently. "Stock is back to where it was before this whole sorry business began, and it looks like it might keep creeping a little higher. Maybe Tristan did me a favor."

"Have you heard from him?" I wondered.

"No," he replied simply.

"Listen, I wanted to talk to you about what we found out in Bhutan: you know, the mission Karma said I was sent here for."

"Yeah," he said, with what sounded like a smile.

I couldn't help my own soft grin. "Is now a good time?" I asked. "Or are you busy?"

"I've always got time for you," he offered, without any equivocation. "Just let me..." he added, as I heard the soft click of a door closing. "Okay," he exhaled. "I'm all yours."

Yet again, joy tugged my lips in a smile. "Well..." I began before repeating the conversation I'd had with Dani. I paused briefly, allowing him an opportunity to express a knee-jerk reaction either way, but one didn't come. "So, I'm wondering what you think?" I added softly. "Is it a good idea?"

"If it's something you want to do, I'll support you completely, you know that," he stated calmly.

"But what do you think?" I persisted, noting that he'd sidestepped the question.

A faint chuckle resonated in my ear. "I think, as long as we're choosy about whom you choose to talk to, it's a great idea," he concluded simply. "Dani's right, it'll certainly give you a much broader audience."

"So, you're cool with this?" I double-checked, smiling.

"Yes," he insisted. "I'm cool with it."

"Thank you," I sighed gratefully, relieved that I had his backing. I could never have imagined him saying no, but I was worried that he'd have reservations, or would say yes only because he thought it was something I wanted.

"No problem," he whispered, as intimately as if he were sitting right next to me. "Listen, I've got a meeting after work, but it won't take too long."

"Selling somethin'?" I asked curiously.

"No, buying," he replied.

"Really?"

"Hmm," he confirmed smoothly. "I figured it was time to start looking for an apartment here in the city."

"Err, you have one of those," I pointed out, chuckling.

"I know," he stated simply. "But I don't want an apartment that's mine anymore."

Shaking my head in confusion, I mumbled an amused, "What?"

"I want a place that's ours," he concluded. "So, I'm meeting this guy who's the best in the business at finding potential properties. He'll give us a few options, and we can look through them later. Sound good to you?"

"Are you serious?" I blurted. "You want us to buy a place together?"

"Yeah," he chuckled. "Why... don't you?"

"No, no, it's not that!" I hurriedly emphasized. "I just... I've..." Exhaling slowly, I paused and blinked. "I'd love to buy a place with you," I sighed, grinning.

***

That night, while Corey and I sat on either side of the couch, our legs tangled somewhere in the middle, we browsed the brochures and listings that his friend had given him.

Sipping on glasses of iced tea, sharing some crackers and cheese, and occasionally pausing to tickle each other, we discussed our favorite architecture and the best location for both his work and mine. Soon, however, the giggles and tickles went from playful to intense and that simmering passion that always bubbled just beneath the surface broke forth.

Legs still entwined, we soon both found ourselves sitting up, staring intently into each other's eyes. His hands moved softly through my hair, the backs of his fingers tenderly brushing my face.

My fingers moved intently and ardently over his chest and his shoulders, massaging his hard, muscles with the firm circles of my palms. His muscles rippled underneath as his arms moved and his hands found every inch of my body.

"So, what do we think?" he asked, not taking his deep, dark gaze from me. "Central Park?"

He was referring to the stunning five-bedroom, 6,000-square foot apartment that came in at a cool $65 million. "I'm not sure I can afford my share of the down payment," I pointed out softly.

"That wasn't the question," he pointed out, leaning forward and placing his mouth to mine in a feather-light kiss. "Do you like the place?" he whispered, his mouth still brushing mine.

"It's great," I told him, allowing my own lips to intimately massage his as I breathed the words. "But I don't earn that kind of money."

"Freya," he mumbled, both hands cradling my face as his thumbs rubbed adoringly across my cheekbones. "We earn that kind of money. We've been married for a very, very long time, according to Karma."

Gripping hold of his shoulders, I tugged him closer and gave into the unbearable urge to suck his bottom lip into my mouth. Slowly, I savored that warm, soft flesh before grazing it a little roughly with my teeth and finally releasing it once more.

"What are you saying?" I asked, before apologetically running my tongue along his lip.

Obviously unhurt by what I'd done, Corey didn't even flinch. However, he did groan sexily. "I'm saying, it's not about what you earn, or what I earn anymore. We're together, my money is your money."

"And my money is your money?" I giggled, knowing that the amount I had must have seemed pretty meager to him, but wanting him to be clear that the offer of sharing was unquestionably a two-way deal.

"Exactly," he whispered, his hands sliding down from my face, caressing my shoulders, my arms and then gradually moving to my legs.

"Oh, Corey," I whimpered, my hips unconsciously leaving the couch as his fingers slid up my denim-covered thighs.

"So," he sighed, smiling as he reached the waistband of my jeans and slowly unclasped them. "Central Park is the one?"

"Is it the one for you?" I asked, lifting myself from the couch once again and helping him slide the pants down to my knees. I left them there, bunched around my lower legs, while I ran my hands through his hair and massaged his scalp.

He was careful to only take my jeans, leaving my white, lace panties in place. "I love it," he nodded, placing his face in the crook of my neck, as his hands began kneading the now bare skin of my thighs. "But it's only my favorite if it's your favorite."

"Corey, right now, I'd agree to live in a yurt if you asked me to," I told him matter-of-factly before placing my hand firmly over his and guiding his fingers to the crotch of my underwear. "Touch me," I urged, coaxing him to stroke my yoni through the thin layers of fabric.

He complied with my request without any hesitation or question. My eyelids fluttered closed as small sparks of pleasure lit me from within. That touch, which had become so very familiar and comfortable, was somehow still exciting and new. He both relaxed and thrilled me; he had the ability to slow my breathing, while elevating my heart rate. His touch forced the tension from every cell, while making me shiver with anticipation.

But suddenly, the spell was broken.

The buzz of my cell phone as it vibrated on the glass coffee table coerced my unwilling eyes open again.

"I'm sorry," I groaned, one hand leaving the back of his hand and reaching over to the table.

The movement of his hand ceased and he slowly withdrew, returning instead to the soothing kneading of my thighs.

"Don't stop," I whined, scooping the phone up.

"It's all right," he insisted. "We're in no rush."

My slightly blurry gaze flicking to the cell's screen, I read, 'Dani calling' and considered dismissing it. "It's Daniela," I told him.

"Answer it," he said.

Shifting my gaze to him, I studied him questioningly.

"I'm not going anywhere." He shrugged. "We can pick this up when you're through."

A little reluctantly, and feeling guilty for that reluctance, I tapped the phone and brought it to my ear. "Hello," I said.

"Hey, hope I'm not disturbing anything," Dani greeted with a surreptitious chuckle. "I just wanted to let you know, since I started putting the feelers out, everybody – and I mean everybody – is interested in interviewing you. Most of them are perfectly fine with giving you editorial approval, too."

"Oh," I responded, shocked that things had begun coming together so quickly.

"I've been pestered by the people at Chelsea Lately and Late Night all day: they seem particularly keen. They're people are even telling me that you can even have veto on the questions."

"Oh," I repeated. "Well... I don't know if I want to veto their questions. They can ask whatever they want.It doesn't mean to have to answer, I just want to make sure that I'm not going to misrepresented."

Gathering that the conversation wasn't just 'girl talk', Corey stilled his hands and peered at me. "What's going on?" he whispered.

"Well, listen, I'll email you the details and you and Corey can check these things out. If you're up for it, they're keen to do it ASAP... like before the end of the week."

Yep, things were definitely moving fast. But, I reminded myself, that was probably for the best. That meant that there was less time to be nervous or to second-guess myself. "All right," I replied aloud and calmly. "Send us the details and we'll take a look."

"Great!" she said excitedly. "I will do that right now."

Bidding her goodbye and goodnight, I handed the phone to Corey and explained that the shows had already been in touch.

He nodded, seeming to understand, without me actually having to ask the question, that I wanted him to cast his more experienced eyes over the deals that were being offered. By the time I'd finished talking, the emails had popped up and he spent a few quiet moments studying the screen. When he lifted his head, it was with a soft smile. "All looks good," he said.

"They're not trying to hoodwink me?" I asked.

"No," he chuckled. "No, they're all above board. So," he added gently, "you want to do this?"

"Yeah," I said, my response coming surprisingly easily. "Yeah, I think I do."

And, within four days, I found myself in a television studio under the bright lights with an audience of about one hundred, not to mention half a dozen cameras. Yet, I wasn't as nervous as I expected to be. Maybe it was that beautiful necklace I wore that reminded me of who I was and everything Karma had told me. Maybe it was knowing that Corey was just offstage, watching me closely with a reassuring and proud smile. Maybe it was simply the liberating experience of telling my story and not really caring what people thought of me. Some would invariably think I was a fruitcake: some already did, thanks to snippets of the story being leaked to the press. I guessed I had some office grunts at the talk shows to thank for that. But, more importantly, others would listen; they would understand that the message was more important than the person delivering it.

"So, Freya," Chelsea Lately began as the applause from her audience began to die to a ripple. "Where do we start?" she asked, laughing.

I smiled and nodded, as the ripple of chuckles filtered through the crowd.

"I know you must be sick to death of being asked the same question about Tristan Lucas, but did you want to set the record straight over that once and for all?"

I gave her a self-effacing nod. "I realize that a lot of people have a certain perception of me, because they know of my broken engagement to Tristan and my relationship with Corey... and that's all they know about me. All I have to say about that is, I made the mistake of thinking that I was in love. My intention was never to use Tristan, and my breakup with him had absolutely nothing to do with Corey."

"And that's it?" she asked. "End of story?"

"Absolutely," I nodded. "Nothing seedy or scandalous went on. Sorry to disappoint," I joked, gaining a rumble of good-natured laughter from the live audience.

"Well, thanks for clearing that up," Chelsea chuckled. "Now, what about this stuff we've been reading in the press?" she added, picking up one cheap tabloid with the headline. 'Goddess?! Wallace's Girl Loses Touch With Reality' She tossed the rag aside with some contempt, before refocusing her attention on me. "So, do you really believe you're the reincarnation of a goddess?"

It was strange. I hadn't even thought about what I would say in that moment. I knew the question was coming, and I could have planned a response, or at least a skeleton of one. But I hadn't. It didn't even cross my mind to. Nevertheless, my reply came naturally and readily.

"I believe that all women have a goddess within them," I offered casually and confidently. "All women have something divine and sacred, and I want them to know that. Every woman should be as lucky as I am, every woman deserves to find a man who not only loves her, but respects her and is able to free her, both sexually and spiritually."

"And that's what Corey has done for you?" Chelsea asked, with a subtle wriggle of her eyebrows.

"Yes," I said frankly, grinning unabashedly. "I was lucky enough to meet the only man on this earth, who could make me truly happy, who could free me and empower me. We don't like to talk about it much here in the States: over here we've got this 'good girls don't' attitude, and we think that sex is predominantly about male pleasure. Every relationship I've had, until I met Corey, I always felt like my pleasure wasn't important."

"And you think a lot of women feel this way?" she probed, a sincerity creeping into her tone.

"I do," I stated, nodding. "I think this is probably ringing true for a lot of women listening right now. And I want them to know that empowerment – true empowerment – comes from sexual pleasure. It comes from understanding that you have a right to be pleasured; you have a right to enjoy sex without any shame attached to that. And above all, you have a right to choose your lovers."

The whole studio had gone silent, you could have heard a pin drop. Every single person in the room was listening enraptured.

"We think that women have achieved equality, and there's no doubt that great strives have been made, and maybe it seems silly to say that the one area of life that needs to change is sex, but I truly believe that repression of female of sexuality is where it begins and ends. Once a woman feels freed sexually, she feels powerful: she knows her worth and she can recognize that divinity within herself."

Chelsea remained quiet as she leaned forward. I watched her absorb my words and I knew she wasn't just hosting a program anymore: she truly wanted to learn everything I had to say. I looked across the studio audience, which was comprised primarily of women. Each set of eyes that connected with mine craved to hear my message. It wasn't some delusion of grandeur: Karma was right about me. I was sent to encourage women to find their own inner goddess, to find the confidence so many people struggle with. And these women, they trusted me. They weren't here to listen to some attention-grabbing media flavor of the day. They were here to learn.

And I was here to teach them.

"At the moment," I continued, part of my brain amazed by the fluidity with which I was able to speak, "the media bombards us with two representations of women: the virgin and the whore. Sexual empowerment, according to pop culture, is usually about getting naked: whether it was Madonna in the 80s or Miley Cyrus now."

"And you don't see that as empowerment?"

"No," I replied. "And I don't think anybody else does, either. I think we all know that's an extension of this perception of sex as a perversion: that women who want sex are 'bad girls.' It exacerbates the cycle of self-hatred that a lot of women live in. We feel ashamed of our bodies, ashamed of our desires, and almost view orgasm itself as an embarrassment. There's no question about it: we need to learn to love ourselves. We need to accept our bodies, imperfections and all. We need to embrace our sexual desires. And for that, especially the last part, we need a lover who understands those things. Men need to realize that, actually, sex can feel good for a woman, too!"

Another light ripple of laughter moved through the crowd.

"Not only that, it's supposed to feel good for women, too. So, I highly recommend that you learn how to please a woman, and how to make sure that she's pleasured before you experience your own pleasure."

"So, it's up to a man to empower you?" Chelsea asked.

"I was lucky enough to find a man who did empower me, who taught me things about my body that I didn't even know. But I don't think its necessary to have a lover to become sexually empowered. Women can do this on their own. First, they have to accept their bodies, and for that I highly recommend getting naked as often as possible," I added with a chuckle. "Learn to accept and love your body – and I mean all of your body. Don't be afraid to explore it: find out what you like, because it's not the same for everybody. Find those sacred parts of you that are able of producing so much intense pleasure. I promise, once you start to appreciate the bliss that be felt, you will stop looking at sex and masturbation as dirty words."

Chelsea leaned forward in her seat. "And now you consider yourself sexually empowered, able to choose your lovers, but you're not choosing a lot of lovers. You're tied to Corey Wallace now, so how does that fit in with your perception of freedom?"

Smiling, I shook my head. "I'm not tied to Corey, nor is he tied to me. We're in love, and we've chosen to be in a monogamous relationship. Don't get me wrong, sexual freedom is not about sleeping with as many people as possible. In fact, a lot of women who do sleep with as many as possible aren't free at all. The reason they're always looking for new lovers is because they haven't found what makes them happy; they haven't found what gives them real pleasure." I paused as I uncrossed and crossed my legs smoothly. "Love and freedom aren't mutual exclusive. Often, love can be freedom. That's certainly the way it's been for me. Corey's never treated me like a sex object, and he's never blamed me for his lust, as so many men tend to do with women. Instead, he's always respected and loved my body, much more than I ever did. Being with someone like that, being taught how to love myself was the best gift anybody has ever given me, and I adore him all the more for that."

A soft, 'ahhh', whispered across a few people in the crowd and I found myself blushing slightly at the way I'd gushed about him.

"So where do you think we're heading?" Chelsea asked. "What's life going to be like for women in the future?"

Inhaling, I considered the question. "It's difficult to know," I admitted honestly. "When any natural force on this planet is controlled or repressed for too long, it tends to become more powerful and persistent. Women's sexuality has been repressed for centuries now, and, whether or not it's still going to be remains to be seen. Simone de Beauvoir would probably tell you that any advancements since 1955 have been window dressing. Sure, we've got singers parading around naked, but we also have human trafficking, brutal sexual violence all over the world, and many of the best jobs still going to men. Women are still not seen as valuable. In some parts of the world, they're still not even seen as human beings."

An oppressive, grave silence had descended on the studio.

"But I do think we're becoming more aware, as a society, of the exploitation of women. And I predict that things will change and change rapidly. My guess is that within two centuries, women will be the recognizably more powerful gender. One thing's for sure: we won't be the 'second sex' anymore."

"You really think that?"

I nodded emphatically. "Yes. After all, patriarchy hasn't always been the norm, and I think it's beginning to become apparent that it's not working. Women are already outperforming men in colleges and universities – something that would have been astonishing a century ago, let alone further back. The fact is, as women become more and more sexually empowered, they will become empowered, period. And that's when we can truly start to hope for a world of equality."

"That's great: we'd love to have you back to talk about this some more." Chelsea smiled. "But for now, Freya Moreton, everybody!"

CHAPTER FIFTEEN

The Surprise

After the Chelsea Lately show aired I was bombarded by many different publishing houses, all of them requesting to sign a book deal with me. After some thought, and some sifting through the many choices, I selected one and determined to write openly about the reincarnation I'd experienced in Bhutan.

Meanwhile, I was being bombarded by emails and phone calls from all kinds of people: advertisers, people I'd been to college with (who just wanted to say 'Hi' apparently), and I even got a text message from Scott. It read, 'Saw you on TV: you look kind of different. I don't know exactly how to describe it. But listen, I'd still love to catch up. Call me, huh?'

I never did.

There were two things about the following week that made me feel wonderful about the whole thing. The first was Corey. He continually told me how proud he was of me, and every night when we made love, he seemed especially attentive, as if publicly acknowledging him as a fantastic lover had made him determined to 'up his game'.

The second thing that made me feel enormously gratified was the overwhelmingly positive response I received. Women (and sometimes men) would stop me in the street in the days following the interview to tell me that what I'd said struck a chord with them. It was all very gratifying, and life was good.

I did a couple more talk shows, all of them similar to the Chelsea Lately one: I also did an interview with Ms. Magazine. And, between that and meetings with publishers, I was a woman on a mission.

It had been almost eight months prior that Corey had asked me to decorate the massive top floor of his Nirvana home in Florida. As a thank you to him, I was desperate to finish it. The problem was keeping that fact from him. I knew I couldn't just fly off to Florida without him noticing, so I had to get all of my plans implemented from a distance. Thankfully, Rebecca was able to put me in touch with some of Corey's Florida-based employees, who were not only happy to help, but amazingly adept at sourcing all of the things I asked for.

Everything was going smoothly. I found myself happy: happier maybe than I'd even been in Bhutan, because I was doing exactly what I was meant to be doing. Not only had I found love, I'd found my purpose, and knowing that I was helping people felt incredibly good.

However, that darkness Karma had mentioned was about to rear its head again.

It was three or four days after the Lately interview aired that I dashed over to Corey's office to surprise him with lunch. I'd grabbed some takeaway sushi from a little restaurant I knew he loved, and I couldn't wait to spend some time with him during my busy day.

When I got to his office, his door, which usually always remained open (unless he was in a meeting), was closed. He didn't have a secretary per se, and Rebecca was nowhere to be seen, so I simply hovered unsure whether to disturb him by knocking or not.

Dithering, I lifted my hand, but I raised voice from behind the door halted my motion.

"You really think this is over?"

It was, unmistakably, Tristan's voice. A tone that had once seemed so honeyed to me now sounded gruff, and so full of venom that it was ugly.

"Tris, I don't want this to go on anymore," Corey replied, his voice calmer, deeper and... sexier. I knew I shouldn't have been going there right at that moment, but I couldn't help it. In every situation, Corey was able to light the fire in me.

"Just because the Senate's got no fucking balls, doesn't mean I can't figure something else out."

"Tristan," Corey insisted. "Man, your clients are abandoning you like rats from a sinking ship. You've lost a shit-ton of money trying to drag my company under…"

"You don't know anything about my money! I'm going to win back all of that money when stockholders realize what bullshit you've been pulling!"

Corey's voice was low. "I do know how much money you've lost. Tristan, you invested everything… EVERYTHING… to ruin me. You'll be lucky if you can make it out of this with a roof over your head. And not a fancy roof, either."

"Fuck you." I was taken aback to hear that Tristan wasn't denying it. Had he really lost everything? Was his hatred so much that he would ruin himself trying to Corey down?

Corey continued. "I hear you're about to be investigated for trying to bribe a senator. Things couldn't much bleaker for you."

"I don't lose," Tristan growled. "I never lose."

"Well, on this occasion, you have," Corey argued. There was no real malice in that statement: it was simple fact.

"No, I haven't," Tristan insisted. "I haven't lost to you, and you know why?"

Corey didn't reply, but Tristan, apparently, didn't need a response, because he forged on. "You haven't won, because I had her first."

"What?" Corey responded darkly.

"I had her first," Tristan vehemently repeated. "I fucked her, Core. How does it feel, knowing that I've been inside her?"

My heart pounding in my chest, and I waited for Corey's reply. My breath was held, every fiber of my being listening to what would happen next.

"Think about it," Tristan continued, chuckling grimly. "Every time you bang her, you think long and hard about the times I fucked that sweet cunt. I had her, Corey. I had her first!"

Flashes of all the old shame, regret and embarrassment flooded over me. I had been used, my body sullied, my yoni desecrated by his disrespect. Trembling, I found my breath coming harder and faster.

"No you didn't," Corey said firmly.

"What?"

"No, you didn't," he repeated, emphasizing each word.

"Yeah, I did," Tristan responded angrily. "If that slut told you she never slept with me, she's lying. I had that whore on our very first date, and almost every night after that."

"You never had her, Tristan," Corey insisted. "You had sex with her, sure. And what?"

"What do you mean 'and what?'. You're not going to tell me it doesn't bother you that I put my big dick inside her before you, are you?"

"It doesn't bother me," Corey responded, quietly but determinedly.

"Yeah right!"

"It doesn't bother me, because it didn't mean anything," Corey continued. "It meant nothing to you, because she meant nothing to you, did she? She was just a trophy to you.She looked good on your arm, and made other men envious of you. I thought you loved her, but you never did, did you?"

"I still had her!" Tristan argued, with what I felt sure was a sickly grin.

"You don't get it, do you?" Corey replied calmly. "You didn't have her, not all of her. You never had her heart or her soul, and you never even spent any of your precious time time trying to get to know those things. You slept with her, but it was meaningless. It meant nothing." A steady pause filled my head as I waited for him to go on. "Every time, every single time I'm with Freya, it means everything, because I know her. I know every silly little thing about her, and I love it all. She lets me see her as she really is. I get that privilege Tristan, not you and nobody who came before you, either."

Tristan's anger had dissipated.Either that or his ability to speak was robbed of him... I'm not sure which.

"I love her, and she shares herself with me. I don't know whether you'll ever realize how incredible that can be. It's so much more than just sex, Tris. You 'had her', huh? You talk like you took something from her. You might think you id, but you didn't. You took nothing, because she gave nothing. And you know the really sick thing? You could have had something from her. If you hadn't been such a selfish prick, you could have had her love. And now, you'll never know. You'll never know how phenomenally good that feels."

"Where the fuck do you get off with all this bullshit?" Tristan grumbled.

"I've got business to attend to, so I'm afraid this meeting is over."

Bolting back from the door, I moved swiftly to the window, turning my back just as it swung open and irritated footsteps swept through the open plan office space. It was a few seconds before I had the courage to turn my head and watch Tristan's back as he marched through the main door and disappeared in the hallway.

Once I was sure he was gone, I turned fully and found Corey's office door ajar. While part of me thought it would be best to walk away and never let him know I'd overheard the conversation, another part of me refused to leave until I'd shown him just how grateful I was for everything he'd said.

Slowly, I stepped forward, and tapped lightly on the door with my knuckles.

"Come in," Corey called.

As I gently pushed on the panel of cherry wood, I found Corey seated at his desk, eyes studying a piece of paper. Noticing me out of his peripheral vision, he lifted his dark head and broke into a beaming smile. "Hi," he greeted me warmly, pushing himself from his seat and rounding the table to meet me.

"Hey," I replied, happily accepting his hug and a brief kiss on my lips. "I thought you might like some lunch," I offered, holding up the bag I still carried. "But if you're busy-"

"No, no," he insisted, shaking his head. "Lunch sounds great," he added, grinning.

It amazed me that he could be so cool only seconds after having such a heated argument. Well, to be fair, he wasn't the one that had gotten heated. But Tristan certainly had been, and that must have riled the love of my life at least somewhat. Once again, his ability to take things in stride amazed me.

His warm fingers brushed mine as he took the bag from me, "What have we got?" he asked. Opening the carrier, he peered inside.

"Sushi," I told him, knowing that he'd already seen it for himself. "But... um," I added, taking a couple of paces back and closing the door. "There's something I want to do before we eat."

"Okay," he responded openly. "Something on your mind?" he asked, a slightly curious crinkle in his eyebrows.

"You could say that," I agreed, nodding.

"What's up?"

Stepping forward, I took his free hand and began to lead him toward his desk. "Well, first, I was wondering if you had business plans this weekend," I said.

As we reached his desk, I took the sushi bag from him and placed it gently on the table. Then, gripping his open-collared shirt, I steered him toward the chair before giving him a firm nudge.

Chuckling, he flopped into the seat with a bump. "Not that I know of," he answered. "Why?"

Leaning over him, I placed my hands on the leather arms of his chair. "I'm planning a little trip for the two of us," I said, placing my face an inch from his. "So, it's more fun if you're there."

Grinning, he lifted his hands to my face and swept back the hair that had fallen across my cheeks. "Hmm, sounds good," he agreed, tipping his head forward just enough that he could kiss me.

When I'd taken his hand and guided him to the desk and started talking, I hadn't really had much of a plan in mind. All I knew was that I felt such a deluge of gratitude for him that I had to let him know how much I loved him. As my lips brushed his, and my tongue drifted forward to taste him with the same enthusiasm that had always existed, the rest of my actions came incredibly naturally.

Pulling gently back from the kiss, Corey looked me in the eyes. "Was there a second thing?"

"Yes," I nodded, falling effortlessly to my knee in front of him. "This," I said, placing both hands on his knees and slowly stroking up and down his thighs.

"Freya?" he asked, a smile still playing on his lips. "Honey, when I said that I had time for lunch, I didn't mean the long lunches we used to have in Bhutan," he chuckled.

"I know," I replied, my voice no more than a whisper. "But there's something I have to do." With that, I confidently took his belt in both hands and unbuckled it while very deliberately keeping my eyes on his.

His elbow resting on the arms of the chair, his fingers remained passive. "Freya," he mumbled.

I allowed my eyes to flick downward, and noticed the steadily growing bulge in his pants. Pleased that he could respond as quickly to me as I always responded to him, I carefully unbuttoned his pants and slowly pulled down his zipper.

"Freya," he said again.

The dazzling white of his boxer briefs was exposed, and the clear ridge of his lingam thrust itself forward enticingly in a bid to free itself. My hands quickly moved to the waistband of his underwear and I looked back up, settling my eyes on his once more. "May I?" I asked softly.

"Yes, of course," he breathed nodding, "But Freya," he blurted, "you don't have to."

Smiling at him, I gently edged his underwear down.

Helpful to a fault, he lifted his butt from the chair, allowing me to shift the boxers from his hips and free the magnificence of his wand of light. Carefully taking his hardness in my right hand, I slowly rubbed him from base to tip and back down again. "Yes, I do," I informed him, keeping my focus tightly on his deep eyes.

He produced a small moan of pleasure before shaking his head. "No, you don't. You neverhave to do anything."

"Semantics," I said, with a half smile. "I have to, because I want to. I need to. I need to show you how much I love you."

"I already know," he gently replied.

Still stroking his lingam, I reached his tip and slowly circled his corona with the pad of my thumb. "I don't think you do," I whispered before steadily leaning forward. Extending my tongue, I trailed the path my thumb had taken just seconds earlier, thrilling as he quivered beneath the touch.

Amazing as it may seem, after over six months of having more sex than I'd ever had in the rest of my life put together, I had never fellated Corey. I'd given him lingam massages, I had caressed and worshiped him with various parts of my body:but I had never given him a blowjob. I'm unsure why I shied away from that particular act. Maybe it was too reminiscent of the way my body had been used in the past. Perhaps it was that one final issue that refused to leave me –

a reminder of all the times men had gained pleasure without giving any in return.

Corey, to his immense credit, had never asked: he had never pushed. In fact, at no point had he tried to urge me to do anything other than what was comfortable.

Suddenly, it felt like the right time. It was the time to pay him back for all those occasions when he'd given and expected nothing in return. It was time to show him that I could be unselfish, too. It was time to let everything from the past go. Corey wasn't like any of those men who had used me for their own gratification: he wouldn't view my mouth on him as his right. He would, I knew, accept it as what it was: a gift, an expression of unconditional love and devotion.

"Freya," he mumbled above me, his hands slowly smoothing over my cheeks and brushing the hair from my face. "You know, you don't-" his words were cut short, when I teased his frenulum with the tip of my tongue.

Feeling heady, I began to giggle, as I lifted my face and peered up at him with tenderness. "I want to Corey," I insisted before dipping my head once more and kissing the crown of his lingam. "I want to," I repeated.Then I parted my lips and placed them around the top of his manhood. I would never be able to take him in entirely. There was no question about that: he was too big. So, I wrapped my hand around his base and slowly massaged the lower half of his wand as I swirled my tongue over the bulbous tip.

"Oh, Freya," he gasped, his hips trembling.

Fighting the urge to smile, I continued at the same pace, bringing my other hand up to gently cup his sack. Tenderly, I rolled his balls in the palm of my hand. I felt them almost instantly tighten, and paused just long enough to look up at him and smile.

He was staring right back at me with eyes so intensely dark they looked almost dangerous. "I love you Freya," he said, his voice a little hoarse.

"I know you do," I whispered. "And I love you." With that, I tipped my head back down. This time, I trailed the thick vein on the underside of his lingam before slipping him back in my mouth. I tried to take a little more of him as I slowly began to move back and forth in rhythm with the motion of my hand.

Meanwhile, the fingers that held his testicles continued to carefully and respectfully massage the warm flesh beneath them.

Just as with every kind of lovemaking had been between us, this was a slow, gentle process. Corey never urged me on, either with his hands or his voice. Instead, he reverently stroked my face and hair while he made gratefully noises and whispered words of love.

By the time both my knees and my jaw were beginning to tire, I felt him begin to tense.

"Freya, honey, you're going to have to stop," he mumbled.

I paused briefly, lifting my head just long enough to say. "It's all right. I want you to come."

"Ugh, Freya," he groaned, as I eagerly took him back in my hungry mouth and began to suck his soft tip. "God, you're so beautiful," he muttered. "I... I...."

Squeezing the base of his shaft, I moved my fist a little faster as I felt his testicles shift upward.

"I love you," he whispered, hips jerking subtly as he began to throb with pleasure.

His essence was, thankfully, not as copious as it had been on many occasions. I suppose, the fact that he hadn't been close to the point of no return several times before climaxing accounted for the more manageable amount.

I didn't hesitate in swallowing him down, realizing as I did so, that there was a sweetness to his taste, nothing like the bitter, salty tang I'd experienced with other men.

"Oh, God," he gasped, his hands still moving tenderly over my cheeks.

As he gradually became still and his body slackened, I slowly lifted my head, not before licking his length once more and then bestowing a light kiss to his now sensitive head.

"Goddess," I corrected him with a smile. I still held his shaft and sack in my hand, fondling them gently. I was glad to have had the opportunity to show him how much I loved him. "Thank you," I whispered.

"Pretty sure I'm the one who should be thanking you," he chuckled. Finding the strength to lean forward, he placed his thumbs on my chin and coaxed my face up to his. Sweeping down, he claimed my mouth in a kiss, allowing his tongue to make a slow exploration before flopping back in the chair and exhaling a deep breath. "Wow," he sighed. "Tonight, I'm going to repay that, I promise."

"You don't owe me anything," I replied, letting my hands slip from his lingam and testicles, so I could go back to where I started: massaging his thighs. "That was for what you did this afternoon," I told him, relenting to the discomfort in my knees and pushing myself off the floor.

Corey stood up too, pulling his underwear and pants back up. "What do you mean?" he asked, as he zipped and buttoned his pants. "What did I do this afternoon?"

"Well, I suppose it's for more than that, really," I admitted, leaning my butt against his desk and reaching behind me for the bag of sushi.

After buckling his belt, Corey tossed himself back in his chair before pulling it closer to me and placing both hands on the desk either side of me. "I still don't know what you're talking about," he said.

"You know, sometimes," I whispered, taking a small plastic container out of the bag, "it's a little overwhelming just how much you love me."

"You know how much I love you," he insisted, smiling.

"Yeah," I agreed. "I do. But sometimes, I get a reminder and it's just... I find myself thinking... wow!"

"Well, that's good," he said, his grin growing wider. "I want to make you think 'wow'... But what did I do?"

"Hmm?" I mumbled, opening the clear plastic box and offering it to him.

"Thank you," he responded, taking his lunch from me. "What did I do to remind you?" he explained.

"Oh," I breathed. "I... I've been here a little longer than you knew," I admitted. "I didn't deliberately listen, but when I got here, the door was closed and then I heard raised voices, and...." Not really wanting to finish the sentence and hoping I'd said more than enough for him to understand where it was heading, I closed my mouth and reached for my own sushi.

Picking up the wooden chopsticks that came with his meal, he looked pensively at me. "Oh," he sighed. "You mean, you heard Tristan? Freya, if I'd known you were there-"

"You would have what?" I interrupted. "Corey, what you said was... well, it touched me so deeply. And I want you to know that you were absolutely right, it meant nothing with him. And it will always mean everything with you."

Giving me a soft half smile, he picked up a piece of his sushi, but rather than offer it to his own lips, he reached out and place it next to mine. "So, that was what you were thanking me for?"

Grinning gratefully as I took his morsel of rice and seaweed in my mouth, I nodded.

"Well, you didn't have to thank me for that," he smiled. "But I'm not complaining about the way you did it," he chuckled. "Thank you," he said, expertly scooping up another piece of sushi and popping it into his own mouth. "And I hope you haven't got a busy afternoon ahead," he mumbled as he quickly chewed and swallowed.

"Why?" I wondered, opening the lid of my own lunch.

276

"Because when you get home tonight, I am going to love you like you wouldn't believe," he stated, mischievously wriggling his eyebrows.

Laughing at him, I scooted back on the desk, slipped out of my shoes and placed my feet on his lap.

***

Trying to keep where we were going that weekend a secret was absolutely impossible. I could keep it hush hush until Saturday:that wasn't a problem.But I knew that once we were on the way, Corey would recognize the route so well that the jig would be up within about an hour at most.

So, rather than try to keep it from him, I was direct about it as soon as we got to the airport.

"A weekend in Nirvana?" he replied, smiling broadly. "Sounds great to me."

"Good," I said as we got out of the car. However, before we headed to the airport, I hovered at Travis' car door. Digging into my purse, I checked my phone, realized I had another message from the publisher, but determined it could all wait. "Would you mind taking this back to the apartment for me?" I asked of the amiable driver.

"Sure," he grinned. "You won't be wanting it?"

"Nope, it's just going to be me and my soul mate this weekend," I enthused, looping my arm with Corey's.

"Hmm," he smiled, using his free hand to scoop his own phone from his pocket. "I guess that means I'm following suit," he grinned, handing his phone to Travis, too.

"Have a good trip, you too."

The journey was uneventful, but I couldn't help thinking about the first time I'd made it – back when I'd felt so nervous about being near Corey; I was so frightened by the intensity of the sensations I experienced around him. What a difference a few months had made. There were no longer any nerves… well, expect for hoping he'd like what he found at the house. There was absolutely no fear about being with him.

The helicopter landed on the sunny lawn, and we climbed out of the air-conditioned craft. Sweltering, humid heat met us as we walked hand in hand across the backyard to the house.

"You think, maybe this time I could persuade you to take a skinny dip with me?" he asked, reminding me of the conversation that seemed almost like a lifetime ago. A lifetime in an eternity of lifetimes, it would seem.

"Try and stop me," I countered sassily. "But first," I said tugging on his hand, "I want to show you something."

"I was kind of interested in what you wanted to show me in the pool," he chuckled.

"Come on," I laughed, strolling under the Spanish-style archway and entering through the open sliding doors. I hustled across the living room, and headed straight for the stairs.

"Where are we going?" he asked, following obediently behind and keeping pace with my eager steps.

"It's a surprise," I replied, grinning. I'd seen the finished pictures the designer had sent just the day before and it was all completely perfect. I loved it and I knew Corey would, too.

It wasn't until we began climbing the second flight of stairs that he seemed to put the pieces together. "You've done something to the room?" he asked. "How did you find the time?" he demanded good-naturedly.

"Well, I have to admit, I had a little help," I said, as we approached the closed door. "It was my idea, but I knew I couldn't put it all into place without a few pairs of hands."

"Okay," he chuckled. "Well, when I asked you to design it, I hadn't intended for you to be lugging furniture, so that's fine."

"Close your eyes," I insisted, taking hold of the handle. I waited for him to give me an amused shake of his head before his lids finally closed. Then, slowly, I pushed the door open and, with one hand still entwined in his, I pulled him into the huge space.

Wide-eyed, I took it all in, before finally saying, "All right, you can open them."

As soon as he did, the smile he'd worn drifted from his face and his lips parted in awe. I watched anxiously as his gaze moved around the murals on the walls, lingered over the blue poppies and the furniture that were all exact replicas of that special room we'd shared in our love nest.

I watched with excitement while his eyes grew absorbing each nuance of the room. The contrast of the neat, white linens was startling against the irregular designs of the Sheesham wood furniture I had imported from India. Stunned, but delighted, he sat on one of the low chairs and dragged me onto his lap.

Although the scenery from the windows was very different from the one of the Himalayas, I'd had a stunning photograph of the view in Bhutan blown up and placed above the bed.

"You..." he mumbled. "You.... You've recreated our love nest?" he smiled.

"I figured, it would be nice to have a little bit of Bhutan here," I reasoned with a shrug. "What do you think?"

"I love it," he enthused, curling his arm around me and pulling me to him. "And I love you. This is incredible."

"I'm so glad you like it," I said, kissing the side of his neck.

We stood up as one as he continued to explore the room. "I just can't believe it," he murmured happily into my hair before gasping yet again. Childlike, he tugged my hand to the wall across from the large bed and stopped in front of the collage I created. Similar to the one in Bhutan he created from snapshots of us in Manhattan, I fashioned this collage from pictures of us in and around our palace. My legs started aching with an odd fatigue as I waited for him to absorb every detail in each photograph and I shifted from one foot to the other.

Finally, he turned that beautiful smile toward me and once again, I could imagine Od's contented face when he looked at his Freya. "There's something you're not telling me," he said slowly, quirking an eyebrow.

"There is?" I asked innocently, happy to draw out my next revelation.

He waited. I knew he was fighting for patience, but I could feel his curious tension in the fingers laced at the small of my back.

"Well…. There is one more surprise," I added, pulling my face back far enough that I could look at him.

"Yeah?" he asked.

"Corey," I began, finding myself shaking, "I'm pregnant."

For what felt like a long moment, he simply looked at me. His eyes bore deeply into mine and then the corners of his mouth began to twitch. Soon, his lips broke into a broad beam. "I'm going to be a dad?" he asked.

"Yes," I replied, chuckling. "You're going to be a dad."

Laughing, he threw both arms around me and swept me up into them. "I love you, Freya," he chuckled.

"I love you," I echoed, giggling at his boyish mirth. "I love you so much, Corey."

As he burrowed his face in my hair, I knew that the difficulties we knew in our past lives had finally come to a conclusion. We were united, and… if Karma spoke the truth… the first of our girls would only bring a new plane of happiness to our souls.

THE END

Questionnaire

For Women Only

B e a part of history by participating in this most comprehensive sexuality questionnaire of modern times. Be honest while answering these questions. Please be over eighteen years old. You will receive by email within 24 hours your full sexual profile. It is important to understand that this questionnaire is for you to enjoy, have fun, and understand where you are with your sexuality. Many women learn a lot about themselves just by filling in the questionnaire.

http://bit.ly/18TPXjF

Did you know? This analysis profiles the sexual habits of American women. Information has been classified according to the age, height, weight, education, occupation, marital status, and the different intimate habits of the women who answered the questionnaire. The survey reveals much about sex in our society. This report is an easy-to-understand overview of the sexual satisfaction and dissatisfaction of American women.

See the results of my analysis: http://www.mysecretquiz.com

About the Author

Jean-Claude Carvill was born in Lyon, France. He is a Beverly Hills Sensuality Intimacy Coach with over 20 years of professional experience. He is also a dedicated Tantra masseur, and, since 1980, when he gave his first Tantra massage, he managed to help hundreds of women to get in touch with their sexuality and become more aware of their bodies. Coming from France, Jean-Claude grew up in a more liberal and free-spirited society and had the chance to understand the importance of one's sensuality in one's life. Wanting to help women experience a fulfilled intimate life, he has traveled through the Middle East, India, Southeast Asia and Australia, in order to learn the secret techniques of Tantric massage. His activity grew through word-of-mouth- marketing and found its main life within circles of women with women who have a genuine desire for the growth and discovery of their sexual fulfillment. His goal is to help them with their journey to better sex, better lives and enhanced self-esteem. As an intimacy coach, Jean-Claude Carvill gives seminars on the awareness of female sexuality, but also coaches individual women that find themselves in a difficult spot in their relationships. Most often, women that come to Jean-Claude Carvill for sensuality coaching find it difficult to reach orgasm during intercourse, feel that they can't open themselves intimately towards their partners or they are already extremely orgasmic but wish to know if there is something more than they already know. Through moral support and Tantric techniques, Jean-Claude Carvill helps these women overcome their fears, become more aware of their bodies and their needs and have a more satisfying relationship with their partners.

Jean-Claude Carvill conducts seminars in Los Angeles occasionally. Jean-Claude has also conducted intimate gatherings for women throughout Australia, Bali, France, Beverly Hills, Chicago and Atlanta.

Question for the Author?

jeanclaudecarvill@yahoo.com

Want to be on Jean-Claude's free Monthly Newsletter?

jeanclaudecarvill@yahoo.com

Need consultation advice?

Contact me at jeanclaudecarvill@yahoo.com

Your review is important it helps to give more sexual freedom to women one at the time.

If you believe your friend will like to read that book I would be honored if you post your thoughts. If you feel one of my books made an impact on your life, I would be grateful if you write a review. Just click the link below you will find my book.

http://amzn.to/11K7Tqs

More books from this Author:

Confessions of a Hollywood Tantra Masseur which is a Sensual Guide for goddesses.

http://amzn.to/14lOh15

Sex Woman First: Teach him how You come first, Prepare to become a Sexual Goddess Forever.

http://amzn.to/126P3jt

My Blossoming Orchid A Neo-Tantric novel. The secret of a very old type of sensuality.

http://amzn.to/15ThEYu

Rebecca Bottom: There is no fantasy about her story

http://amzn.to/1IyZYDx

Guide to Licking and Sucking - How to Impress Him with the Best BlowJob - The Best Illustrated Guide to Oral Sex - The Ultimate Techniques

http://amzn.to/1DKUG8O

The Desires of Anais And her Stirring Sexuality

http://amzn.to/1IeVIwh

Dead Drunk - A Mystery and Erotic Thriller

http://amzn.to/1xOLUFK

Available online at Amazon, Kobo, Goodreads, Smaswords, Barnes & Noble

www.ingramcontent.com/pod-product-compliance
Lightning Source LLC
Chambersburg PA
CBHW070352290526
45790CB00004B/1451